MARTIN KARI

Copyright © 2025 Martin Kari.

All rights reserved. No part of this book may be reproduced, stored, or transmitted by any means—whether auditory, graphic, mechanical, or electronic—without written permission of both publisher and author, except in the case of brief excerpts used in critical articles and reviews. Unauthorized reproduction of any part of this work is illegal and is punishable by law.

ISBN: 978-1-63950-368-1 (sc)
ISBN: 978-1-63950-369-8 (hc)
ISBN: 978-1-63950-370-4 (e)

Because of the dynamic nature of the Internet, any web addresses or links contained in this book may have changed since publication and may no longer be valid. The views expressed in this work are solely those of the author and do not necessarily reflect the views of the publisher, and the publisher hereby disclaims any responsibility for them.

Writers Apex

Gateway Towards Success

8063 MADISON AVE #1252
Indianapolis, IN 46227
+13176596889
www.writersapex.com

# CONTENTS

About the Author ................................................................. v
Dedication ........................................................................ vii
Acknowledgements ............................................................. ix
Notes ............................................................................... xi
Prologue .......................................................................... xiii

**Germany** ........................................................................ 1
**Finland—Wedding** ........................................................... 7
**Germany** ........................................................................ 13
    Work in Heidelberg ...................................................... 17
    Work in Karlsruhe ........................................................ 25
    South Africa ................................................................ 31
    Life in Transvaal .......................................................... 36
    Life in Cape Town ........................................................ 50

**Brazil** ............................................................................ 66
    Life in the State of Sao Paulo ........................................ 66
    South America Tour: Brazil ........................................... 90
    Uruguay ..................................................................... 91
    Argentina ................................................................... 92
    Chile ......................................................................... 99
    Peru .......................................................................... 104
    Ecuador ..................................................................... 108
    Colombia ................................................................... 116
    Venezuela .................................................................. 121

**Germany** ........................................................................ 128
    Life around Stuttgart .................................................... 133
    Transylvania ............................................................... 136
    Greece ....................................................................... 150
    Spain and Portugal ...................................................... 176
    Portugal ..................................................................... 182
    Spain ......................................................................... 190

**Australia** ................................................................. **213**
    Melbourne—Brisbane—Perth ..................................... 213
    Kabul-Tur (Caboolture) ............................................... 215
    Glass House Mountains—The Legend ....................... 216
    Work on Own Property, Home, Hobby Farm ............. 218
    A Natural Life Shared with an Australian Nature ........ 225
    Possibilities for our Young Generation ....................... 231
    Australia- "A Big Real Estate" .................................... 232
    Australia, a Magnet for Visitors ................................... 234
    South-East Queensland, a Natural Treasure ............... 238
    Re-Connecting to the Rest of the World ..................... 240
    Outback—Australia—Tour ........................................ 253
    Outback—Poem—Trial ............................................. 253
    Home-Stead Visit ........................................................ 257
    In Eighty Days Around the World in 2003 ................. 268
    Hawaii ......................................................................... 269
    Canada ........................................................................ 281
    USA ............................................................................. 287
    Alaska .......................................................................... 298
    Canada ........................................................................ 303
    NIAGARA (Fragments) ............................................. 306
    Germany ...................................................................... 308
    Finland—Norway—Sweden ....................................... 314
    Norway ........................................................................ 322
    Finland ........................................................................ 325
    Sweden ........................................................................ 335
    Finland ........................................................................ 337
    Germany ...................................................................... 340
    France ......................................................................... 344
    Back Home ................................................................. 355
    Retirement—As a Writer ............................................ 358

**Epilogue** ................................................................. 363

# ABOUT THE AUTHOR

The author Martin Kari was born in Transylvania during World War Two in 1941. For the first 26 years, the author has "travelled" in a *"Journey Of A Lifetime, volume 1": first as a* refugee in Germany, then going through different education-leels, work-life, travels and many hobbies. Another 40 years, volume 2, takes the wife and the six children stepwise on board.

A long period of a lifetime started in Australia in 1981, which is expressed also in *"Australia—a Migrant Experience"*. Australia has given back the writing-pen, too.

# DEDICATION

To my beloved wife, **Arja Kari**—

This second chapter of my life belongs as much to you as it does to me. From the first days of our love to the beautiful chaos of raising six children together, you have been the soul of our family and the heart of every adventure.

Through countless journeys across oceans and continents, it was your courage that kept us moving forward, your laughter that lightened the burdens, and your love that made every strange place feel like home.

You are more than my companion—you are my safe harbor, my greatest joy, and the reason every road we traveled led not just to a destination, but to a life filled with meaning.

Arja, this book is dedicated to you, with all the love a man can hold—for the life we built together, for the family we cherish, and for the unbreakable bond that has carried us through a lifetime.

Forever yours,

Martin

# ACKNOWLEDGEMENTS

I'd like to express my special gratitude to the Publisher for the opportunity to have my writing published. It is the team-work that makes it possible to bring out a dialogue with a reader, which otherwise hardly could succeed. The guidance of the editor together with the design input and the printing have considerably contributed to my own writing efforts, for which I am very grateful.

# NOTES

*Some of the personal names included in this book have been changed, or only first names have been included, to protect the privacy of those concerned.*

The book cover shows life emerging even out of the ashes in the East Coast Botanical Gardens on The Big Island of Hawaii.

# PROLOGUE

"Journey Of A Lifetime—Volume 2", is a continuation of a life with a family and also a document of a specific time.

We are all a product of our time and therefore have a story to tell. By doing so, others can connect to the story and become more aware of their own "life story". We do not have to be declared famous to relate our own stories because we are unique in our existence and, therefore, already "famous". The " journey of another lifetime" can assist us in recognising our own story and that not everybody reaches the level to put his experiences into words.

Life should be seen as a journey. This Volume 2 continues the emphasis in Volume 1 of detailing the landscape of other countries and the lifestyles of their people, my family and I have experienced. We need only to connect with people of other countries to share their knowledge and to exchange our knowledge with them. Life has been always our best teacher!

I suggest that the narrations here supply a picture that a reader can co-experience a country and its people without having travelled there. Personal events and their outcomes in this book should be seen as a bigger picture of someone's life. We learn first, then go out to learn more on a journey. We then sit back later in our lives and ponder "what have we really learned?" What matters is the end result—and there are as many ways to reach the end as there are people.

To come to a conclusive "Journey Of A Lifetime", a pre-requisition is to keep records in a diary throughout the whole of your life. Only then is it possible to give a true account and personal recommendations, which should be the essence of the story of a "Journey of a Lifetime".

The endless number of "little things" in our lives should primarily be our concern, the "big things" rarely happen and, if they do, they are more difficult to "control". With this in mind, our "Journey Of A Lifetime" continues in Volume 2.

# Germany

Our engagement party in Finland was detailed in my book *Journey Of A Lifetime—Volume 1.*

My fiancée, Arja, and myself had just left the Finnish port of Turku by ship with a big farewell from the family—this time we did not need an icebreaker to forge through the icy sea.

We were heading back by train from Stockholm to my hometown Ettlingen in Germany and hoped there to win the hearts of my family—a keen undertaking as this proved soon enough.

Our plan was to start the new study terms together at Heidelberg University. I did not have a room in Heidelberg since my friend had reclaimed his room after a year as an exchange student in Scotland. I had happily rented his room during that time.

Raising money had to be given priority during the few weeks before starting university. There was no better choice than to stick to the local company that had previously afforded me excellent income opportunities.

Arja stayed for a while with my step-parents so that they could get to know each other. It didn't work out, however, because curiosity and re-education attempts were mainly on the agenda. My step-parents had the unshakeable belief that this daughter-in-law was not good enough. This was the unfortunate preconception. Arja maintained her Finnish "sisu", which means, she held a quiet, unshakable determination that my parents could not understand. They were not used to dealing with people outside of their traditional German boundaries. "You should marry a German girl," they said.

This was enough. We moved out of their way to give them time to better consider where they really stood—whether they wanted to isolate themselves from us or get to know Arja.

They were rejecting first what they didn't know because of personal insecurity—and this is an old human trait.

Arja started nursing work at a hospital in the nearby town of Karlsruhe. This allowed us to organise our lives better. Always Arja remained strong and kept her Finnish cool, remaining unshakably on our common path. She moved to Karlsruhe and I moved to a student hostel in Heidelberg to continue my studies. We would visit each other on alternate weekends.

Controversy teaches us a lot about our fellow citizens. It is a privilege to get to know somebody for the duration of a lifetime. This process never stops—it is ongoing. We never know ourselves, nor others, unless we embark on an unconditional mutual understanding backed up by constant efforts to uphold it.

Towards the end of 1967, during the Christmas break, we joined my boyscout group for a holiday in a Black Forest cottage called "Devil's Mill" for a couple of days. There was a heavy winter snowfall that transformed the area into a fabulous winter paradise.

The snow was so deep in places that we could hardly move around, as we did not have any skis. Most of our time was spent inside the cottage in front of the fireplace. We also practiced singing madrigals for an upcoming Pentecost event.

We all had to leave "Devil's Mill" on foot to reach Alb Valley because the road up to this higher part of the Black Forest was impassable with the snow masses.

Before Arja joined me in Heidelberg, she went back home to Finland for a visit and brought back more personal belongings.

In February, while she was still in Finland, I had an opportunity, through the university, to gain a ski teacher's licence in Davos, Switzerland.

The skiing tests with the lessons were a "piece of cake" under the grand scenery of the "Matterhorn". On the first night of our group's arrival there was such a big snowfall that we could not leave the house until machines dug out passages along the roads. All the cars on the side of the road had disappeared under the snow. The next day was clear and sunny with the sun reflecting intensively on the ice-crystals' white surfaces. The heavy, new snow presented a challenge, in particular, for slalom skiing and it was little wonder that some students ended up in plaster. These plaster casts had plenty of comments written on them—this was a common skiing tradition. The main thing was that I was spared from this "privilege".

Before leaving Davos, a farewell party was held to thank the organisers. I contributed by composing a song and playing the guitar during the party.

Having a Swiss ski-teaching diploma opened the door for very good opportunities to teach and excellent money to be earned.

Returning from the white splendour of the Swiss Alps, I was surprised to find no snow in the lower regions. At that time of the year everything looked dark and dead: trees without their green leaf 'crowns' and, with the snow missing, light was especially in short supply.

After pre-exams back in Heidelberg, nobody could hold me back from visiting Arja in Finland and I spent a week there with her family. This time I even gave an old Finnish tradition a try and rolled myself in the snow straight after a sauna. This is a great way of ensuring that you are in good health because any disease would be frightened off after such a shock! But I passed on the ultimate test of a swim in an ice hole. Finns do this on a regular basis. From that point I am not a Finn yet!

With that new experience from Finland under my belt I could return in a better shape to Heidelberg. Arja was to follow in April. We kept in close touch during this time. Not only did Arja receive my letters from Germany, but also (as I was later told) letters from my step-mother urging: "Arja, you better stay in Finland and do not disturb Martin in his studies".

It was amazing, how something could be so twisted. All of a sudden there was a concern about my educational future, but my step-parents never came to the party with real financial help when required.

I hope I keep an open mind now that I am in my older years and not to be "blind" like my step-parents—there are always people trying to do the "right" thing by their standards, but they don't recognise the isolation of their own experiences. They often get caught by their own limited vision towards the lives of others. There is a little bit of this in each generation.

After accommodation at the student hostel had been organised, Arja came back to Heidelberg and also started at the university. The large number of students accommodated in different buildings created a problem of its own for effective studies. My room colleague Raoul, who came from Venezuela, did not pursue his studies with priority. His busy social life impacted on our living area and so an agreement was reached that he didn't disrupt the night with female companions—as was the case next door.

Somebody wanting sexual instruction had only to visit the room next door. It was bizarre that at one desk a physics student was absorbed in his studies, while behind him "instructions" took place. Nobody was complaining—some students must have been advanced in those times. In this case the "party" was disrupted when parents from France turned up at the room obviously worried about their underage daughter's wellbeing. However, the daughter had a major reprieve because the boyfriend was quick to disappear.

The only way not to become disrupted in studies was to escape into seminars at the university. Too many different characters came together in a student hostel that you could not maintain a study atmosphere. What a difference to private accommodation! But that was in short supply in Heidelberg.

Anyway, the agreement with Raoul secured a reasonable night's sleep, at least for me. He slept during the day and was busy at night away from the hostel.

Life allowed Arja and myself to get together for a break on weekends. One time, we launched our folding canoe on to the river Neckar, which passes through Heidelberg. My friend also brought along his new girlfriend from Scotland—thus the number of canoe occupants was four.

The time of the year was late May 1968 and the weather was unseasonably warm—a good time to cool down with a boat ride on the river. We did not have to wait too long for that: soon after all four of us climbed into the canoe, it tipped over, throwing everybody into the water. Our first reaction was naturally excitement, until we found out very quickly that my friend's girlfriend could not swim at all. My friend knew it and was therefore the first to dive into the river and pull his girlfriend, with our assistance, from the bottom of the river.

Gasping for air, she recovered quickly and found her tongue again: "Why did you take me into the boat? I can't swim, I could have drowned".

It was a bit late by then to inform us. We were all free to make our decision, to enter the boat.

Special circumstances often reveal hidden personalities. This boating tour quickly came to an unfortunate and unpleasant end. We were not prepared to accept any blame, especially when we helped to save the situation and Arja did her best to comfort the Scottish girl.

This incident helped to seal my affections for Arja. She had remained calm without losing her joy—and this became a strong indication for me. Life tests us constantly, we all have to learn to respond appropriately.

Meanwhile, our lives in Heidelberg asked for extra efforts outside our studies to maintain a minimum budget. Arja was keen to contribute and didn't mind working for a few hours in the household of a Heidelberg family.

Also, on many weekends Arja usually cooked "Berliners" (donuts) in the modest kitchen of the student hostel. This regularly attracted other male students from the building.

The kitchen was the place where students from different rooms met—many of these students were from foreign countries. On one occasion a student expressed his views on Israel and its Arabic neighbours. An Egyptian medicine student was also in the kitchen at the time. After hearing the comments, he lost his senses and took a knife from the kitchen, attacking the other person. Fortunately everybody present could keep them apart before something serious happened.

This incident shows, regardless of intellect, people are not the same and, therefore, think differently. We are always well advised to take into careful consideration other people's sensitivities, because they are a crucial part of human nature.

In our student life we did not have many possessions. Besides our studies, we had plenty to discover and share in our lives. Early in summer 1968 came the news from Finland that Arja's sister was going to get married in August.

We quickly decided we would join the wedding.

# Finland—Wedding

One year after our engagement we were on a good track to manage our lives together. We also knew we wanted children in our family later on. So we gave the green light to seal our commitment with marriage—and to enjoy a double wedding with Arja's sister.

Finnish culture and German culture were not that far apart from each other, despite their different languages.

As I realised over the coming years, many proverbs are similar in both languages—a phenomenon we were not yet aware of. Are similar life experiences responsible for similar proverbs? One source could have been during reformation time, when the Finnish reformer Michael Agricola was a student of Melanchton and Martin Luther, the German reformers.

I would like to introduce three synonymous proverbs here in a sequence of German-Finnish-English: The German and Finnish proverbs have exactly the same wording and meaning.

"Eigenlob stinkt "— "Oma kehu haisee"—"A man must not blow his own trumpet".

"Alte Liebe rostet nicht"—"Vanha rakkaus ei ruostu"—"Old love never rusts".

"Der Apfel faellt nicht weit vom Stamm"—"Omena ei putoa kauas puusta"—"He is a chip off the old block ".

It can be easily recognised in those three samples that German and Finnish proverbs have a common meaning, most English ones are different.

With the support of common meanings in our languages, Arja's parents wrote a German invitation to my step-parents announcing the date of our wedding in Finland on August 11, 1968. The successful formality was well received by my parents: "We rather see you married than live on your own, the Finns are also decent people".

Rather a sparrow in the hand, than the pigeon on the roof? Was this their understanding? My parents offered to drive together with us to Finland, an offer not to be missed.

The family tour went ahead, leaving early August. Dad wanted to see for himself how paper was manufactured in Finland. His chemistry engineer background followed him with persistence—probably still nourishing his hopes to get me into his footsteps.

Dad had slowly distanced himself from the pressure of his working life having retired for almost one year. My step-father appeared more at ease and started to be more sociable, especially towards Arja.

On the other hand, my step-mother became hooked on matching me up with other relatives in the family. There is a reason relatives have the name "relative"—that's because they often pretend to know "relatively" more than others could anticipate. Many years later, an aunt in Brazil point-blank said: "I always thought that Martin would marry the cousin Constance". What a perverse logic relatives can unleash! Is there always something more behind thoughts and behaviours than we can see?

The wedding trip to Finland also took us to Stockholm where our romance had started three years earlier. Driving through Stockholm, dad was still in command of the steering wheel, never thinking to get relief from driving all the way. On a bend of a road he nearly missed the curve, and if I had not grabbed the wheel we may have had an accident. The danger over, dad said to me: "Keep to yourself and don't interfere with my driving". Having said this, he was not prepared to admit that by driving against the high border of the road, we would have turned the car over. The "storm" calmed down before we boarded the ship to Finland with the car.

My step-parents found the long, sunny day on the ship's deck an excellent holiday opportunity, where heated moments from the past were easily settled.

At 10pm the sun was still above the horizon, dipping and rising again only three hours later. Coming closer to Finland, an archipelago of islands underlined the beauty of this area with massive naked granite boulders emerging smoothly out of the sea and Finnish forests hanging on everywhere.

On our arrival at Turku harbour, Arja's father grabbed me by the arm and initiated a dance full of fire to take the stiffness out of the welcome.

My parents could only watch in surprise as to how the family here in Finland "worked".

The traditional welcome in the Finnish sauna did its part soon. My step-mother could only mention to her future daughter-in-law: "I never saw my mother-in-law naked"!. Whether mum and dad wanted this or not, they went through a transformation in their lives, even if only for the moment! One cannot teach older dogs new lessons!

Arja's parents made big efforts to make the double wedding of their two daughters a memorable event.

Mum and dad had the city apartment completely at their disposal, so they could move around freely—which they did. On his excursions in the south of Finland, my step-father visited paper manufacturing facilities. He could not have anticipated that, 25 years later, a Finnish company would buy the German paper manufacturing company that he had directed for many years.

(We were living in Australia, 25 years later, when Mum phoned us to give us the news of the company buy-out. "Can you imagine, Finland has bought the company dad led for so many years," she said. What she neither said, nor knew, was that the Finns shut the place down in

Germany so as to supply their own paper. It was something Dad could never have dreamed of.)

After visiting the Finnish companies my step-father commented: "Finland is very advanced in paper-manufacturing technology". The country is also advanced in other technologies! The electronic giant Nokia is also Finnish! Many people around the world have no knowledge about this fact.

*Double-Wedding, Turku-Finland, 1968.*

Coming back to the preparations of the wedding ceremony: Mum and Dad just made it from an excursion in middle-Finland to be back for the event at St. Michael's church in Turku. Father Petteri walked through the church centre with both his daughters at his arm to the altar where, in front of the pastor, the two bridegrooms waited. The brides stood out in their white wedding gowns. The pastor surprised everybody addressing the gathering in German as well. My parents were especially delighted witnessing this courtesy.

Finland is mainly Lutheran, only a small number of Orthodox and Catholic live in the country. The population has a practical view towards religion. It is a tradition to help its people in many ways.

The pastor asked the bride and the groom: "Do you want to take Martin/Arja as your lawfully wedded wife/husband and honour him/her in health and in sickness until death you depart? If you agree, say: "Yes I do. To seal this commitment I give you the symbolic ring to put on your bride's finger".

The grooms kissed the brides and then the road of their lives together received its green light with the explicit support of all guests present. Tradition also helps here to fill in the gaps of what we don't know.

With the church ceremony over, everybody moved through town on a perfect, sunny Sunday into the festive premises of a special school for deaf and mute children, of which the other father-in-law was the director.

I was spared a speech—there were enough others to give their point on the occasion. Dancing, eating and conversations made the time of the day pass happily.

Father Petteri had specially built a bridal hut where we sought refuge while the party went on well into the night. On first inspection of the hut, as I carried the bride over the threshold, we were surprised by a funny bloke who had already made himself comfortable in the room. Arja was very determined to throw the intruder out.

We spent a few more days in Finland that allowed a real holiday with the whole family. We enjoyed family visits, sight-seeing, relaxing, swimming, not to forget the sauna and plenty of Finnish food. Even Dad was surprised when he tasted Finnish "piima" (butter milk), which he had never tried in Germany.

Finland had a small population of only four million people compared with Germany's many millions. This kept the country's environment still very natural. The air was not polluted and people could enjoy its healthy environment with large forest areas and its 66,000 lakes. Summer is a gift in Finland with an average of 20 hours of sunlight each day. Winter, in contrast, gives back time for a good long sleep when the long nights take over.

# Germany

Arja and I and my step-parents arrived back in Germany "in one piece". Soon the realities of daily life caught with us up again—but we moved in different directions. We "battled" life in Heidelberg, whereas Mum and Dad returned to their pensioner's life in Ettlingen. For a few weeks we still lived in the student hostel. At that time we had to live in separate buildings—there was no provision for married student couples.

It was, however, quite common for students to find a way to bend the rules—married or not.

Our days at the university were running on different tracks and Arja also met Finnish students. One special encounter was with an astronomy student called Kalevi on a city tram in September 1968. He had in his pocket a Finnish newspaper, which Arja recognised and started to talk to him: "You must be from Finland with a Finnish newspaper in your pocket? I live with my "newly-baked" husband in the student hostel. Would you like to come and taste my freshly made 'Berliners" (donuts)?"

Kalevi was happy to accept the invitation saying he had just returned from South Africa and his wife, Pirkko, was going to join him from Finland soon.

From this first meeting, slowly developed a friendship that has lasted our whole lives—and that's something special in anybody's life.

In student circles it didn't matter how you were furnished. Arja produced by her "own magic" Berliners with a cup of tea to create a perfect atmosphere to welcome people.

It was natural for us to bring other people into our lives who we had met on the way.

One weekend I filled the position of a referee during a tennis tournament. At the end of the tournament, I was approached by Marion, a student, who turned out to be the daughter of a relative living in Stuttgart. She was also studying in Heidelberg. She told us about private accommodation soon becoming vacant. The only way to find accommodation in Heidelberg at that time was through personal contacts. The landladies were two sisters—one a seamstress and the other a private kindergarten teacher. They both accepted our application. The one-and-a-half partly-furnished rooms were not quite flash, but we transformed the place very quickly into a nice living area. Self-made bookshelves, wall pictures, rugs, chairs, fridge and stove completed the picture. As soon as we were ready, a house-warming party was arranged and Marion was also amongst our guests.

For the first time I didn't use the break in my studies to work in my hometown of Ettlingen. Luckily the big company Bosch offered me a job to sell their range of hobby machines. Through this connection I had access to their in-house special deals for a fridge and stove that fitted ideally into our new accommodation. The weeks in this job were interesting and lucrative as well.

I moved around between Heidelberg, Mannheim, Frankfurt, Pforzheim, Karlsruhe and Stuttgart selling a record amount of machines. My own sales strategy paid off, giving me a substantial income in return.

Bosch wanted me to continue with them, but I declined the offer. After all, I could not find personal satisfaction in convincing other people to buy these products—whether they had money or not. My own sales psychology could have fed back into our own backyard in only a matter of time. Success is not necessarily always good.

Our place in the "Rahmengasse" (Frame Alley) must have reached an appearance that even thieves became interested in making their move. Waking up suddenly one night, even though it was dark, we knew something was wrong. The window shutters were open. Luckily nothing went missing because our few possessions like a record player and tape recorder were permanently fixed on to a shelf—so that they could not be taken away in a hurry.

We reported this incident to the landlady who immediately improved her dwellings with security devices, but did not upgrade our accommodation. All I could do was to make sure the shutters could not be opened from the outside anymore. Life continued otherwise steadily in Heidelberg.

Arja found a job besides her studies with an elderly couple as an occasional housekeeper. I supplemented our daily needs teaching guitar lessons to people from very different backgrounds including a professor's wife.

I also met a former classmate from the high school (gymnasium) who had followed the "normal" education path and had just finished his medical studies. Bernd was always a very bright student, but he could also be a bit extravagant. As we exchanged memories, he expressed his surprise to find me in his ranks—me, the former "little rogue" of our joint class in Ettlingen.

Not long after our meeting I received the news that Bernd had passed away. He had followed the example of many medical professionals—"doctors are usually the worst patients". In this case, Bernd had ignored his condition of diabetes and had suddenly succumbed to it. This is a stern warning to everybody to pay good attention to their own wellbeing.

Humans are oddly-behaved "animals" mainly because of their "intellect" which leads them to believe they are above Nature's course and ignore the fact that we are bound to it like all other living forms. We have an equal responsibility towards our existence. Nature does not discriminate with good or bad, we are the ones creating the views towards it.

The case of my classmate touched me because of our most interesting meeting only short time before. Nature tells us also, life continues and this was the message I took on board.

Meanwhile, at the University of Heidelberg terror activities by the first generation of the "Baader-Meinhoff" group continued to disrupt teaching. One bizarre disruption occurred during my studies when I handed in my seminar work and received an unexplained total rejection. Investigating further, I found out accidentally that my work had produced "a conflicted situation" with my lecturer.

I mention this because this situation had far-reaching consequences. If I wanted to finish my studies, there was no way around this lecturer who had marked me on his black-sheep list. Again here, our human nature played its role. In other words, I must have been at the wrong place at the wrong time. The lecturer had dismissed the matter and swept it under the carpet, leaving me high and dry. I had no intention to rock this boat any further and soon stepped out of it for good.

The last straw came when I was rejected for a scholarship on the basis of my parent's wealth. Uni fees were in place during that time and I would have liked to have relief from such fees. In my opinion, Germany in those years still had one foot in the "dark Middle Ages". How do we classify a selection criteria for medical studies when decisive admission points are based on your parent's professional background? How could you justify in a modern society that somebody independent like me, at the age of 27, was still made dependant on his parents?

At the same time, parents had a duty in Germany by law to supply the offsprings with equal educational standards like theirs. Such blindness is a flagrant disregard of children's genetic succession which rarely follows in the parents' direct footsteps. There are too many inherited genes behind the scene to justify such an absurd claim.

The official response from the bureaucrats to my application suggested: "You have to enforce your rights through the legal system". Who in this world would take their parents to court? Not me! Although I knew that a fellow schoolmate had done this successfully.

I only ask, where was the legal system standing here? For the time being, I "remained in the boat" to see what could still be achieved and not jeopardise my time and efforts at the Uni.

I was wrong again, too many odds were against me. A decision "to leave the boat" ripened once and for all—slowly but surely.

Everybody has his limits in what he is prepared to take. A move into another direction of the Pedagogic Academy proved too unrealistic so I was quick to leave it alone.

The location of our residence was pretty much central to everything in Heidelberg. It was close to the river Neckar, where we had long walks along its grass banks enjoying the views across to the historic settings of the city centre along the hillsides.

Winter arrived early in November 1968 with snowfalls. During an early morning walk in the fresh snowfields in the upper forests of the surrounding hills, Arja could not follow our normal walking speed. She didn't say anything about not feeling well. All of a sudden, she fainted in front of me. I looked into her eyes as she instantly gained consciousness and helped her to come slowly back on her feet. My first question was: "What happened to you?"

I held her in my arms assisting her and it took her a while to break the silence: "I might be pregnant", she said. Wow! What a surprise! We walked home slowly and I reassured her that we both were happy about the situation.

A new era had entered our lives and we were more than happy to adjust ourselves to it. Our lives with our family became, from that moment, more important than anything else.

## Work in Heidelberg

In the coming months I decided to bring my studies to an end and move back to my original profession. Heidelberg had not much industry, but I did find a small hightech company manufacturing precision drawing instruments. They offered me good employment and our lives continued well from then on.

From one day to another we left all the uncertainties of the university behind, finding a better direction.

Arja looked after our modest home while I went to work. We arranged our lives in this old-fashioned way: Arja was the "minister for our internal affairs and I for external affairs". This has worked well for the whole of our lifetime.

An elderly retired lady lived above us in a small backyard hut. Steep stairs led up to her room. A stove in her room was heated with briquettes. It was only natural that we helped her to get the briquettes from the cellar up to her room. To us, she was Aunty Lotte. When Arja prepared coffee, the smell encouraged her to join us. Having problems with her legs, Aunty Lotte needed assistance to come down the steep stairway. The water pipe through the house served as an internal telephone for her. Her knock on the pipe told us: Aunty Lotte wants to join us. We didn't mind as she was one of the older generation who the modern German 'miracle' economy could not reach. In her lonely life she needed somebody to talk to. It is amazing how much so little can make a difference in somebody's life. Aunty Lotte regained her confidence in our coffee circle and talked endlessly about her previous life.

Despite having been a central figure in the area distributing the newspaper for many years, she had only one other person she called a friend. Aunty Lotte didn't trust many other people—she had her reasons.

One day she came down the stairs by herself. She was totally upset. "I don't want to live anymore," she said. "My only friend betrayed me with my bank account. The money was for my grave-stone. Now I don't have that anymore."

It took us a while to calm her down and find out what had really happened.

This "friend" had the guts to use her signature and trust. She continued: "She has a stove, fridge, washing machine and TV—all new from my trust account. Whom can you trust in this world? What I cannot understand is that she and her husband go to church every Sunday."

The bank could not do anything to recover the money because the text of the trust with her signature left all options open. This is an unfortunate incident, but not an isolated one. In how many cases have people "come out of hiding" just in time to cash in on somebody who is leaving this life.

Not so long after, Aunty Lotte came to our rescue and helped us out of a situation—and thus put some sense of meaning back into her life. In September 1969 our landlady disappeared for a while. We received a registered letter from her that demanded that we leave her premises immediately. The only explanation: "Your rented room is not meant for a family, but only for two persons". The strangest thing was that one of the landladies had her own private kindergarten.

Hearing this message, Aunty Lotte promised to help our case. She knew all the people around from her newspaper run and let everybody know of the kindergarten teacher who could not tolerate a young family with a child. I was not sitting and waiting either. I organised the biggest newspaper in the country, The Bild, to come and report on the matter. They ran a front page story on our plight with a photo of Arja and our newborn boy, Risto. At the same time I approached the local federation of lessors to find out about the legality of this demand and they organised me to report on the matter at their next general meeting.

The landlady must have received notice of a "storm" brewing. She suddenly arrived from her holiday place in Austria and offered to withdraw her demand, offering us to stay as long as we liked. One only condition was sought—that I should not publicly report on the matter. The case was settled for us and we had no further intentions.

During this course of events, I had also spoken to the owner of the company where I was employed. He immediately offered me a dwelling on the company's premises.

With this in mind, we approached the landladies and told them that we were leaving their premises. The new dwelling was a vast improvement in our living conditions. We were lucky to receive this offer, because it was close to impossible to find accommodation overnight in Heidelberg.

The case became settled and Aunty Lotte enjoyed this outcome with us. Once a week we visited the old place to see how Aunty Lotte was going. She enjoyed our baby boy Risto, who always came with us. Painful memories surfaced for Aunty Lotte because her only child was still-born and her husband had died of an illness at an early age.

Why have some people got to suffer so much in their lives, while others turn their lives upside down and still get away with it?

The birth of our baby boy Risto was quite routine, despite the rather ancient delivery procedures of the hospital. Progress in Germany often happened slowly—tradition putting the brakes on.

Our first-born became quite an experience for both of us. Arja supported this event quite rationally with a correct lifestyle and lots of swimming activities. The very first bath and nappy change at home came close to a nightmare without harming the little fellow. Like all babies, he turned out quite robust, teaching us how he liked best to be handled. The first child is a significant event in every family, turning all the attention then to the new family member. In an offspring, we really recognise ourselves for the first time.

Our first visit from Finland was Arja's friend, Tuija, who since early childhood was her best friend. Tuija worked in a transport company in Finland and turned up one day while we still lived in "Rahmengasse" (Frame Alley). Her accommodation in our limited space had to be unconventional, but that didn't matter between friends. Where there is a genuine will, there is also a solution. Our solution was that we all slept in the same bed with Arja in the middle. Finns are normally straight forward practical people. Arja had enough time to catch up with Tuija on our new lives and there was no denying that we were happy. This message would go back to Finland, without any doubt. This visit also showed that Finnish people stick together and care about each other.

Other friends and relatives paid us visits in succession and baby Risto enjoyed plenty of attention. Looking at him during nappy change, though, one had to make sure not to receive a sudden "shower". My parents also made the journey to Heidelberg one day, not forgetting to bring along all their "good advice" which they could freely take back home again. They had, of course, other ideas about the name of their first grandchild, which they impressed upon us unmistakably.

From Finland, Arja received a big bunch of flowers with a note attached saying that we should spend Christmas in Finland with her family.

The news of Risto's birth reached Finland with a telegram, starting a funny family discussion. Arja's sister, Raija, first got the message and started spreading the news. Talking to father Petteri on the phone she announced: "Congratulations on the birth of the second granddaughter". There was a big silence on the other side! Raija continued: "I was only teasing, Risto is born".

Petteri became so excited and happy that he straight-away had to visit mother Tysse at her workplace telling her: "Do you know, we have got a son!" The joy was real and unstoppable.

The end of 1969 arrived, and we planned our trip to Finland. This time we took the ferry-ship from Lubeck to Finland, the fastest ship in the world at that time with a travel speed of 45 knots. Finland was also emerging as a strong industrial nation building the best ships, especially the outstanding ice-breakers.

Our shipping passage offered luxury to everybody—there were even facilities for babies on board. Risto and his cousin, Sanna, were the stars of the family in Finland, everybody wanted to win their hearts.

Santa Claus still calls Lapland his home in the north of Finland. He brought Christmas fascination also to us. Fascinations are a gift in our lives—before the realities take over. They help us with our imagination to get past realities and enjoy a "better world".

Christmas is celebrated in Finland in a similar way to other Protestant parts of Europe. The snow usually banishes part of the darkness that reigns during most of the winter time. Warm rooms create, as a contrast, a cosy atmosphere at each home. This is reflected in the high standard of home construction with their well-known taste of Finnish design: combating the simple harsh realities of nature with fantasies in equally-simple expressions.

After "refuelling" with Finnish cordiality, I went back to Heidelberg the way I came, while Arja spent a bit more time with the family in Finland. My Finland visit also included a sauna that was good as it allowed me to return much cleaner.

When Arja was preparing to return to Heidelberg, she encountered a problem: she could not return by sea to Germany because of a smallpox outbreak in Hamburg. Air travel became the only way to return to Germany.

In February, I was also confronted with a problem—a sudden health problem. For years "specialists" had diagnosed me with a stomach ulcer, despite my telling them that this was not the case and they were "fishing" in the wrong spot. My appendix was positioned higher than normal, and since 1964 I had regularly suffered symptoms that were totally wrongly diagnosed. Doctors are not more intelligent than any other person, they can fail in their duty like anybody else.

In February I came to a point that I could not be sure any more if I could survive the colic symptoms related to an acute appendicitis attack which I suffered six years before in Southern France. It was there that I had been in hospital under observation for the first time.

Now I could follow up, personally, how our medical system worked. First I made sure that the chart going with me into surgery was mine and not somebody else's. The surgical departments being stretched to their limits was nothing new to me. My surgeon worked another five hours flatout with his team on my case after having already been on duty for two full days without a proper break. When I saw him for a few moments, I wished good luck and said: "I'd like to live for a bit longer". His surgical outfit was wet on his back all the way through. One could only wonder how these people could stand up to such demands. Mistakes could only be a natural consequence from such an environment. I knew that my case went well when I woke up and heard: "Welcome back to the world of the living".

Another chance had been given to me to continue with life. It took me many months to regain my strength after this operation and rebuild my immune system.

Arja's mum came to see us in the summer of 1970. Just before her arrival, I finished a special cot for our little boy Risto. At first I made the bed with high legs, but I soon cut them shorter when the boy fell out of the cot. In the middle of this confusion, mother Tysse arrived by car with Arja's cousin and his wife. She could see past the problem, bringing her kindness into our world.

I can always remember her smile; if only everybody could be like this beautiful woman. I was privileged to have her daughter as my wife.

The first weekend during her stay we showed her around Heidelberg. We also visited my step-parents in Ettlingen.

Mum was not present at the time as she had made a big decision to see her brother's family in Brazil—a once-in-a-lifetime journey from Germany into a very different country. Dad was keen to stay where he was. Brazil was, for him, too far and uncertain. My mother-in-law's presence must have brought out his generous side because he offered us his car to show Tysse around.

The well-known town of Rothenburg, east of Heidelberg, became one destination in our tour. Even today, the town reflects history dating back centuries: stone-paved alleys allow modern traffic to move slowly between historical building sites. You feel transported well back in time, before the Middle Ages.

History has fortunately been preserved in other places in Germany after towns destroyed by the war were rebuilt to their original appearance. In Germany, tradition has always been a strong cultural element. However, it can produce a side effect of a reduced understanding of other people who do not follow such tradition.

During this trip we faced an unpleasant experience in a restaurant. When we entered, only locals were present at the time. I knew we had to look for a table of our own and not to make the mistake of taking a seat at the table of regular patrons. The Finnish conversation between my wife and her mum was apparently something new for the proprietor. Our lunch finally arrived on the table and little Risto could not wait any longer, accidentally pulling a plate off the table. The waitress took the opportunity to make a big fuss out of it: "You have got a very expensive son and illbehaved monster into the bargain"! I went with her to the bar to settle the case away from my mother-in-law, not wanting her to experience any discomfort.

The restaurant owner gave me a broom and dustpan, telling me to clean the floor and adding: "If you don't clean it up immediately and pay for your mess, I will call the police".

This became too much for me, my patience ran out and I replied:

"You call the police, I am waiting here for them".

He didn't, of course, call the police. They wouldn't have known what to do with a one-year-old "offender".

I settled the case by paying part of the amount asked for, just to get out of the situation and stop any bad impressions from reaching our Finnish visitor.

Economical considerations should have their limits—decency should take over. I doubt this would happen in Finland. Our tour continued leaving behind these memories where they belonged.

The more I travelled the world, the more I realised that everything is possible. Fortunately we have the freedom to make our own choices and leave behind what we disagree with.

During our time in Heidelberg, our son Risto didn't fail to keep us busy. He even managed to lock his mum out on the balcony of our residence. Through the glass door she had to watch how the little son developed his idea of a freedom in the kitchen. Arja's attempts to explain, through the door, how to operate the lever, didn't much bother the son inside. He cleaned the table instead, pulling everything on to the floor, leaving mum outside high and dry.

The house co-tenants were not at home and everybody else was at work. Once the table was cleared, the son climbed on a chair and on top of the table. The son danced with joy on top of the table while Arja could do nothing but watch. The next level of activities inside the kitchen was directed towards pots and pans on the shelves. Thankfully, help arrived when somebody came out of the factory and heard Arja's plea for help: "Could you please get my husband because I am locked out and can't get in". Arriving on the scene, my key delivered the access to the kitchen and I instantly secured the little fellow to prevent him from doing any harm. Arja was relieved as she walked through the balcony door into the kitchen.

Thanks to heaven, nothing really happened and we got away with our scare. Parents must have luck when raising children! It is difficult to comprehend how much could have gone wrong during such an incident.

## Work in Karlsruhe

A former boy-scout mate had started a business in Karlsruhe in plastic-injection moulding with the help of his family. He was looking for somebody to help him in his business. When I learned about this through a friend, I did not hesitate to contact him. We came surprisingly quickly to an agreement, which helped to improve our living standard.

Plastic-injection moulding technology was about to explode in its developments right across all industries. Good prospects showed up on the horizon. There was no way around it, we had to move from Heidelberg to Karlsruhe.

Before this move, my wife accepted employment with a family to look after their five-year-old daughter Astrid, whose both parents were orthopaedic surgeons. An offspring of this old Heidelberg family later became the tennis champion Boris Becker.

Moving while we are young should be part of our learning process. We don't learn much staying idle in one place. Fortunately not everybody has this understanding. What would the world be like if everybody was on the move?

But this is also how intellects differ from each other by supplying this colourful image of mankind around the world.

An immediate accommodation was not yet available in Karlsruhe, so we decided that Arja and Risto should go home to Finland in January until we could move into a new home during April 1971.

Christmas could still be spent with my parents. Our little Risto helped to keep relationships good between us and my parents. It was good to see the older generation enjoying our younger one.

In Finland, son Risto kept mum Arja on her toes. On arrival, he climbed the table in his full winter gear, showing off to everybody: "Here I am!" Once everybody in our Finnish family branch had taken notice of him, Risto went straight over to his next surprise, dismantling in only a few seconds the door bell keeping the door shut and showing his achievement to everybody. It must have been the early signs of his mechanical talents! Risto also investigated the balcony which was covered with a layer of snow. This was straight after his bath and Arja had left him for only a few moments.

The cold air from outside entering the rooms made Arja aware that something was not right. She was not even dressed properly. She rushed from the bathroom when she realised Risto had thrown snow over the balustrade from the balcony. Arja could not be quick enough to stop him from climbing the balustrade. With luck, this challenge remained in narrow boundaries.

During April 1971 our residence in Karlsruhe became a reality and Arja and Risto returned from Finland. We managed to set up our dwelling in a comfortable way with our personal touches. The accommodation was in a big housing estate, belonging to the owner of the company where I was employed.

Our family life returned again to a routine. In our section of the house there were no other children. It was interesting to watch how children made contact with each other. In the neighbourhood there also lived a boy slightly older than our Risto. The two boys made eye contact through the window, partly escaping our attention. Encouraged by the neighbour's child, Risto threw his toys from the window down to him into the backyard. As long as there were toys going one way into the yard, their play rule worked. Fortunately we became aware of this game in time, before it might have turned into a much bigger problem: what would they have done with no toys left?

The windows became permanently locked, but still the toys couldn't find their way back. Slowly a toy collection consisting mainly of Lego building blocks started to rebuild and nothing went missing any more.

One child in a family asks for a lot of attention. Two children occupy each other for a certain parent's benefit.

August 1971 was the time that our second child joined our family. Risto welcomed his sister Raija. His initial interest in this new addition to our family promised a good start for all of us.

This was not the case with our dear neighbours, who had different ideas. The economical "miracle" in Germany had made very little provision for families with children. The new stress for progress in the society could not handle additional demands at the time. The occupants below us made this very clear. No matter how hard we tried, they would rather have had no children in their neighbourhood. They turned their TV up so loud during the night that we had no trouble listening to their programs. This noise disrupted the children's sleep and made them irritable during the day. Summer 1971 was also unusually hot, which affected my wife just before the birth of our second child. During shopping she fainted and needed immediate assistance. I took time off from work to help her during the remaining days before the confinement.

The animosities around us didn't stop. As a couple from different nationalities, we could not find acceptance during that time. Arja's obstetrician had nothing better to say than: "You shouldn't have a second child so soon after the first one".

Family allowance was only available for the "better" part of the society—the public servants. Everybody else received assistance only after their third child. It was very difficult to understand the logic behind this. In the Middle Ages, the population was kept large to support the few privileged in their demands.

Germany always had its class divisions. Efforts had to come from a majority basis to run their "show". These were the relics of an antiquated feudal system. The ones benefiting from it were always reluctant to share with others, until it turned into a political instrument.

I accept that by using commonsense, we can only deliver in a society what can be provided. Traditionally, we have many problems with changes in society levels and are reluctant to give away any of our privileges. It is like a tug of war, depending on which side one stays—on a giving or receiving side. When the latter becomes dominant, like the social system has developed over the years, it can make a "boat" unstable—if not sinking with both sides on board. Everything in our lives is dependant on a balance.

In our case, we were often on the side receiving the build-up of "downsides" which led eventually to a political correction.

I am not complaining here. These were facts which, sooner or later, triggered decisions for changes in our lives. There are people that can take things at their face value and never ask questions. But there are those who aim for changes to improve their lives. It is not difficult to see on which platform we were standing.

The allotment gardens on the other side of the road had a monthly club meeting with music, beer and dances throughout the weekend nights.

Germans like their clubs. Everybody identifies himself at least with one of these institutions and there are hardly any limits to such a choice. Even if we wanted to take part in the monthly get-togethers to deal better with the noise, this did not suit our small children. They could not sleep and neither could we. Our weekend became stuffed up because a majority of club members decided to have fun their way.

We soon came to a point where we realised this was not the life we wanted. Before a final decision was made, other "shit stirrers" crossed our path. One day, Risto caught a bad stomach bug and had to stay away from other children. We asked my step-mother for help and she sacrificed her time and joined us. Her presence didn't help much at all after she started pulling out "old garbage". During the course of this event, my step-mother said all of a sudden: "Go to Transylvania and see how your brother is doing". This was something new to me. I had never before heard that I had a brother. The situation escalated and my step-mother made more and more accusations towards Arja. I could not tolerate this any longer and asked my step-mother to leave.

If things in our lives stay hidden long enough, they will come out in a way we don't necessarily like or want. The relationship with my step-parents reached an all-time low.

Trying to leave behind what happened, we invited my step-mother and her sister to visit. But that was a bad mistake. She couldn't resist the temptation to bring up past discords again. This time, however, in front of other visitors, giving them a seal of disapproval once and for all.

How strange human beings can be! We tend to often know more than we can put into praxis.

In a search for new horizons, we directed our views to overseas. Our application to the South African Embassy received an immediate positive response. Before making our final decision, we wanted to find out about possibilities in Finland.

Dissolving our household in Germany went surprisingly well. Our self-made furniture attracted a lot of interest and we achieved better-than-expected prices.

Before heading to Finland, we found it appropriate to visit my step-parents. They again had other ideas, turning our farewell into an unpleasant situation.

My step-mum wanted to have her last word with Arja. We finally found ourselves locked in the cellar room overnight, probably with the intention of stopping us leaving. But what was the alternative? The next morning, I said from behind the locked door: "This way you can't stop us from going away". My parents had no answer for this comment, so they returned to the "negotiating table". We understood their concerns but asked that they give us more of their understanding.

Our farewell was on sour note.

It was in August 1972, when we all moved first to Finland.

With the assistance of my father-in-law we looked around for work for me in Finland. We did not, however, look in Middle Finland and so probably missed an opportunity to join Nokia's business at a very early stage.

It was impossible for me to stay in Finland without work, despite the family wanting to keep us there. Arja also decided that we should move to South Africa. So I left for South Africa alone to prepare the move for the whole family. Arja was in the best care with her aunt in Tampere.

At my farewell emotions accompanied the words of my father-in-law: "I won't see that guy anymore. Who is going to pass away first, the old dog Sepi or me?"

"Don't talk like this dad, you are still young and strong," we said. Did Petteri already have an idea that cancer would take him away in May two years later?

Decisions are made in life to be followed up. Our Finnish friends from Heidelberg, Kalevi and Pirkko, farewelled me from Helsinki on my first leg to Frankfurt, where I would catch a long-distance flight with South African Airways. Boarding the big 747 Boeing aircraft, I realised that I was heading into a different world, a new and possibly rich one.

Despite not having sympathy for the current ruling in South Africa, I left this for others to sort out. It was beneficial for the country to take new people in from outside to help towards achieving a normalization. I came on a professional mission to the country with a work contract, which was to be finalized on arrival in South Africa.

The flight was fully booked out and with its payload the huge plane took off safely from Frankfurt heading to the islands of the Canaries thus avoiding the airspace over the African continent. African nations barred South Africa from flying over their territories in protest of its "Apartheid ruling".

This was also my first long-distance flight. The Boeing 747-400 cruised steadily high up in the atmosphere. Only around the equatorial winds did the plane shake for a while. These early "Jumbos" showed on their workmanship with rivets on the surface, whereas in 2008 a "Jumbo" has a totally smooth surface.

Over South-West Africa, Namibia, the plane entered African airspace. From the cruising height we had a totally clear vision right to the ground. The colours of the land gave vivid first impressions. Only just before our arrival in Johannesburg, did the reflection of house roofs add to this colourful image of the Southern African continent. These colours gave indications to geologists about the nature of soils with its mineral distribution. South Africa has one of the richest mineral deposits known on earth. Its mining industry is the backbone of its immense wealth.

## South Africa

The plane made a perfect landing at Jan Smuts International Airport. One interesting note could be added here: the flight from Frankfurt to Johannesburg required a stopover in Las Palmas, whereas from

Johannesburg to Frankfurt the plane managed to fly non-stop. A plane had less to climb to reach a cruising height in

Johannesburg because the starting height was already 2500 metres. The climb from a start close to sea level can take up to 40 percent of all fuel that a plane has taken on its flight.

Johannesburg gave a warm welcome with crystal clear sunshine, rarely seen in Europe with its cloudy skies and pollution. A registration process at the airport went without much of a delay and this gave good first impressions. At first glance it became obvious that the black population was recruited mainly out of tribes: Bantu, Zulu, Xhosas and Herrera. They displayed their friendly nature, but with caution. European descendants were on the official side of public services, but most basic work was covered by the black population.

A small bus took me from the outskirts of the airport into provided hostel accommodation, right in the centre of Johannesburg. On this route, some city parts looked modern along a road varying in its condition, others looked as if they were never finished and patched up in a hurry with whatever was available.

At first, a rest became a necessity, since I ended up with a bad flu possibly due to being in a plane for many hours in a closed environment with plenty of other passengers. One of my first activities was to organize a whole box of fresh oranges to help me get over my flu. With my condition improving, I started to make phone calls to get in contact with the company in Krugersdorp at the West Rand of Johannesburg.

To give Arja a call in Finland was a timely problem. South Africa had only a cable connection to overseas with a limited transmission capacity. I had no hope of getting through with operator assistance. I sent a telegram instead announcing my good arrival.

Most telephones were not working properly—this was one of my first lessons. When the coins dropped and no connection appeared, everybody knew the telephone didn't work!

When I finally got through to the address in Krugersdorp, I was told that the German manager was in Germany at the very moment and was expected back in two weeks time. I had started off well! People were obviously not in a rush, telling me to come back in two weeks time.

With this in mind, I started with my own investigations first in the city centre and moving further out each day. The railway was the main people mover and buses connected to the black townships of Soweto and Orlando around Johannesburg. On a Friday afternoon I entered a train packed with people. Some public transport did not show the 'Apartheid separation' signs where only white Europeans could exclusively use the transports. Africans were not allowed to join. They had their own transport, where white Europeans were also excluded.

I learned quickly on that Friday afternoon that it was not a good time to use public transport when people had received their weekly pay. Standing near the entrance of a packed train carriage, I got a big scare by watching an incident that happened just in front of me. One black passenger shut the mouth of a co-passenger next to me with his hand. In his other hand he used something like a knitting needle, forcing it from the back into his body nearly unnoticed. A brown envelope was taken forcibly from the victim. Nobody around seemed to have seen anything, because he could have become the next target. On the next stop, I left the scene as quickly as I could, mindful that the victim's body had fallen on to the train floor. Everybody else was also busy fleeing. Nothing was said, the scene remained silent. The train continued its journey and it was left to somebody else to find out what happened.

After Europe, I could not believe what I had just witnessed. It did make me one experience richer, but in my first letter to Arja I was not sure whether to stay or not. She replied: "We should look further and make sure we gain something for ourselves. Therefore it is better to stay where you are, because I want to see the world as well".

The black townships around Johannesburg reflected the problems of the different societies living together in South Africa. A black township was practically a no-go zone for other groups of the society that included Europeans, Coloureds and Indians. Coloureds and Indians lived more in Durban on the east coast. Cape Town had a population of Coloureds and Blacks as well as Europeans.

Referring to the townships, they represented a constant problem in their set-ups. It was hardly possible to bring its inhabitants in line with government ruling. The conditions were imposed and not accepted. Measurements by the government never fell on fertile ground for that reason.

Even when complete new housing estates were built after shanty shelters had been bulldozed down, no efforts were made for a common ground. The township population did not produce the respect, which the government expected in its isolated efforts. Often the materials of windows, doors and floors of new accommodations were used in cooking and heating fires.

Once most was used up, they moved out and rebuilt their shanty shelters. It also happened that an economical advantage was pursued by renting the new accommodation to others and cashing in on the illegal rent, while moving back into free shanty accommodations. A no-win situation for a government.

What was missing here were unconditional efforts towards an education. It had to get worse first with the turning tide at the end of the 20th century in South Africa, before anybody could expect something better. It is probably only natural in human terms that previous underprivileged parties in the society turned against the once-ruling party.

A first outcome had to be a violent transition.

According to a physical law of a time-balance between action and reaction, it is likely that a process towards a normalization will take the same time it took to build apartheid.

During those first days in South Africa I met people from many different backgrounds. A recently-arrived migrant explained to me how he started. He invited me to join him for a dinner, unveiling at the table how he had already made his first million. To support his claim he walked with me afterwards into the city centre to a fenced landmark surrounded by high-rise buildings, informing me: "This was vacant land with full-grown trees until I investigated at the Lands Department as to who owned it. No owner could be traced, so I just registered the land in my name and went straight to a real estate agent and sold it for two million rand. That's the way to make money in South Africa". I asked him: "Do you know another place like this to make big bucks quickly?"

"Things like this don't wait for us," he replied.

My first impressions of South Africa started to become more and more colourful.

Here, in the southern hemisphere, Spring started with first storms after a dry winter period. The light blue bell-like flowers of the jacaranda trees with their blue carpet underneath transformed streets and gardens into a marvellous sight. Jacarandas are highly drought-resistant maintaining their flower cycle.

Meanwhile the time drew closer to again contact the company in Krugersdorp to find out about my employment. The new manager had just arrived from Germany leaving behind the previous one, who had already employed me in Germany. Before I started work, I used my time to organize accommodation for my family, who were waiting for the signal to join me. Renting a house was easy.

Every day after work I spent time cleaning inside and outside the house. During my first night in the house all sorts of unwanted pests emerged out of the cracks in the timber floor making my life unbearable. A radical elimination process followed, preventing me, however, from occupying the house for at least two days. A workmate helped me out with a room in his house.

The company also gave me a car to move around more easily. Basic furniture was organized, making the house more livable. At the home's entrance, a table with benches around filled the veranda area. Time passed quickly towards the end of the year.

## Life in Transvaal

My family arrived at last on December 6, 1972 in Johannesburg including our new-born baby daughter Mirja, who was born at the end of October. An emotional welcome took place at the airport after such a long separation. We all did our part for this family reunion.

Everybody was happy with the space in the house and garden. There were no complaints from nearby about the children's presence. Our lives could develop without transition into a regular pattern. We also had enough room to keep a pet. First, a young German shepherd joined us from the neighbourhood. The dog didn't listen, however, and was killed by oncoming traffic in front of the children, as I walked with them across to a park.

"This can happen when you don't listen," I told them. To help the children forget this incident, we immediately organized another German shepherd puppy. Not long after a black Labrador-cross turned up on a cold morning outside in the ashes of a previous fire and happily joined our family. We kept an eye open, however, to ensure the dogs were treated properly—especially by the children. There are simple rules: a dog must always come to you, and, never disturb an eating or sleeping dog.

Our eldest son, Risto, liked having his dummy to go to sleep when he was in Germany. In South Africa, however, I realised he had abandoned this habit. Arja told me how this had happened back in Finland. Her aunt looked after the children one evening when Arja was invited to the theatre by her cousin's wife.

As the aunt forgot about the dummy when putting Risto into bed, she was wondering, why he didn't sleep. Next morning he didn't fail to ask for the dummy. The aunt's "magic" gave a helping hand here. "There is snow outside and it looks like a mummy dog has picked up your dummy and given it to her baby, who is certainly more in need because you are a big boy now," the aunt said.

In our South African backyard was a hut for a black servant as was the case at every house. We could neither trust such arrangements being new in the country, nor were we used to employing somebody in the family for a very low income. Some people claimed that this was the way they gave employment to the black population. In most cases they did all the housework, while the lady of the house could spend her time on other activities, very often in the social field of a school or church. Generally speaking, life looked calm on the surface—but there is always a "calm before a storm". It occasionally came to our attention that these employment arrangements didn't work out allowing theft and violent crimes to take foothold. Employing somebody in a family is a trust situation which, in my view, cannot be dealt simply with a cheap labour arrangement.

People have their expectations and if it is not met, they will resort to other means in their power.

At work we employed mainly the black population. German companies had a reputation in South Africa for reasonably fair employment conditions. We also trained people on a job, giving them incentives to learn and perform. A learning process offered in a tailored way that they could understand, made them quite reliable workers.

You always had to stay in communication with them to avoid any quiet build-up of tensions that may suddenly explode into violence.

Black people are, generally speaking, nice as long as they feel understood. A low threshold of stimulation can quickly turn around into aggression, which is quite natural in our human behaviour.

Two single incidents at work highlighted the general situation of that time. As stated before, we employed mainly black people with the exception of a few Europeans like myself. A sudden dispute erupted in the workshop and nobody knew exactly what had happened. One black employee grabbed a chair and was about to hit a European worker but he escaped from the premises.

No discussion took place, the decision was: the European had upset the peace at work and so he was the one packing up and leaving the premises.

On another day, a gathering of black people from the nearby township took place in front of the company building. Watching this from inside I noticed that our Bavarian employee from Germany had packed up in a hurry and disappeared through the back of the building. It was not difficult to conclude that something had become too "hot" for him. And indeed, talking to a representative of the outside gathering, it was revealed that a pregnant black woman had come with her supporters to claim the fatherhood of her unborn baby.

During that time the law in South Africa prohibited all relations between its "white" and "black "population. A written law was one thing, the reality was something else.

Quite a number of black women actually wanted to have racially-mixed babies out of desperation to improve their living conditions in an enforced white rule.

Racial-mixed people enjoyed, for some reason, slightly better status than black people during the apartheid. However, hatred sowed discord between the different races in South Africa. The government didn't fail to put in place paper legislation for "offenders".

The crowd outside the company was advised that the "offender" they were looking for was not with us any more. Any decision had to be considered very carefully, especially as we were in the proximity of their township.

A "wrong" decision could have easily spilled over into untold violence—that being one of the realities in South Africa at that time.

Something less serious, but with not less of a disturbance, also happened one day. In summer we had to keep a close eye on snakes from the surrounding bush making their way into the factory building. They were after a hiding place in the cardboard boxes stored in the dispatch.

If a snake turned up, mainly the black employees took off in fright and didn't return into the building until the scene had visibly been cleared.

One could also observe that Africans liked to wear a talisman around their necks. This was a bit of a refuge towards their origin, often from outside of South Africa, where a chieftain with his medicine man still ruled.

Africans were often foreign workers with permits to stay in South Africa bearing the transition from an ancient tribal tradition straight into modern economical demands. Somebody dealing with Africans in those days had to take facts like this very much into consideration.

One day it was not a snake in the factory premises, but a huge python creeping outside along the building. The moment the employees saw it, the whole place became alarmed. Nobody could stop them stabbing, crushing and burning the beautiful six-metre long python. This was not the end of the incident, all Africans left the place, because in their understanding it was a bad sign.

Next morning everything was forgotten, like nothing had happened.

Manufacturing in South Africa was of a fairly high standard and therefore a lot of money was made available for new investments. Despite the stigma of apartheid, good practices were in place and these are worth noting and not rejected all together with apartheid. Politicians rarely learn to use the positive sides in order to change the less positive ones.

South Africa also centralized the income of its minerals wealth, using it mainly for new investments. The wealth then created new activities for its working classes, whether Europeans or Africans. One bonus came out of it: people paid very low taxes.

The cost of living was also very cheap with the strong currency of the Rand. People with qualifications could make a good fortune with hard work.

Farming could also return a good income. I met individuals who worked subcontracting during the day in high-tech places earning good money and then after hours, including their weekends, worked their farm with all sorts of businesses like cattle, pigs and specialized crops.

Wheat farming remained more traditionally in the hands of the Boers, the Dutch descendants. They had brought to the country their own Afrikaans language that was mainly found in the government administrations.

The Boers built on the strength of their relationship with the black population to protect themselves from foreign interference. Farmers had agreements in place with their workforce and additionally remunerated workers with goods like: one suit per year and other clothes in between. In most cases, the Africans had the understanding that they were being looked after—as long as they were not told any differently from outsiders.

In the farming sector, there were fair and unfair elements. One of the unfair elements was the introduction of apartheid, a measure taken typically by somebody who was pushed by a foreign interference. In their self-determination, the Boers overlooked for too long the changes entering South African society. Their pertinacity sent them into an isolated state from where they lost touch with the new realities.

There were "good Boers" and "less good ones". The "less good Boers", however, brought down "the good ones". History has demonstrated this with the abolition of apartheid through Nelson Mandela, who gained the upper hand with the vast majority of the African population.

Despite all the good intentions, it appeared that South Africa first had to turn to the worst under apartheid, before emerging into a better system.

What initially happened was a change in roles, introducing the African majority with its own "good" and "bad actors". History will hopefully help to settle this conflict in South Africa for a better future for all parties.

This won't happen quickly or easily. A lot of lessons from the past and present have to be learned in the process with new sacrifices carried across the whole society of South Africa.

On a personal note, a letter reached me in South Africa from the International Red Cross that, for over 20 years, they had unsuccessfully tried to get in contact with me on behalf of my biological father. My step-parents had blocked all these efforts. Now I understood why the mail to their address was strictly their concern. Nobody else was allowed to look into the letterbox. This letter from my father made me cry—and that was the first time my wife had seen me like this. For the first time I knew that I still had a father and five siblings. In the letter was written: "At last I have found my stolen son! "

My biological father Michael had re-married the sister of my mother, who passed away at my birth. I could not understand what my step-parents were after. New wounds opened being now so far away and receiving this message. They couldn't stop any more letters from reaching me.

I started planning to visit Transylvania,where my father still lived. Why do we have to bear all these problems in our lives? There are much better ways in our lives,if we could use our brains more efficiently.

Life at home in South Africa unfolded without television at that time. People didn't know about TV, so they couldn't miss it. Some years later TV did make its entry into South African homes.

The mining activities high up in the Witwatersrand around Johannesburg left obvious signs with the big dump hills. The deepest underground mines were here. A vicious system was here in place: the main African tribes had been in discord right throughout history, therefore a mine employed opposite tribes engaging them in the first place in a case of likely disputes, before reaching the "European bosses".

Work generally stopped in South Africa on a weekend. The exceptional sunshine at a height of 2500 metres invited us to explore the African bush with its famous wildlife which could be found just outside of our town Krugersdorp.

Apartheid could not reach Africa's nature.

Contrary to other countries of the world, you were not allowed to keep your personal identification documents with you. There were too many foreign workers from neighbouring countries on limited time-permits trying to get hold of permanent identifications in the country. This was one of the main targets in an ambush, which occasionally happened outside towns. You were asked to present your documents at a police station within 24 hours, when identification was requested.

Crime was similar to the "wild west scene". Most Europeans had firearms but Africans were not officially allowed to have any. You had to be very cautious in dealing with uncertain situations. As the "liberation-process" shows today in 2008, nothing stops people in South Africa from pulling a gun anymore. Where societies failed necessary adjustments in the past, violent crime is taking a foothold. All that remains in these conditions is the hope of not being in the wrong place at a wrong time.

Coming back to the South African sunshine, there were wild-life parks,where people could drive through fenced-off areas of bushland and experience from a close distance antelopes, rhinos, wildebeest, zebras, giraffes,ostriches, lions and cheetahs.

*Old Lion in the bush—South Africa.*

*Cheetah—South Africa.*

*Rhino—South Africa.*

*Giraffes—Transvaal.*

Elephants are only found further north in Krueger's Park where there is enough vegetation for these "scavengers".

Out of the relative safety of a car, visitors could watch the animals up closer than in the wild, often coming in direct contact. People were also told not to leave their cars, because it would be a risky undertaking to escape from a lion. It is a special experience to come that close to wild animals in their natural habitat. The animals are more relaxed in such a controlled environment, having been regularly fed. Their hunting instincts to survive were not challenged here.

On one excursion, a curious zebra paid us a close visit. While looking along the windows of our car it reached the knob of the small swing-out window in the front. In a split-second, the knob disappeared in the zebra's strong set of teeth. Next in line was the mirror, which followed the same way. The zebra realised quickly that this food was no good, so parts of our car ended up on the side of the dusty road.

I moved the car out of the zebra's way before the windscreen wipers and the antenna received "another expert opinion". The zebra followed us in a typical zebra-gallop for quite a while. Our children in the car enjoyed themselves quite a lot.

The mainly dry weather of the Transvaal region favours, in some areas, the growth of cacti that rises to tree height. In this bushland you had to be alert because of snakes, which are no danger as long as you give them time to escape. Giving the snakes a warning is best done by knocking the ground with a stick. It is rare for someone to be bitten by a snake—driving a car in today's traffic is more dangerous.

A natural lake resort near Pretoria created an environment of more abundant vegetation. Luxury homesteads along its shores were well fenced off, barring access to the public. High walls, electric fences, warning signs and big dogs expressed the residents' safety concerns already evident in those years. This showed where wealth was hiding. Many houses outside city centres didn't show such safety features and often had beautiful gardens open for everybody's view.

Very rich people tend to live in isolation, afraid that something could be taken away from them. We definitely had no such concerns.

As life teaches us: "Every fate is equally formed, we all get our share."

Winter in Transvaal was special: during the day there were warm clear sunny skies while at night the temperatures dropped considerably below freezing point.

In evenings we usually had the old kitchen stove going full throttle, heating the house up to 25 degrees Celsius for a few hours. If we left a bucket with water in the kitchen overnight it was frozen solid by morning. It was so freezing in the morning that hardly anything could be done before the sun started to warm up. This was particularly uncomfortable in workplaces with tinshed constructions. Here, the first action of the day was lighting a fire in a jerry-builder which workers sat around to catch a bit of warmth. With the sun's regime back, the cold was quickly forgotten and daily work could begin.

A challenge waited at my workplace. The new manager introduced his ideas with a good amount of sophisticated politics. He backed himself up with support from the company's headquarters in Germany who wanted him to "sweep the company with a new broom". Whoever had connections at home in Germany, had a better chance of survival. The new manager established his regime and dismissed everybody he didn't like. It was also decided not to manufacture here any more, the company only being a distribution outlet for goods coming in from overseas. This was not something entirely new in the business world—but with manufacturing not required any more, I also became obsolete. I decided to leave this power game and move on before engaging myself in any political battles.

I had no problem finding other employment immediately, thus sparing any worry about how to keep living in South Africa. We still had a good deal of personal freedom here—which was very different from where we came from. We had no problems with the neighbours—children were regarded as an asset receiving respect and tolerance from everybody. They were the main considerations for staying on in South Africa.

A brief visit to Cape Town informed me of a new employment prospect. The surrounding Cape Province area had boasted the natural beauty of the mountains, grasslands, rugged coastlines and vineyards. There was also a more relaxed atmosphere than the pulsing city life of Johannesburg and its surroundings.

A move to Cape Town also meant an improvement in our environment. After my return to Transvaal, we thoroughly organized our next move with the assistance of my new employer. The relocation of our household was left with a removal company.

We could not see all the interesting parts of Southern Africa, because of our small children. From reports of other people and written information I formed this image of South-West Africa/ Namibia: The country being under the cooler influence of the Atlantic Bengolea current from the south is very dry most of the time. Specialized plants and the African wildlife have adopted to the harsh conditions. Sunshine is the rule there, rain is very rare.

A South-Western gentleman told me a funny story about when he visited Germany. In South-Western Africa it was common to ask: "Have you had rain this year?" The gentleman, arriving in Germany, also asked this question prompting his German counterparts to burst into laughter: "Asking for rain in Hamburg is the same as asking for sunshine in the Sahara, we haven't seen the sun for quite a while". In Germany, rain was the rule, rather than the exception. Only a Namibian explanation helped to bridge the gap in understanding: "We have waited seven years already for rain in Windhoek".

Despite its dry conditions, Namibia can offer a surprising diversity in its rugged nature: ancient mountain ranges, dry grasslands, desert stretches, struggling bush-forests, dry salt lakes in the Etosha Pan, tough African wildlife sharing the ground together with the ancient tribes of the Bushmen, Berg Danas, Nama, Hottentots and Hereros.

Europeans had mainly settled around the coastal towns of Swakopmund, Wavis Bay and the inland capital of Windhoek. During history, the country saw a short German rule that had left behind a lasting influence, mainly in Windhoek, with its buildings and some residents with a core of German descent.

Mineral wealth supports a relatively small population. The dry climate supported the exposure of minerals through erosion and its preservation during a long geological history. Gemstone lovers found a paradise here. Petrified wood pointed to an exceptionally old geological age of the area.

Upholding its principals, the UN had thrown another apple of discord into the political scene of Namibia. The UN couldn't see the realities that South Africa was protecting the northern border to Angola stopping the guerrilla war entering Namibia. The three official languages of Afrikaans, English and German point towards the special status of Namibia. A traditional connection to South Africa could not be denied. A majority ruling imposed by the United Nations did not take into consideration the construction done by all groups. Finally, the different representations of Namibia's society struck an accord even without the UN—an event with historical dimensions.

We decided to travel to Cape Town in our VW Kombi with our two dogs and a kitten. Traffic outside Witwatersrand, to the south, changed from heavy to almost non-existent. Wide, open grasslands welcomed us on a narrow bitumen road only wide enough for one vehicle. One had to stop on the side of the road to let oncoming traffic pass. Here was traditional Boer country. Single farm properties made a living out of these grasslands with large wheat fields. Not even bushland could take a foothold here. The next bigger settlement was Kimberley with its famous "big hole" from diamond diggings. A museum here showed the biggest diamond found in the world. The mining of diamonds was still current with respectable profits. Some substantial income found its way back into the region with investments towards big cattle and sheep stations.

Most of the year, these highlands remained dry under the intense South African sun. The little rain turned most of this country into brown-yellow colours. Wheat crops had to grow quickly to a harvesting size after starting with only little rain. Not even the African wildlife was visible in the barren conditions of these highlands where only the Boers could make a living. It was only further south in Cape Province that the green vegetation started to come back between the mountains. Wild, ridged mountain slopes surrounded the most southern tip of Africa, leaving only small passages to descend to the coastal plains around Cape Town.

*Lions Head—Cape Town.*

## Life in Cape Town

*Cape Of Good Hope, South Africa.*

*Camps Bay, Cape Town (1973).*

Cape Town's centre is dominated by the colossal formation of Table Mountain in the background. The Lion Head goes out to the Atlantic with the Twelve Apostles Mountains continuing to the east along the coast.

The city follows on the foothills of Table Mountain in front of a bay harbouring ships. This must be one of the nature's greatest displays on Earth!

Our arrival in Cape Town was accompanied by a hiccup with our car. On the last leg, the motor went on strike, refusing to work any longer. Where is a will, there is always a way out! A towing service helped us to overcome the last hurdle and get to Cape Town. With time we settled into a new house with views towards Cape Town and its Table Mountain. The house was only recently built in a new area of the south-western outskirts of Cape Town.

The sand around the house indicated the proximity of the Atlantic Ocean and the beach. Our household arrived in one piece but in a very strange fashion on an open wagon towed behind a truck. Our new home soon gained our personal touch. The two dogs and the children found a chameleon outside the house that took permanent residence on the arms of the chandelier in the living room. It was camouflaged there with its colour changing to the light-intensity of the day and in relation to the environment. No flies nor mosquitoes could be seen any more in the house from now on. The long specialized tongue of our chameleon was constantly on the lookout for passing insects. A chameleon can remain totally immobile, while its two protruding eyes move 360 degrees focusing on the insect. When the distance is exactly tongue length, the tongue shoots out of its mouth in a split-second. The very tip of this tongue is equipped with a highly-efficient organic glue, which makes any insect stick to it. Once an insect is caught, the tongue rolls quickly back into its mouth with the trapped insect inside. Depending on the insect's size, one could observe how the eyes of the chameleon moved further out to give the inside of its mouth more room.

You won't see anything escape from the chameleon's mouth.

It then takes the chameleon all its time to digest its prey—this food had to last for an unpredictable time. And, noticeably, the chameleon never received one drop of water. It is an amazing creature. I am sure the chameleon watched us in return.

Our son, Risto, visited the local nursery school where he learned both current languages—English and Afrikaans. The latter was basically Dutch with elements from English and French.

You were well advised to learn some Afrikaans if you wanted to be heard in South Africa at that time.

One day, I caught an Aurora snake in one of the premises at work. I put it into a cardboard box with a clear plastic window enabling us to look at the snake for educational purposes. At home I showed the children the snake in the box and told them: "This is a snake, have a look at it. If you see something like it, leave it alone and move away. A snake can bite, causing lots of pain". The lesson over, everybody had a look and then the snake in the box went into a spare room. The snake was forgotten there for a number of weeks.

One night the dogs' vicious barking from the kitchen woke us up. I went to have a look but saw nothing so I calmed the dogs down and went back to bed. A couple of minutes later the barking started again, even louder. This time my wife went to have a look and yelled straight back from the kitchen: "There is a snake in the kitchen". Off I went to the kitchen to catch a glimpse of what was going on.

In a corner of the kitchen, the snake from the box raised its head into the air, hissing and spitting at us. One dog's hair stood up while barking relentlessly at the snake, but he remained a good distance away.

The broomstick became the first "weapon" I could get hold of in a hurry and I tried to push the snake out of the kitchen door. As the snake became more agitated, it started to spit its poison towards me and the dogs. A minute splash of this poison in the eye would have meant certain blindness. The snake had a sudden change of mind and sought refuge in the gap left behind the built-in cupboards of the kitchen. What did we achieve now? The situation had turned to the worse. Removing the fixed cupboards was not a quick solution, neither was the use of fire. In the heat of the moment, I grabbed a bucket of boiling water and poured it along the edge of the wall behind the cupboards. We could first hear the snake escaping into the furthest corner, from where the boiling-water process started again in reverse until the snake cautiously appeared at the cupboard's outside wall. With the end of the broomstick, I smashed the snake's head bringing the chase to an end. After disposing of the snake, we could only try to get some sleep for the remaining few hours of the night.

Our minds were kept awake thinking about what could have happened, if the snake had moved either into our or the children's room—or gone hiding somewhere in the house. The snake had escaped from the box by using its saliva and tongue to make a soft spot in the cardboard and then it pushed itself through. The doors inside the house had a gap on the bottom that allowed the snake to move around the house. The fact that the dogs had a higher body temperature than us, determined the direction of the heat-sensing snake. The weeks in captivity had rendered the "aurora" extremely poisonous. Fortunately the children were not aware of this night's spectacle. The dogs barked from now on at every branch on the ground that looked like a snake—they even barked at bones.

One weekend the family decided to pay a visit to the French aircraft carrier "Jeanne d'Arc" which was docked in Cape Town harbour. The ship's arrival was announced on radio and in the newspapers, as there was yet no TV.

Driving through Cape Town, we were stopped at the traffic lights when a uniformed pedestrian asked us for directions. At first glance, we realised that the gentleman was a high-ranking officer from the French aircraft carrier. The gentleman's question was in English, and I answered in French: "Why don't you come on board with us and we will show you around Cape Town, if it's okay with you". The aircraft-carrier commander responded: "This is very kind of you. I'd love to accept your invitation but only, if you come to my ship after our sightseeing". Our trip went ahead on a typical clear sunny summer's day making it a memorable event for our guest.

Entering the exclusion zone around the ship with the commander Monsieur Moktaki it became obvious that our toddler Mirja required a nappy change.

The first officer said: "Our kitchen would be the best place to change baby nappies". On the way to the kitchen the commander ordered two of his officers to fulfill the task.

Everyone joined in judging the "special performance" on a warship. Everybody had a good laugh and many comments were made. The "operation" indeed succeeded and the nice-smelling toddler changed hands on deck.

*Monsieur Moktaki and Risto.*

Commander Monsieur Moktaki showed us around on the nuclear aircraft carrier. At the end of our visit, after a special photo with our eldest son Risto and the commander, we suggested that we continue with our sightseeing. We stopped at our home and offered our special guest a cup of coffee. To make our guest feel more comfortable, we invited over our French-Belgian friends. Then it was time for the commander to be back on his ship.

The nappy change on an aircraft carrier, a guided personal tour of the ship by the commander, an organized sight-seeing tour and a welcome at our home was a special experience for everyone.

The year could not have enough weekends to explore the beautiful Cape Province. A visit to the game park High Noon became a special event because of its rugged mountainous terrain that featured a colourful flower splendour in fresh green meads during spring and early summer. A peaceful country atmosphere welcomed visitors in the midst of a wilderness where you could drive for hours watching African wildlife from inside the car.

*Baboon in front of our car.*

*Zebra, taking a bite.*

*High Noon, Cape Province.*

*High Noon, Cape Province.*

Beasts of prey were kept in fenced-off areas well apart from zebras, antelopes, giraffes and wild birds. A number of mild-mannered horses waited in the entrance area to show visitors around the vast natural reserve on horseback accompanied by a guide assistance. The children also experienced their first horse ride. The natural beauty was just amazing.

Besides the game reserves, other breath-taking scenery was to be enjoyed along the coastline.

Near our residence, small individual bays along the Atlantic Ocean offered a relaxing beach life. Even in summer, the water remained rather cold in the area. In a naturally-protected pool near the sea our two dogs played in the water where they could reach the ground while our children played in the shallow surf of the sandy beach. The dogs stopped the kids from going further into deeper water, giving us time to relax on our own.

Following the coastline past the Cape Town bay and its harbour, other beautiful bays like Camps and Hout Bay followed towards Cape Peninsula.

The road led through a wildflower paradise. The proteas call this area their home. Cape Point nature reserve was also home to indigenous animals. Baboons roamed about the rocks of the coast. They disrupted traffic, easily jumping on to a car and trying to get something off the passengers. Despite warning signs not to feed the baboons, people still fed them. That attracted the baboons to the road. These ape species have particularly long, sharp front teeth enabling them to inflict severe injuries.

When we passed through the area, one of the baboons jumped out of the blue on to the front window of our kombi. By the number of baboon carcasses around, it was obvious some baboons perished this way. Our baboon decided to reduce my view by hanging on to the windscreen wipers. I immediately slowed down, not wanting the animal to fall off—with the result that the baboon ripped both wipers off.

It couldn't have much fun trying to eat them. We quickly left the scene—retrieving the wipers was no option.

At the furthest point of Cape Peninsula, high rock cliffs broke the fury of the oceans. The Atlantic to the west and Indian Ocean to the east meet here in a straight outgoing foamy line of surf. The Indian Ocean is warmer than the Atlantic creating an extreme weather pattern. In summer in the southern hemisphere horrific winds raged here in the midst of a clear sunny sky. A cloud band rolled off the edge of Table Mountain—a phenomenon found only here which is called the Black Doctor.

One time we experienced these hurricane conditions in the city: concrete-filled barrels were placed in regular distances linked with a heavy rope. This gave pedestrians something to hang on and not be blown away. This was a mighty display of the nature's force.

The bays along Cape Peninsula were of a particular beauty and featured the rugged Twelve Apostles mountains in the background. But swimming in the bays was dangerous due to the ocean's rip currents, which could pull a swimmer out beyond help. We pre-ferred to stay away with the children.

A visit on the cableway to the top of Table Mountain was also a great experience. Breath-taking views in all directions accompanied a walk on its flat top. To the south, vertical rockwalls fall down to a lower height where pine forests gain a foothold in the difficult rocky terrain. At the end of this vegetation line, a road was cut into the wall of Table Mountain giving views over the entire city.

Table Mountain drops to the east on a slight inclination continuing with the formations of the Twelve Apostles. You could also see a natural water-reservoir in the distance.

Lion Head mountain, which runs off Table Mountain towards the Atlantic Ocean, became a subject of our visit on a New Year's Eve. Only the last section of the mountain required a bit of climbing to its top. Upon arrival, we were alone, surrounded by the starry southern night sky above us—underneath us an ocean of city lights sent its reflection into the dark ocean. A unique New Year's adventure.

The seasons of the year were marked distinctly: in Transvaal, the north of the country, winter was the dry season, whereas in the south in Cape Town summer was dry.

With a view towards a unity in the country, the South African Parliament had two seats, one in its north at Pretoria and the other in Cape Town. It was not accidental that Parliament-time was chosen in line with the dry, fine weather season of each location. South Africa didn't spare the cost of moving its Parliament from one "resort" to the other in the name of unity.

Other worthwhile excursions around Cape Town were Stellenbosch and Paarl, renowned for their long tradition in the wine culture. They are located in the north-east of Cape Town on the foothills of mountains, both protected by a valley behind the Table Mountain. Long established cultivated vineyards produced outstanding wines under ideal climatic conditions. These wines carried the names of the locations Paarl and Stellenbosch.

A traditional conservative attitude had also left intact cultural marks on many buildings of Cape-Dutch architecture. Vintage festivities took place in March when locals were invited to witness the grapes going into wooden barrels and receiving the first "foot stamp" treatment.

A few weeks later in autumn, young wine was drawn from the wood for tasting in the guesthouses next to the vineyards. A huge wine-storage of stainless tanks including wooden barrels stored the vintage of each year, before ending up in bottles for the market.

The winter rain-season prepared seeds of wildflowers for spring showing up in colourful carpets everywhere. I remember one early Spring day, the mountain range of the Drakenstein-Berge was covered with snow on its upper levels while the surrounding meadows proudly showed their spring-flower carpets—a rare natural display. There are many beautiful scenes around Cape Town. The University of Cape Town, with its rugged mountain background, was surrounded by forests and green meadows. This was one of the most magnificent university settings in the world.

The beauty of this area could not divert from less pleasant realities. In Cape Province, "Whites", "Blacks" and "Coloureds" lived side by side. This co-existence worked as long as a tolerance level allowed it. The crime rate was at that time much lower in Cape Town than in Johannesburg. There was more tolerance than acceptance between the different groups.

This was occasionally demonstrated in daily life situations, especially during our weekly trip to a shopping centre close to the city. My wife was doing our shopping, while I did a couple of other purchases in the area. Returning to the shopping centre I waited in the car on the side of the road with others in a row. In front of me a utility was parked. On the footpath in front of the shopping centre there was quite a large number of people. The woman from the utility was on her way into the shopping centre. A tall black man walked on her side and removed the wallet from out of her handbag. The woman did not realise it, but her husband in the utility did.

He walked out towards the thief. All I saw was the thief trying to stop the farmer from coming after him. This turned out to be a bad mistake, because the farmer was much taller and bigger. He punched the thief in the face, grabbed him by the neck and upper leg, and threw him hard onto the ground. The thief's resistance had come to a quick end. The farmer picked up the obviously unconscious thief from the ground like a "flour bag" and tipped him into the back of his utility. As I had witnessed this altercation from my car, the farmer asked me: "Come with me to the police station across the road and witness what happened, will you?"

We drove a short distance to the police station. The farmer dropped the unconscious thief on the desk. The policeman said: "Get the bastard off my table, this is where he belongs," and he pointed to a corner fenced off with steel bars. The culprit didn't exactly land smoothly inside. The police listened to the farmer's story. The case was quickly closed with our two signatures and adjourned until further notice, if any.

Cases like this were dealt in South Africa in a very harsh way—it largely depended on which side of the population you stood. The police did not "muck around" to enforce their rule.

On a more positive note, in November 1974, our family welcomed a new addition with our son, Peter. This made two boys and two girls. An interesting comment reached us at the discharge of my wife with our new-born baby from the hospital. As we went past the administration desk to join our waiting children in the car, I was told: "First money, then the goods, this is how you are shopping, we make no difference to this rule here."

I must admit, such openness took me by surprise being reminded with such a comparison to pay for the birth of our child. They must have had their reasons to make a demand this way.

Everything went quite well at work, until I had to learn another lesson.

During our time in Transvaal, we met a young couple—the man having sound technical skills, which I would have liked to incorporate into my team at work. The owner agreed to make the contacts.

I didn't get any feedback and then was bluntly informed: "Your friend starts work in a week's time with us". I couldn't see anything wrong with that. The day arrived when the new addition started work. But he did not work with me—he worked close with the owner. As I had started over one year earlier, I still could not see anything wrong. I only learned from private contacts that our new man had started with much better conditions than I had. Politics was introduced again. This friend even followed the recommendations of the owner's wife to marry his girlfriend because: "In South Africa we don't accept relationships without commitments. If you want to succeed with us, you better get married". The quick marriage helped our "new addition" visibly to succeed in the company. I started to ask myself: "Why did I prepare the ground for this "intermezzo?" A clear answer emerged: do not mix your private interests with professional requirements. "The cuckoo always pushes another egg out of the nest." Before things could turn ugly at work, I withdrew most of my support from the "cuckoo"—giving him his share of responsibility.

Meanwhile a friend of mine lured me into his business, which the company owner didn't like. He thought he could have it all his way and still enjoy a "dance in both camps". The "cuckoo" could not hold his position and the company also ended up without him. "Who sets a trap for others, usually gets caught himself".

As I could see no future in the scarce employment possibilities at that time in Cape Town, I followed up the advertisement of an international company in Port Elizabeth.

It appears that where it is nice in the world, there are always less opportunities—by creating our problems, we also provide the employment to fix it, a perfect roundabout!

The trip to Port Elizabeth introduced me briefly to a multi-national company environment. While I worked on a test project, the people in the department "stuck their noses" unnecessarily into my presence suggesting all sorts of "political dirty tricks". I decided not to join this crowd.

Are big companies directed by capital with all its human resources, whereas smaller companies, especially family-owned ones, are they sometimes driven through the conflict within the different parties? Only throughout a lifetime can one get closer to an answer.

It is also, by all means, personality driven that some deal better with the "downsides" in life than others. Are we mainly on a receiving side in our lives? Opportunities come to us, bad and good ones, and we have to reflect on this. The main thing in our lives remains still to stay on track with a positive outlook!

In May 1974, news reached us from Finland that Arja's father, Petteri, had passed away from cancer. His prediction was unfortunately right as he said on my farewell: "I won't see that guy any more". Do some people foresee what life holds for them?

While we were still living in Germany, my step-mother's brother and wife from Brazil had visited us. During conversations they asked: "Have you ever thought about coming and living in Brazil?"

This memory surfaced now in South Africa tempting us to reconnect to it. Our first contacts were so promising that we couldn't resist giving Brazil a try.

Brazil's economy was at that time still booming. Qualified technical personnel were said to have good opportunities. The idea developed more and more in our minds. A language course in Portuguese was organized with very good success: each night the tape recorder was left running with the language course for one hour while we were falling slowly asleep. This method proved to be highly efficient. During the day, we remembered whole sentences in Portuguese and within weeks we were able to communicate in basic Portuguese. This certainly helped us in our contacts with the Brazilian Embassy in Cape Town.

We were about to burn our bridges in South Africa. Everything was ready for Brazil. Most of our possessions were boxed and we sold other possessions we didn't want—and we tackled the paper-war mainly with South Africa. Brazil came closer when we entered the Varig 707 Boeing plane from Johannesburg to Rio de Janeiro.

Our flight path went over Angola to its capital Luanda, but nobody on board actually knew this. We received this information only when the plane flew so close over treetops in bushland that the passengers became unsettled. The plane's crew and pilot remained calm and friendly. While we watched wildlife on the ground rushing away from the plane's appearance, our two older children received an invitation into the cockpit to have a look at the instruments and have a bird's-eye view of the flight. The door to the cockpit remained wide open. The relaxed Brazilian lifestyle was already welcoming us on board the plane.

When approaching Luanda airport, the situation became less relaxed. Everybody knew that Angola was in the middle of a civil war. Senseless killing took place here in a power game waged by only a few ideologically,sidetracked individuals—the result of past colonial arrogance.

We touched down under military protection. Our plane was flying low to avoid becoming a target. As soon as the plane came to a halt, everybody had to rush into the protection of the hangar. Despite this serious situation, most people remained calm.

After the plane was ready to take off, the military escorted us back to the plane with visibly more people than on our arrival. Our flight was scheduled to take paying refugees out of the country. Our children had to sit on our laps to provide the extra passenger seats. Tanks, which were supposed to protect our plane from rebel fire, moved to the side of the runway. What an introduction into Brazil! The plane took off steeply to get out of this troubled area. The pilots must have been well versed in this situation. Initial anxiety on board disappeared quickly when the plane reached its routine cruising height. The plane didn't show any signs of having a problem with its extra payload. Its four jet engines delivered us safely to Brazil. We arrived in Rio overnight passing above the coastline with a sea of lights underneath, bordered by the sea and the inland mountains. When samba music was turned on in the plane, everybody knew we were about to land.

The air smelt very different here—hot and humid. After leaving the plane, we didn't know who was a passenger and who was staff. The plane to Sao Paulo had left already. We had to find our way on to another plane and make sure we caught the right one.

People were less concerned about our enquiries and more interested in our kids. This was the first sign that we had arrived in a country where children were the "kings".

The next plane we boarded in Rio arrived in Sao Paulo. Through the night, the few passengers were kept awake with full-of-fire music. Our children walked in and out of the cockpit, picking up their first Portuguese lessons.

# Brazil

## Life in the State of Sao Paulo

My step-mother's relatives were as confused as we were upon our arrival. Nobody knew exactly where we would arrive, either at the Congognas City Airport or the Viracopos International Airport. To cover both eventualities, our welcome party had split into two—some at Sao Paulo, the others closer to their home in Viracopos, where we finally arrived.

Our clearance at the airport went fairly quickly, because the formalities eased substantially when our family welcomed us and they had already paid the required attention to the authorities. It is important, in Brazil, whom you know. The country doesn't keep doors open for new arrivals unless they have the right connections.

My uncle's son-in-law, whom we met for the first time, welcomed us. The Brazilian family's house stood in the countryside on a chacara—the smallest countryside property up to one hectare. The next size property was a sitio, while the largest properties were called haziendas.

The driveway of my uncle's "Chacara Austria" was a drive of more than 100 metres uphill before we reached the front gate.

The house had a granny flat next to it, where we were comfortably accommodated.

Until the second party arrived from Sao Paulo, we were introduced to the two housedogs, Susie and Baerly.

*Risto and Chica—Brazil.*

The family's pet "capybara" (the largest rodent in the world which lived in the jungles) was already asleep. Therefore we had to wait until the morning to be introduced to Chica. My uncle's eldest son had brought home all sorts of animals including an anaconda—the largest constrictor snake. Pets were not common in Brazilian households. That society did not have much regard for other living forms as pets.

From the first moment, we felt at home with my uncle's family. Their two grandchildren, Andrea and Alexander, made friends with our children straight away. They had waited for this moment to welcome playmates from Africa, the home of lions, elephants, giraffes and zebras. It was amazing to watch the children and how they got along despite initial language barriers. This is something we lose when we start to work on our "formal education",which is often used to distance us from others in a search for superiority.

The next morning the sun welcomed us to Brazil. Being in a higher location, the sun was considerably warmer than in South Africa. We were told not to worry right now about our next steps in Brazil. Our two older children spent one day in Sao Paulo with my cousin and her children, but they came back with the symptoms of meningitis from the heavily-polluted city atmosphere. From that moment on, Sao Paulo was declared a no-go-zone for our kids. Some others might have no option but to live there and bear the consequences. My cousin was therefore keen to visit her parents and to eventually move out of this city. We considered it a privilege to live with the support of a friendly family for our first days—and out of the pulsing life of a Brazilian metropolis. It turned out particularly good for our children to adapt slowly to life in a new country.

There was plenty to discover already on the chacara: lemons and oranges in the trees, beautiful flowers of frangipani, poinsettias, islands of bamboo and palm trees. During the first weeks we also helped to clear the high grass around the property as fire prevention.

My aunt proudly introduced us to the locals in the nearby village of Vinhedo, a typical village with its "praca central" (central place) in the shade of old-grown elm trees. Tables with benches underneath in the midst of gardens invited people to meet here after the heat of the day had given way to a cooler night breeze. This tradition can still be found in Portugal and Spain, where many Brazilians originate. Today Brazil is considered the oldest multi-cultural society—and has its old problems as well. Everybody in Vinhedo now knew that some African imports had arrived. All the people were friendly, forthcoming and ready to help. A simple life could be found in Brazil but a majority of people were deprived of a good living standard. Poor people are used to helping others—its the only way for them to survive. Rich people are often too busy to do so.

Our German shepherd, Mars, arrived in Brazil not long after us. The other dog, Pluto, we had to leave behind. Mars was very shaky when he first left his special box from the plane. No wonder after such a detour from South Africa via Germany, then to Argentina and finally Viracopos. The main thing was that Mars survived this long-distance flight, probably because of the high insurance we paid.

Once recognising us, life visibly returned to Mars and the joy on both sides became so great—a feeling only experienced between the best of friends.

We had to keep our dog well controlled and away from the dogs of the house. Once, though, they got stuck into each other. My cousin, Thomas, interfered in a dangerous way in trying to pull the dogs apart. He was lucky that our dog was still recovering from the flight tranquilizers.

Before life could start for us in Brazil we were required, within a fortnight, to supply our fingerprints at the nearest police station in order to receive identification documents. This was the first indication of the level of crime in the industrialized parts of Brazil. Even we were not spared from coming face-to-face with crime, but that did not become apparent during our first weeks there.

My first visits to manufacturing companies revealed, how low the income was. The currency of the "cruzeiro" was traded so low internationally that one US dollar equalled 2000 cruzeiros. In other words, an average income of 4000 cruzeiros per month represented 2 US dollars.

Naturally the cost of living was also very low, so people still managed to make a living out of an income. A big number of people without an income had a struggle on their hands to survive—and this included crime.

My technical experience enabled me to find a company where I started work as a draftsman. Not long after, I moved my family closer to work. We bought a small hobby farm with a modest house on a country hillside. The price was 1000 US dollars which at the time was quite affordable. I could even lower the price paying in foreign currency.

*Our Chacara Finlandia—Brazil.*

People in Brazil could normally only buy what was produced in the country. Only a selected number of people had access to foreign currencies that enabled them to buy expensive foreign goods.

The economy of Brazil in those days had some good directions with a competitive domestic production, but the government could not stop corruption with foreign investments and goods. Money was especially hard to get for ordinary people. The higher inflation rate compared with the interest rate of borrowed money secured a profit for everyone, who could get money from a bank.

My job also included a company car as an additional bonus and this helped us move more freely around.

Despite a high depreciation of the Brazilian cruzeiro towards foreign exchange rates, life in the country didn't become affected to that extent. Prices also moved up here, but not to the official high inflation rate. The price-wage spiral was kept down during those years under the military rule. A social movement in the late 1990 abolished the internationally enforced low level of Brazil's currency to replace it with the "real" which was initially equal to the US dollar.

This move also hit the secret foreign currency reserves of many people living a privileged life.

Our lives on the new property were, in many ways, extraordinary. We had a lot of work to bring the property up to standard.

When we first looked at the place, it was obvious that there was a conflict of interest between the younger and older generation of the owners. The elderly couple enjoyed their retirement away from the hassles of the city, while the younger generation wanted to sell the place and get hold of the money. Trying to spoil a deal, the elderly couple must have dumped all their rubbish around the house, making the place look less attractive. Ignoring the situation because I wanted the place, I looked past this artificial mess. A deal came together and the transaction was documented in the local court register.

We spent every available moment cleaning up the place. The company where I worked urged me to use the cheap labour of a "caboclo"—a Brazilian farm worker. Most of them were mixed between Europeans and Blacks brought in from Africa during early colonization. Brazil created their own slogan for their dominant human race: "café com leite", meaning: coffee with milk. The light chocolate colour of their skin, mainly females, attracts a lot of

Carnival visitors to Rio from around the world in January.

Brazil has a gentle, friendly population, which most of the time ignores the problems of poverty surrounding them. They know exactly how to enjoy their lives. Such an observation from outside should not ignore the fact that the high crime rate in the country is also a release-valve for its poverty-stricken population. Brazilians have learnt to live with poverty, they are good actors. They know that it has always been like this and will not change in a hurry. It is however essential to be careful, not to be in a wrong place at a wrong time.

Coming back to our "caboclo" called Deus, he did what he was told, as long as he felt comfortable. After receiving his pay he disappeared into his shanty town near the city, returning only when he had no money left.

People can have very different mentalities around the world. Economical, social measures have to take those differences in consideration; what is applied in one place, doesn't necessarily work in another.

In Brazil wages were not entirely paid to one person, there were different regulations: for married couples the wife often received the husband's wage through a bank account in her name; single incomes were often not paid in full, part of it was put into a savings account to educate people to manage their income. In the case of "caboclo" Deus I did the wrong thing paying him the full amount. A couple of weeks later he turned up asking for work again and realised that I had taken on somebody else. The second labourer was a Black with the name Nelson. He looked strong, but he didn't apply his strength at work. He didn't know about the existence of our German shepherd, as the dog remained quiet in the house. One day, however, I just prevented the dog from ripping Nelson into pieces when he tried to sneak into the house. I also realised that he had a pistol with him. I sent him straight off my property, warning him not to set foot on my land anymore. From that moment I didn't bother to employ anybody any more.

In the eyes of a "caboclo", we also belonged to an "elite" in Brazil—but this was a wrong perception. As a matter of fact, there were conflicting attitudes about who could lay claim to being "elite".

During our time in Brazil we were invited into real elite conditions. The host lived in an exclusive double fenced area, where armed guards controlled the area day and night. Depending on who paid the most—the landlord or the crime syndicate from outside—the guards maintained their vigilance.

The host was proud of his luxury set-up in isolation expressing this: "From where we come, we are more intelligent, that's why we are the bosses here". These were the words of an international company director's wife. We distanced ourselves in a Brazilian way ignoring those people with their comments.

Before we really could continue on our property, I went with the owner to the International Plastic Exhibition at Dusseldorf in Germany. We needed to make new business contacts. Despite a serious connection to religion in their lives, Brazilians were very open in bilateral human relations. They like their "amisada", an enjoyment including both sexes. It didn't take long to find this out about Brazil.

Many "meninas" (young females) believed it a privilege to become a central-point in men's lives, even for a short time. Such free enjoyment with others surfaces specially during the Rio Carnival season—make sure you are not caught in the wrong way. After the work at the exhibition in Germany, my Brazilian boss took me to porno film screenings and eventually to the red-light district. A local tried to introduce us to a "compliant lady". I cannot forget the look on her face, when I told her: "My wife looks much better". My boss didn't like the occasion spoilt like this, it was certainly not the Brazilian way!

On a positive note, by sheer accident I met an old friend in the middle of a crowd at a railway station. We could only have a short conversation, because we were about to organize our return flight to Brazil. At the exhibition I also met a friend from Cape Town, who expressed his interest to move from South Africa to Brazil like we did. It is sometimes amazing, how distances in the world seem to shrink and bring people unexpectedly together.

Returning to Brazil, we had a stopover in New York to catch a direct flight to Sao Paulo. The flight path was over Greenland. The plane's captain announced that this was a rare moment to have clear skies over this part of the world. Green fjords became visible along the coastline limited by snow and ice masses on emerging sharp-formed mountains.

On our stopover in New York, the "New World" showed us its busy face with its modern progress. Every person,who arrived in America was fully registered and on departure deregistered again. Here I received confirmation, if you were not deregistered within three months, one could have been called to do military service in America.

Earlier, when the Vietnam War was raging, I declined a job offer in America, because of this regulation.

Outside Kennedy Airport the big "yank tanks" caught my eye. America displayed its wealth everywhere but there was not much cultural background visible. Outside Europe many countries had their pride in new developments, building on a traditional image still for many years to come.

Whether their developments will reach that far, remains to be seen in an increasingly faster developing world.

Back in Brazil, I received notification that our household removal goods from South Africa had arrived in Santos, the coastal shipping town in the State of Sao Paulo. Everything to do with administration in Brazil had to be directed by a "despachante". They were registered agents who dealt with Government administrations on behalf of private people and businesses. It was a relic of the past, when the majority of people couldn't deal with administrations because of a lack of communication and writing skills. A fee paid to a "despachante" usually started with a request. The amount paid and the supplied references determined the speed in processing the request. In my case, I had a strong connection through my uncle's son-in-law, who had a high-ranking position in an international company. This connection helped to get our goods out safe and quickly from harbour customs. I was allowed to wait for the clearance. While waiting, it did not escape my attention how other shipping consignments were treated. The key to success in Brazil was money and connections.

The harbour town of Santos was very hot and humid, not really a good place to live and work. While there, I paid a short visit to the beach. The water was very warm—much warmer than in Cape Town. A surrounding steep coastline blocked the heat with the humidity, creating an unpleasant sauna-atmosphere during summer.

The road climbed here in many serpentines to a high plateau, where many trucks slowed the traffic down, giving everybody behind an incredible taste of a diesel pollution.

This narrow passage was many years later redesigned in a perfect traffic solution—a new highway cuts straight through this steep coast in one line high above ground. It is a civil engineering masterpiece. There was also a new highway being constructed from the city of Sao Paulo. I experienced the first real huge city atmosphere here.

Sao Paulo is located in a wide depression of a high plateau, which doesn't allow its pollution to escape easily—the whole city was a dangerously polluted area. Its 20 million population of that time, a constant traffic chaos, high-rise buildings as far as the eye could see and slums on its outskirts, created the basis for an environment with many question marks. Here was a perfect example:

We create our own problems, which asks again for solutions to keep up the circle of our activities.

In a concentration of dimensions like Sao Paulo we find everything we can think of: a concrete jungle, a natural jungle around Butantan Research Institute of antivenoms for snake bites, mostly incredible hidden wealth, poverty beyond imagination, devoted religious expressions, brutal senseless crime, state-of-the-art industry, a huge soccer arena, an airport, the "favelas" (the millions of poverty-stricken, disappointed migrants from Bahia in the north of Brazil), broad "avenidas", skyscrapers with washing lines hanging across the whole facade, parks… you name it, you will find it in Sao Paulo.

It was most of all the sheer number of people and motor vehicles filling this city to a bursting point that left an impression. It was quite normal not to use your own car in Sao Paulo, because finding a parking place was a "lottery situation" and if you found one, somebody was most likely to take it forcibly from you.

I left this "inferno" and returned to the undisturbed life on our property which was located not far from where Brazil's "mato-grosso" (great forest) started.

In time, we changed the house inside and outside as much as we could do ourselves: new timber walls and ceilings, floor tiles, paint work inside and outside including the roof tiles, granite "foliettas" for garden walls.

What we could not change was the water supply coming out of a well which was safely located inside the house. The well was 60 metres deep tapping ground water from our hillside. The pumps and pipes never worked properly at that depth—we had more water supply from the tropical storms out of the sky. They were so regular in summer that people used to say: "Do we meet in town before or after the storm?" Our problem with the water usage did not stop with the well, the shower in our bathroom supplied good electrical shocks, if not used in the Brazilian-way: stay out of the shower, turn the hot water on and then go under the shower. Not following this procedure and standing first underneath the shower gave you a "decent" electrical shock by turning on the hot water tap. This indicated that electrical installations were to a "special standard".

I remember one of our German visitors rushing out of the shower promising loudly to never use a shower in Brazil again. By the way, he was an electrical engineer!

Electrical fuses were very easy to fix: a paper-cylinder filled with sand with a wire in its centre; as long as a fuse-wire remained thinner than the supply line, anything could be improvised to overcome a power failure.

Outside the house, on the lower side of the property we had 80 citrus trees equally spaced. The trees were kept in a good shape, so we had more than enough fruit for our own use and to give away. On our boundary we grew a row of banana trees. Tall bamboo grew also in the bottom corner of our property. Where we lived the climate was tropical.

Despite the altitude of 900 metres above sea level, we had still to be cautious because of health risks. The children were better not to run barefoot on the dirt like they could do in South Africa. The dust here contained microscopic larvae of bloodworms, which could easily enter our system and cause serious health concerns. Grubs from the "bicho bern" (screw fly) waited invisibly on leaves to be transferred just by a touch of the skin, from where they worked their way underneath. Within days an ugly swelling of infested maggots could develop in any living form. The dogs knew about this and became immediately alerted, when they heard the deep sound of a screw fly buzzing in the air. The flies are always out depositing their minute eggs.

It was recommended to have a "medical clean-up" of our system at least once a year to prevent serious health risks, which were widely responsible for the low life-expectancy in Brazil. Nature was still dominant, despite all human civilization efforts. Our children could watch newly-hatched birds in their nest between banana trees being devoured alive by masses of black ants. In nature's terms, the nest was in the wrong place and everybody else was well advised to leave the black ants alone.

I had to learn another lesson with other ant species when digging with the shovel in the garden—half the soil was full with ants. One species was so small, it could hardly be seen. But when disturbing them, they made you instantly aware of their presence. They are called "lava pes (wash the feet).

The first you know that the ants are on your feet is that you feel like you are standing in a fire. When this happened to me, I don't know how high I jumped to get out of the place and shake off the "pest" as much as I could. The pain reminded me of them for quite a while longer.

It is not the case that danger is waiting in nature for you everywhere. It is more important to know what to expect,when doing a wrong thing by nature. Spiders and snakes cause danger, when they become disturbed in their habitat.

Living outside of populated areas like we did, begged for extra caution, especially when there was no phone available. At that time people were actually buying houses to gain access to a telephone. We had no hope to get a phone in our area. There was no " jeitinho" (bribe) big enough!

Brazil's wealth included tropical timbers that were used without any knowledge of their value. I saw with my own eyes on a concreting job, a cinnamon-timber being used. This should be declared a "sin". Even valuable timber like "embuia" used on houses was often painted in pink making the natural beauty of the timber disappear.

The colour of many houses pointed towards the Portuguese heritage, but back in Portugal tropical timbers were not ready available like in Brazil. Tradition had its influence that way.

I bought myself various timbers to make my own beautiful furniture out of embuia, peroba and Brazilian cedar. Peroba was available in lighter and darker colours. The expert could tell which one to use and not to use, but not being an expert, I learned my own lessons.

Light peroba could not be worked on after it was dried, only when it was freshly cut.

If timber were used with more care towards its proper use, we could save a lot of timber and not have to cut down so many trees. Only by running short of something, we usually wake up and realise its value. Quality timbers were very cheap in Brazil at that time. Trucks bringing raw timber from the jungle often sold their load on the way to a first bidder saving them a troublesome drive into cities. You could buy a truckload of tropical timber for 10,000 to 20,000 cruzeiros, which amounted to 5 to 10 US Dollars. What an irresponsible waste of nature's treasures!

In its central State of Minas Gerais, Brazil had large deposits of manganese-iron, which was exploited to earn foreign currencies. The same area harboured a wealth of gemstones. People with a gemstone hobby found an "el dorado" here. In my collection with my eldest son I still have beautifully-coloured Brazilian agates, one enclosed with visible pre-historical insects in water. A rare discovery!

In the local European community the news circulated that musical instruments were practiced in our house. This brought us in contact with people of similar interests without moving around and looking for them. In time, our house boasted an ensemble of different musical instruments, including a guitar, and we mainly played baroque music.

The dirt road to our house became impassable after heavy tropical rain, therefore these meetings were good-weather events.

One night, our neighbours, a Lebanese family, needed our help to get the wife into a hospital, because her baby announced its arrival. In the haste of the moment our kombi slid off the road and got stuck. In the pouring rain, a neighbour further down the road was called to assist in getting the woman to the nearest hospital. Our joint efforts paid off, because the woman arrived in time and delivered a healthy baby. Such nightly interruptions were quite common when living outside a town next to the Brazilian jungle.

At work I learned about the skills of Brazil's workforce. Its workers were always ready to learn something new and their skills were remarkable. Brazil's fast-growing population created its own competition pool. It was especially the young people who made big efforts to advance themselves.

I remember a couple of cases where engineer candidates stayed back late on their own accord just to get an opportunity to be taught in a specific technical field. They were grateful students, the kind I only met again in Australia later on, as I was also training refugees from Vietnam.

Going to university was for most people impossible. A secondary education system was instead used to reach academic standards. This was of a particular interest for me, because also I came from such a background, but from Germany. When thinking that I had done my share in efforts back then, I had to learn what efforts a number of young people did here to advance to an academic level.

One student worker went every day after work on the bus to Sao Paulo, a 120-kilometre trip one way to attend secondary night education at Sao Paulo Technical University. He returned home next morning to have just three to four hours sleep before starting a new day's work.

He never appeared to be tired though, he was always full of energy and attention.

There is a reason behind the slogan of the Brazilian flag which encourages with "Ordem e Progresso" (Progress through Order) to move into the future.

Just when you thought order was not the outstanding identification of this nation, you would be surprised to find perfection here and there, though not widespread; typical for new developing societies competing in a global market. They are often more energetic and flexible in pursuing their goals than traditionally accustomed-societies. However some individual demands could be left in limbo.

I mention here that when I eventually returned to Germany from Brazil, I received comments like: "The banana bender is back ". They will also learn in Germany that other nations are not "sleeping" and they better watch out that they do not fall behind. Economies like in Brazil are more driven by their powerful needs, where everything follows stricter rules. This was reflected in many ways when talking about skills in Brazil: stonemasons worked in Brazil for "peanuts" yet their work was so good that one could ask what drives them to perform to such an excellent standard? It can't only be the poverty surrounding them! There was a pool of willingness and skills waiting for their future to surface in time. The granite flags that were delivered to my property were one example. They were nicely worked by hand to exactly even sizes of 50x200x400 millimetres with the top and bottom surfaces smooth and the outside roughed. The grey Brazilian granite with its black spots is by all means very hard! And then considering the price of 500 pieces for 5000 cruzeiros made you to think how they could make it so cheaply.

Colourful granite was often used to shape double kitchen sinks, including the benches, out of one piece in a mirror finish. And don't forget, this was done in hard granite. A stonemason working with a wrong approach on the veins of a granite block would most certainly not be able to finish a sink in one piece. I cannot recall having seen somebody in Europe doing this kind of skilled work. In many parts of the world we boast of progress without realising that we have lost many creative skills. Computer assistance often helps today to undermine skilled creativity and "give the less-privileged a chance".

Looking at Brazil's health system, it left a lot of questions unanswered. The only straight answer was that medical professionals enjoyed a status to such a degree that the majority of people could never afford to see one of them. Brazil had helped itself with by a liberalization in medical treatments directly through the pharmacist. His advice didn't cost anything and in most cases, his medicine kept patients alive. Many pharmacists had developed, in my view, a very good understanding of medical conditions and helped people in real terms. We experienced only once a serious medical condition, when our children quarreled outside the house and one of them was pushed on to the sharp edge of a granite flag. My wife acted rationally and calmly to bridge the time until I came home. There was only one quick way to the nearest hospital. The treatment my son Peter received did not impress me—only his stamina helped him to get through this ordeal.

An absurd thing happened also to one of our friends: she turned up for a routine consultation, ending up unknowingly with an operation accompanied by a hefty bill. If her husband had not been employed by a large international company, that paid for these expenses, he probably would have had to sell his house to cover this huge bill. Sometimes we have to give in, we can't win all the time? Especially in front of a powerful institution like the medical one. Luck is often the best helping hand.

The company I was working with initiated a couple of dirty business tricks, of which I became only aware when three months had passed without wages. One bank manager had facilitated loans for real-estate transactions. But when he was suddenly removed from his position, the money-laundering scheme fell apart leaving a financial mess behind. I was not prepared to share this burden and moved to another overseas company. If you knew the right people in Brazil, you were never let down. Word of mouth usually carried you further.

Business in this new place dealt more with the industrial powerhouse of Sao Paulo. On various business trips I learnt more about this "hubbub".

The old highway to Sao Paulo, called Via Anhanguera, was constantly under repair, before the new highway could be commissioned. Traffic to Sao Paulo was like "hell on earth"—there were big, dangerous holes in the road and sometimes dogs would cause a traffic hazard. Many dogs were killed attracting the "urubus" (vultures), which caused more traffic chaos. One day, in front of me I watched how bits and pieces of the "urubus" flew up in the air in front and between cars.

In this rushed business world of Brazil, animals in general didn't enjoy much respect. Business came first. I was amazed how little damage these big birds of prey inflicted on cars.

The only thing that really stopped the traffic was the police. Nobody dared to argue with them, they had all the back-up of the military government. Nobody talking about it, but everybody knew that a money note in the back of a driver's licence could help a lot when dealing with the police. Neglecting this point wouldn't get you far. The police could also establish something wrong with your car to make you pay what they asked for. The country's police force was definitely not overpaid.

Coming closer to Sao Paulo after leaving the dogs, urubus and police behind, it was better to keep your car windows closed when passing the city's sewage plant. Shortly after you passed the shanty town called "favela" which sheltered cardboard, timber, tin and newspaper dwellings used by an unknown number of people living here in an incredible poverty. Many came from the north in search of better living conditions. They were here in their millions. Not being able to find work because of their lack of qualifications, they waited to see what their destiny held.

"Favelas" were a no-go zone for other people because no guarantee of a return could be given. Brazil had a huge problem with this migration from its northern region of Bahia. This was unfortunately also the result of an early deforestation, which created large desert-like areas taking away the living conditions of the people. The deforestation hasn't stopped—the desert is growing also in Brazil. We have to wake up and stop such trends.

A flight to Europe during daylight hours can show you how the Amazon River mouth pushes into the Atlantic and that starts off the Golf Stream that continues through the Caribbean keeping most of Europe ice-free because of a regular supply of rain. It can be also seen here "that all we on Earth are one and in the same boat". Deforestation in the Amazon area will eventually bring the ice back to Europe. Our lifespan is unfortunately short and we can't look much beyond it.

The misery in the "favelas" on the doorsteps of Sao Paulo was hard not to notice. Straight behind this mass of poverty-stricken individuals rose the end of the airport runway—a different world started here all together. The take-off and landing of aircrafts could not disturb this world of poverty any more. Who was to blame for this situation? Was there anybody really concerned? In private comments with my boss about these conditions, he had only to say: "Don't look at it, look away from it, this is not my concern, Brazil is not only like this".

He was right until we were with overseas visitors in Sao Paulo crossing a busy intersection filled with a massive crowd of people. A lad in his early teens violently got hold of my boss' arm and ripped off his hand bag, disappearing into the crowd. I looked at my boss. We said nothing knowing that he was actually lucky not to be confronted with a knife or a gun. This lad was most likely from one of the favelas bringing something home to help his family to survive. Thus, it was evident that their problems easily became other peoples' problems.

Disproportionate wealth in countries like Brazil, in itself, appears like a crime. As it is well known, different polarities attract each other, not necessarily in a wanted way, but this eventually unleashes crime. The indifference on one side of a society creates a strong vacuum on another side. We should aim for a balance, where fewer people are left behind.

An incident I experienced during carnival season demonstrates how close I came to being involved in a crime scene during our last year in Brazil. It was January and I was driving to my boss' address in a VW beach buggy he had lent me the night before. I had to pass through the outskirts of a shanty town. A bar with a coffee shop had a couple of tables and seats positioned partly on the road. The place looked busy with an untold number of onlookers around. When I drove past it, a tall black man with black long hair, a full beard, his shirt and trousers in a "sorry" condition, rushed suddenly onto the road in front of my car raising his machete towards me. Whether he was drunk or not, didn't matter for the moment. What did matter was, how was I going to stop this confrontation. Slowing down my car, I watched the man to move to my side. I stood no chance of defending myself—the car was open on its sides and top. The man stepped to the side. I accelerated and hit him with the side of the car and he flew through the air. I didn't stop to find out what happened. Three hours later, on my way back home, I chose to take a long detour home to avoid this place. I later learned from the neighbour's "caboclo" (farm worker) Chico that the offender received on-the-spot harsh punishment from the people in the coffee shop. Believe or not, they used the offender's machete to cut his right hand off. This was taking the law into their own hands, with the result that the offender had no hand any more to swing his machete against anybody. I avoided the area of this incident from then on—not wanting to get involved in any revenge attacks. The case must have disappeared fairly quickly from people's memory. What a harsh reality!

The sheer size of Brazil meant there was a big supply of natural undeveloped spaces. The country's first endeavours to decentralize from the coast to further inland started in 1891 with the first settlement of Brasilia. In 1960, it was decided to develop Brasilia into the capital of the country with its ultra-modern architecture. The main architects, Oscar Niemeyer and Lucio Costa, worked on a concept to advance Brazil into its future, leaving everything else aside and creating something totally new with its capital Brasilia in the Goias-Highlands.

This initiative has not gone far enough since to turn the whole country around into a wider progress.

Other initiatives like the "Transamazonica" became too much of a challenge for the present time. Maintaining a highway through the Amazon Jungle proved to be impossible. Nature with its "mato-grosso" (jungle) closed in faster than the road could be kept open.

Social problems of Brazil reduced the dimension of new initiatives as well. New political moves towards a democracy absorbed more and more attention for a fast-growing population. It appeared also in Brazil that social demands restricted new development concepts. Were Brasilia and the Transamazonica been just a one-off? At least they were in the last millennium.

Brazil moved into hostile territory with its environmental issues in those days. A new supermarket chain demonstrated a typically-successful business: with their profits they bought land in the Amazon interior and paid to cut down the forest for new cattle stations. The meat from there ended up in the supermarkets, a clear cycle to control the profits better. People who stood in the way of such developments reportedly got shot by contract killers. International organisations didn't perform much better in saving the indigenous Amazon tribes to gain access to their land with or without the knowledge of the authorities in the country.

Demands for progress from within and outside Brazil have put non-proportional measurements into the place to succeed, disregarding losses of its natural resources to which indigenous people also belong. We know this happens all in the name of progress with its attachment of a profit. When can we learn to change to more sustainable forms of progress? Will this be only when it is too late and we are forced to adjust? We can only hope this won't be the case.

Advancing into our third year in Brazil, we learnt that even the private preschool had its own problems in store. Our children developed from others purulent head skin infections. At least our eldest son was spared this experience at a private primary school. We stopped sending the younger children immediately to preschool in the expensive taxi transport—school buses didn't exist in Brazil.

I have to admit, people in Brazil had to put up with their problems and eventually succeed in their goals. They must have been better primed for their problems by knowing nothing else. We always relate to what we know!

In our case, we had reached a point of moving on from here to the disappointment of the many friends we had made in Brazil. One special friendship with the neighbour further down the hill brought us together for many exchanges of philosophical thoughts. Maria and Romeu lived on their "Chacrinhada-Nona" in their retirement. They were always very friendly and helpful. They came to our rescue one day when I was at work. The kids were playing in the garage and one of them had got locked in. The heat of the day demanded quick action. My wife's first thought was to put the culprit in through the window so that he could open the door from inside. The plan did not work. Our neighbour, Romeu, was called to the scene. Despite being in his late seventies, he easily found the solution by pushing the pins out of the door hinges and removing the door. The situation was finally saved. A poetry booklet by Romeu is still with us today in Australia. His words represent the kindness and sensitivity of the Brazilian people—a contrast to the country's realities. Can strong beliefs, not finding fertile ground, feed on crime? He put this dedication in the book: "Ao meu culto e feel amigo Martin, ofereco como pura da minha sincera admiracio"—Jundiai—18-9-1977.

*MENINA POBRE (a religious devotion)*
Maos postas, ajoelhada aos pes da Virgem,
Ao Pai Noel sua boneca pedia
E baixinho tambem rogava ajuda
Do meigo Jesus e da Ave-Maria.
E quando a aurora do Natal surgiu.

*NATUREZA EM FESTA (a devotion to nature)*
Numa noite serena muito clara
A natureza alegre quis brincar.
Convidou as coisas do ceu, da Terra,
A virem as belezas exalter.
Muito sofrega a brisa ja soprava.

(Note: Translating poetry is quite difficult! With some Spanish or Italian language knowledge, a reader could understand the essence.)

Brazil and its people were mostly a great experience for us at our home base. But we were not prepared to share in the long-term circumstances surrounding the people. Brazil had already moved for too long away from a migrant country with a pioneering attitude. The country was in the firm grip of its own problems. We learned a lot in Brazil—good and less good lessons.

One lesson was a wake-up call for us. While taking steps to sell our property, we hit a "snag". The property was still in the name of the previous owner, despite all the legal formalities being done. I became very determined to track down the previous owner, dragging him to court and making him register the property in our name. Somebody must have initially bribed the procedure. I was lucky to locate the previous owner after two years and get him engaged in a new procedure. If I hadn't found him, I could neither have claimed ownership of the property, nor sold it. Brazilians used to say: "If everybody is out for a " jeito" (bribe), nobody bribes anybody".

Regulations for leaving Brazil were under a very complex military rule. Our friends tried to talk us out of it, because hardly anybody managed to get out of the country without "feather plucking". Over a period of six months I was visiting authorities daily, as well as locally in Sao Paulo, paying fees and " despachantes" (middle-men) to arrange our departure from Brazil.

The company helped me with the dispatching of our household. Once the sale of our property was over, we were ready to move on. The family in Brazil was understandably not very happy with our decision, but we looked into the future and this was how we wanted to deal with it. Brazil was another lesson with good outcomes as well. The people of Brazil had given us new ways of looking at life, so we moved on with more wisdom.

To get around a mountain of regulations, we left the country with our car, including our German shepherd. The dog did a good job keeping everything out of the property. If one of the neighbour's dogs dared to pay us a visit, our Mars grabbed the intruder on the neck regardless of the size, shook him and made him to leave the property helter skelter. One night, our dog became entangled with a "Vila Brazileiro", the biggest and most vicious dog on earth. He chased this intruder off the property, but not without harm.

Another German shepherd from a German migrant's property became the only dog accepted on our property when he sought refuge after a vicious knife attack from the German's servants. The dog, Alfa, received only compassion from our Mars. Alfa recovered under our care but one day was forcibly taken by his owner, who rarely was at home, from the spare room of the house, while we were away. He was well advised to keep away from the rooms in the house where our Mars stayed. What a "great" understanding between countrymen! Alfa was never seen after that.

I'd like to mention that of my step-mother's relatives came to Brazil in 1930 with a lot of enthusiasm. Leaving problems of our civilisation behind, they escaped into the jungles of Brazil hoping to live a more simple life. Many people dream about it but very little is known of an outcome in such a move. These relatives worked incredibly hard to provide their basic needs. They succeeded first, but couldn't progress later on. The new problem of isolation caught up with them in a tragic way. This doesn't mean that escaping from the demands of our daily lives will necessarily have a tragic outcome for everybody. Leaving progress behind will always be harder than going with it. We can only change the nature of problems—they are with us, their existence is caused by ourselves. There are many reasons supporting a view that we are hardly better off than somebody else. "The ups and downs in life make us more equal". In the case of the relatives, their destiny went little by little from hardship to tragedy. Wrestling a living from the jungle meant also, pulling rocks out of a river, cutting trees by hand for housing materials, collecting and cultivating what was needed to feed themselves. This was a never-ending demand, where an exchange in work and goods was abandoned. Finally after years of relative success, they faced a turning point in their lives. Health became the biggest challenge. An injury in a tropical environment is the biggest danger. These relatives were also intellectually motivated keeping in touch with the outside world through the language of Esperanto. Aunt Erika was an international tutor for Esperanto. Tragically, their only son succumbed to a snake bite. Not long after the father Alexander passed away due to ill health.

The circle of events didn't stop there. Their jungle property was submerged in the floods of a new hydro-electric project. Erica went back to Vienna after living 50 years in the jungle. She tried to build a new life for herself at the age of 90—a life that could not last much longer. How could somebody face such a lot of personal tragedy? When we move in our lives, we can be never sure of the outcome. The same happens, when we don't move. Life was never meant to be easy.

Our preparations to leave Brazil went according to plan: our self-constructed container was picked up first for storage in a "safe" place to be delivered later to our new overseas address. We bought a station wagon with enough room for the whole family. A closed trailer was hitched behind the car carrying our belongings and food for the duration of our South American tour.

Once the family, including Mars, had taken their place in the car, the tour started in early October, 1977. My uncle received our furniture as a small consolation and thank-you for their support. He only retrieved some of the furniture, however, because the new owner of our property wouldn't give him access once he moved in. Who does not come in time, will miss out eventually.

## South America Tour: Brazil

Driving to the south inland first, dense forests changed into more scattered forest areas with bushland in between. Trees in yellow and red flowers announced springtime—the rainy season was not far away. While in Brazil, we had hardly looked around the country. Brazil was not yet ready for tourism in its wide territory like South Africa at the time. Our plan was to experience the country and the whole continent of South America on a tour after nearly three years in the country.

Still inland in the south of Brazil, on the border of Paraguay, lie the Cateratas de Iguacu (Iguacu Falls), the largest water cascades in the world fall from the river Parana into a long deep trench, which continues into Paraguay and Argentina. The river mouth is in Rio de la Plata around Buenos Aires. The suspension bridge across the canyon was a "Red Indian" construction able to take single courageous visitors, but no groups. This deficiency later turned out to be a disaster with an increase of visitors—people fell into the raging currents of the gorges. Keen explorers could even gain access behind the water cascades running from the river out of the canyon.

Going back to the coast, we met with cities again. Most areas on our way were unpopulated. Influences of German migration could be seen in the more moderate climate around the cities of Curitiba, Blumenau and Florianopolis. The road leading along the coast revealed the last tropical flora with special banana trees, of which the little bananas tasted like apples. For that reason, they are called banana de maca (apple banana). One bunch went on board with us feeding everybody for a while.

A tent in our trailer was abandoned here because of the heavy rain. Its installation turned out to be so complicated that we preferred to sleep in the car. A small incident, which should never have happened, reminded us to park our car at the end of a day in the direction we wanted to continue on the next day. Driving one morning along the coast, we realised that the day before the sea was on our left side so how come it was now on our right side!

Further south in Porto Alegre we visited my cousin, Purli, and his young family. On our arrival the car had to be locked away overnight to keep the local car thieves away. Parking in the street was no option. Purli had a good relationship with the locals—his collection of rifles on a stand next to his bed demonstrated this. We also met his father-in-law, an Englishman whose wife was Brazilian and Purli was Austrian-born, a good Brazilian mixture.

Our tour went ahead from here along coastal lakes to Uruguay. On the border Brazil confiscated the number plates of our car, not allowing us "to take Brazilian property out of the country". Thus we had no official identification for our car anymore. We encountered problems dealing with this situation from time to time as we continued our holiday tour.

## Uruguay

Sunshine welcomed us in Uruguay and we dried up from all the rain from Brazil. The wide flat grasslands reflected a calm atmosphere but this was only on the surface. The country was in the grip of Tupamaro rebels, destabilizing it unpredictably. But during our visit we did not experience any problems.

We stayed for a couple of days in the capital Montevideo in the south on the shores of Rio de la Plata. In contrast to Sao Paulo, Montevideo was a large "country town", quiet with not much visible activity. People were more relaxed and friendly. In a music shop we were invited to sign a guest book and were given lots of useful information about South American music, best represented with a guitar. The shop owner accompanied us to other shops helping out with his local knowledge. Houses in this beautiful city were very well built in a southern European style with white walls, arched veranda passages and stylish half-round tiled roofs.

Montevideo must have seen good times. Conditions seemed to have turned around here at that time. The Tupamaros challenged the authorities resulting in an increased stagnation of its economy, mainly of wheat and meat from the fertile flat country.

Buenos Aires, the capital of Argentina lies across the wide Rio de la Plata delta. Before leaving Uruguay, we celebrated a family birthday in a Montevideo restaurant. The meal turned out in a typical way, one huge piece of well-done meat on each plate and nothing else. The taste of the meat was the best impression the country could give. It was, however, too much to eat.

## Argentina

A ship took us across Rio de la Plata. Custom officials in Argentina inspected our trailer that carried most of our personal belongings plus a range of groceries. Everybody remained friendly, while we made conversation in Spanish. Only in Brazil do people speak Portuguese, because of their colonial history with Portugal. The differences are not that much. They can understand each other, if wanted. Argentina was another country in the grip of its own rebels at the time. The effects from it became more visible than in Uruguay. Bad news of abductions and murder sprees had reached overseas. Not long after our arrival we found out that people were highly intimidated by the events in their country. An uncertainty lay heavy upon people's otherwise joyful, open character. The much larger size of Buenos Aires did not appear much different from Montevideo with its low level of activities.

In Brazil we were given a useful "black-market" address to change Brazilian currency into US Dollars and German Marks. The exchange place reflected the tricky nature of such a transaction in the middle of a volatile rebel situation in the country. Mainly "insiders" from the industrial powerhouse of Brazil used this address weekly to exchange currencies—but only for two hours on a specific day.

The address was top secret. It was only passed on in certain circles, and not without risks. Guards with machine guns protected the entrance and the interior of the private residence. Argentina needed Brazilian currency in an economical exchange with its bigger neighbour. Therefore it was possible to access foreign currencies only here. Once inside the address, I had to clearly identify myself, progressing then to a table where I put my currency down, surrounded again by a number of armed guards. My money was closely inspected before it was passed through a trap door into another room from where only other machine gun barrels could be seen. A piece of paper with handwritten figures came back from the trap door asking me to accept, which I did. I was not sure whether I would lose my money or not. When the exchange came through, I knew we had made a good deal. Securing this success, it was best to leave the area as fast as possible.

Our tour through South America and a new start somewhere else depended very much on the outcome of this transaction. It showed again, the right connections in Latin America meant everything. Criminals were also in Buenos Aires on a constant lookout. While driving out of the city centre, I asked another driver at traffic lights for the direction of the address given us by friends in Brazil, whose parents still lived there.

The gentleman in the other car indicated for us to follow him—he would show us the direction. After one hour's drive on a highway we were still in Buenos Aires. He stopped on the side of the road and came towards us: "We are not far from my home, I would like to invite you to my family, before showing you the address which is close by. I am from Scotland, do you speak English? How did you arrive here in Argentina?"

For the rest of the day we were guests of this family. The wife was from Argentina; their children were two boys and one girl in their teens. We all had a lot to talk about and with night closing in, our hosts insisted that we should stay in their house overnight.

People with special qualifications could still live in Argentina relatively well, even during these troubled times of internal terror. All South American countries were under military rule—democratic initiatives were nipped in the bud with a brutal guerrilla-style war. One had to be careful not to get caught in such actions.

Next morning our host family showed us to the address we were seeking. We had a letter from our friends to introduce us to their parents. However, nobody answered the doorbell. We decided to wait across the road under some shady trees. We did notice movements from behind the curtains in the house. It appeared that somebody was home. Some moments later, an elderly man came halfway towards us out of the house. As I handed his son's letter to him, he spoke briefly to us in German, expressing his security concerns with the neighbourhood. The elderly couple was under constant fear of being denounced by somebody. All their children had fled to Brazil and Europe to escape from random prosecution in the country. Our meeting on the road remained brief, the gentleman was afraid of receiving visitors from outside Argentina. Here we experienced two opposite cases of people living under the same conditions. The Scottish gentleman and his family just went on with their lives, despite the constant threat around him. The elderly couple, like many others, possibly got caught in their own fear. The real situation in the country could most likely be judged halfway between those cases.

It was better to do our shopping in town by leaving our car with the family on the outskirts of this huge city. A quite modern transport system had been put in place here. A train track was built suspended in the air to allow traffic on the ground to remain undisturbed. Using this train link brought me well and truly into the city centre. Leather clothing could be bought quite cheaply. I was not keen to buy at my first encounter with a retailer, who approached me on the footpath. I began bartering with him, but he bluntly rejected my first offer. I walked away and then the retailer caught up with me again offering a new price.

Offering to pay with US Dollars reduced the price to a degree that I could not resist. Our transaction of goods had to be completed inside a building, off the road, to keep the money exchange out of sight from any witnesses. With the rest of the shopping done, I returned on the train to the city's outskirts, where my wife with the kids had spent their time in a nearby small park.

The day had turned already into late afternoon and we decided to continue our trip rather than spend another night on the side of the road opposite the elderly couple's house. Just before we left, the elderly couple came out and invited only me into the house that I witnessed the wall-photo-recollections of their past life in Germany and Argentina. Their stories told of the better times the country and its people had seen.

*La Pampa, Argentina.*

Despite night closing in, we got on our way and moved out of Buenos Aires. The road led through flat and vast Pampas country—the bread basket of Argentina. Ancient black soil supports here a rich harvest. The weather had changed from sunshine on our arrival in Buenos Aires to steady rain throughout all the Pampas. As soon as we left the city behind, the traffic reduced to nil, especially during the night. Thinking we were alone on the road, we started to speed up, but not for long. Having just settled into a steady progress on the road, I could not have stopped quickly enough to avoid a huge black bull in the middle of the road. His black colour made him difficult to recognize. I came to an emergency stop just centimetres before him. I was anything but calm at that moment—just like the bull. He looked sidewise through the front of our car without moving as if wanting to say: "What are you doing here?" Driving into this massive bull would have spelled disaster for us. Even when I drove around him, the bull remained firmly in one place with only his eyes visible in the darkness of the night. I instantly reduced my speed to a safe visible distance.

While driving the children could sleep comfortably in the back of our Brazilian Chevrolet caravan. Our German shepherd had his place on the floor of the other front seat, where my wife assisted by entertaining me with conversations and tape music. We stopped a couple of times during the night while the rain continued uninterrupted. We passed the city of Mercedes with the first cautious daylight coming through heavy clouds. The weather did not invite us to stay. At this time of the year—October—Springtime in the southern hemisphere brings the rainy season and when it has started, it stays around for a while.

Petrol was very cheap in Argentina, the country was self-sufficient with resources spreading from the south to north in Chubut, around Mendoza and in Jujuy. With the mineral resources and agriculture on top of it, Argentina could be considered a very rich country. It is a pity that internal conflicts had thrown the country into an economic downturn.

Argentina's cool south with its mountains and forests to the east can be compared in its beauty with alpine European areas in Switzerland or Austria.

Fireland, its most southern point opposite the Antarctica is a very difficult sea passage for shipping with its unpredictable sudden weather changes, accompanied by ferocious storms. Until the shipping passage of Panama in Central America was finished in 1914, all shipping went through Fireland from the Pacific to the Atlantic Ocean and in reverse. The name of "Fireland" originates to the early days of shipping in the area, when the first passage of the Portuguese explorer Magelhaes took place in 1520 and he saw the fires of the Red Indian tribes, probably signaling each other about the arrival of foreigners.

Bariloche in the State of Rio Negro is a world renowned ski resort.

The rain had followed us all the way to Mendoza and on the foothills of the Andes the rain rather intensified. A two days' rest was decided. We watched the rain persisting from a park house with a workshop and petrol station. When lining up for fuel, a young service attendant quickly put the petrol nozzle into our tank but did not turn the pump counter back to zero. Watching this, I got out of the car and read the figures on the pump. I didn't know how many people had filled up before. According to the figures, it must have been half of Mendoza's population. I went straight into the office complaining: "My tank doesn't take that much petrol. I am not paying for what your pump shows." After lots of talking, the boss asked me: "How much are you prepared to pay?" I replied: "I won't pay more than my tank can take even though it was not empty". The pump could now wait for the next "blind" customer.

The clouds before the Andes hung very low obscuring the area's vineyards which were situated on the foothills of the Andes and produced the best wines of Argentina.

Not knowing if the weather would improve, we decided to continue our tour. To get to Chile, we had to cross the Andes which reach a height of 7000 metres in the area of Cerro Aconcagua. A great experience lay in front of us. Soon after Mendoza the road followed narrow winding valleys first up and down, before starting to climb uninterrupted. Steep rocky mountain slopes cut into the sky, no trees could grow here. The area is ecologically too young, rocks are the only materials. The Canon Del Rio Atuel breaks open a view in the highlands before the mountain peaks appear covered with eternal snow.

We were alone on the road, stones and dust took over from the bitumen. Up to Uspallata, before the Chilean border, a railway line also climbed up, parallel to the road. A number of tunnels cut through steep mountain slopes protecting the track from avalanches.

*Border, Chile, Aconcagua (6940 metres)*

## Chile

The border control at Uspallata lies at a height of 3800 metres next to the majestic Cerro Aconcagua, the Andes' highest mountain. Its peak showed no cloud, the rain remained behind us. At that height winter ruled all year around. Our border clearance went without problems. Chile received us at the height of Pinochet's "war of power". An incredibly steep concrete road led on the Chilean side down through a deep cut-in valley. Rock boulders on the road indicated that the mountain slopes were not stable. One eye on the road, the other one in the air helped in avoiding being buried by a rock avalanche.

The road quickly descended, leaving the snow behind in the higher region. Green valleys started to take over and small forests appeared in lower parts.

Single houses surrounded by gardens and trees resplendent in spring flowers were a touch of "paradise" after the harsh Andes. When the road entered open land, the capital Santiago came into close range.

Canola fields with their yellow were in spectacular contrast to the naked stone background of steep rising mountains.

The increase in traffic and people announced well ahead a pulsing life in Santiago.

Like the previous countries on our tour, Chile also went through a phase of military rule led at the time by President Pinochet, who spread uncertainty with fear through his claim to power. Our stay in Santiago was only of a short nature. Its people were not exactly forthcoming. Shops in the city along many broad avenidas offered everything at prices which apparently most locals could not afford because they failed to be part of a normal busy city scene.

We couldn't make any contacts at the time, people in the streets kept very much to themselves, probably a reflection of the wide insecurity in the country. Paying a visit to the hard ruler of this country was definitely not on our minds! Having finished looking around the city with its modern and traditional Spanish face, we carried on with our tour to the north. We were unaware that Pinochet's Secret Service had noticed us. We spent our first night away from the road outside the city. Our dog bayed in the middle of the night, throwing everybody suddenly out of sleep. Two police officers knocked on the car's side window and demanded to see our identification documents. The dog had frightened them initially so they had first their pistols ready. The presence of our children saw them approach us in a friendlier way. After having thoroughly examined our passports, they finished their investigations. This interrogation ended peacefully and we were left alone for the rest of the night.

The plateau, where Santiago is located, drops to the north through a rocky canyon down to the coast. The vegetation suddenly changed here to dry bushland. On the Chilean coast the long Atacama desert owes its existence to the Humboldt Stream from the Antarctica which creates extreme dry conditions. Clouds from the east cannot reach this area as the Andes mountain chain stops them. Control points on roads leading to the capital were introduced by the military junta.

On our arrival at the northern checkpoint at the entrance to the Atacama desert, a plain-clothed man approached us and followed us to the checkpoint. He must have known that I had a German passport because he addressed us in fluent German. It was suggested that we follow the gentleman's car for our own safety. Another two checkpoints came up within a few kilometres and the presence of our official company allowed us to pass without any hassle. We didn't ask any questions. We mainly watched to see what else would develop.

With the night drawing closer, we were asked to stay in a government work depot in the desert. The depot and its many buildings were surrounded by a wall. We were free to accommodate ourselves for the night, but were cautious with food offers from other people in the camp. The night passed quietly. When being told in the morning that we were free to continue our travels, we realised that the gentleman had observed us and didn't see any suspicious circumstances.

From now on we could start to pay attention to the unique area we were travelling in. The road changed between bitumen, stone, dust and sand. Rock boulders lining the road were pushed out, when they tumbled down from the mountain slopes. The steep Andes limited this coastal area, the road was always close to the Pacific Ocean. Its cold water current boasted lots of fish, which the flocks of pelicans constantly demonstrated by diving into the sea and visibly pulled out a load of fish in their large beaks. Sometimes their beaks became so full they could not close them, losing part of their catch. Sometimes the cheeky seagulls stole the fish from the pelicans' beaks while they were still flying.

The early morning hours here were very foggy. Exactly at 11am, the sun broke through the fog, creating brilliant clear views for the rest of the day.

An olive-green bush vegetation with hard leaves appeared occasionally. The colours in the area changed from yellow to reddish and black sands, white spots were saltpetre, brownish stone was copper.

It is said that it never rains here. But when it does like in late 1970 after more than 100 years, this world's driest desert becomes an explosion of colourful flowers, of which the seeds were dormant waiting only for the rain. People from all over the world came then to witness this miracle which lasted only for a few days. New seeds went again into the ground, waiting for the next rain.

*Japanese around the world cyclist.*

We met not one vehicle on the road. From Santiago to the border of Peru in the north covers 2000 kilometres with only a few hamlets in between. Antofagasta and Arica on the border are the only significant settlements with a small human population of mainly Inca descendants.

In this solitude of a desert world to see a Japanese bicycle rider was like seeing a mirage. We had to stop and engage into a long conversation. The young man had an orderly appearance. He was organized to the last imaginable detail with his bicycle and back-packs. Asking him, if he was in need of anything, he bluntly refused and told us: "Accepting help, I could become dependant and risk my tour around the world". This was something to think about and we began to especially appreciate our South American tour.

North of Antofagasta are the richest copper deposits known on earth. We stopped for a break at a small resort in the area. Some rich people from Santiago had their summer residence there. A servant of a nearby villa told us: "The owners are very rich, they can afford to share their luxury with somebody else, but you have to be out before the weekend." To make his decision easier, I gave him a bonus, which he visibly appreciated.

We also used the break to re-organize ourselves after the wet days in Brazil and Argentina. The temperature in the area was a pleasant one and this misled us to thinking, it was okay to expose ourselves to the sun. Less than one hour in the sun was enough to cause bad blisters on the skin. I first realised this, when I saw our children's backs—but it was too late, we were all sunburnt. The dry air must have been the cause of such intensive sun radiation. Marks from this incident have remained with us to this day in the form of freckles. In later years, when looking at each other's freckled back, we had a standard saying to explain it: "Chile!" Our stay was quite relaxing until the owners of the beach property arrived unexpectedly on the Friday. Their distrusting faces appeared as if wanting to say: "What are you doing here?" Initial scepticism turned soon into curiosity, opening the way for discussions: "We have never had visitors from Germany or Finland here in the Atacama, you are welcome as our guests." The Chilean couple expressed their joy to have visitors in this isolated place and asked us to stay longer. They arrived in Antofagasta with their own plane. It was good to see that people in Chile had not lost their kindness, despite the recent political upheavals by Pinochet's military junta. Everybody had to be vigilant and not give cause for an interrogation, which could easily have led to a prosecution.

With a permanent sunburn and good memories we continued our journey further north. Every now and then a checkpoint turned up in the middle of nowhere. The officials asked for identification and the so "generally beloved money".

In Arica we arrived at the border of Peru. Still on the Chilean side, we heard the National Anthem begin broadcasting on the radio.

Every person at the border was asked to stand ready for the salute, including us. Nobody around knew what the occasion was. It must have been one of those measures from the military rulers to test the loyalty of the population.

If somebody did not stand and salute, he was most likely reported—a vicious instrument of intimidation!

## Peru

On the Peruvian side of the border nothing seemed to happen. Hardly anybody was there and nobody was in a hurry. A pile of transit papers was destined to keep us busy for a while. After all the paperwork was done, nobody wanted to check it, because the boss had not yet turned up. Lunch-time passed in beautiful sunshine and still no trace of the boss. The rule was, as hardly anybody turned up at the border crossing: "What we can't handle today, tomorrow will be another day". "Manana". If this applied in general, I lobbied for exemption and convinced one official to ring the boss and let him know that there were four little kids waiting for his clearance. The boss suddenly turned up ending our waiting period.

The road into the country first went high up into the Andes, where the desert continued with no vegetation around anymore and the road cut through rugged rocky mountain areas. While there were only a few settlements along the road in Chile, the picture changed here with many settlements of the mainly Red-Indian descendants, the Incas.

Hamlets could be found here in the middle of the desert surrounded by reed-fences in order to protect their living areas from moving sands. "Cabanas de totoras" (huts) were properly built of reed mats, completely enclosed with only a door opening. The more we advanced into isolated areas of the Andes, the less the Indians took notice of us! The bad memories in their legends from early contacts with Europeans are still passed on today.

They tended to ignore foreigners, but still maintained their vigilance. Only in city areas or certain tourist places did they show their "kindness" as part of a tourist-business strategy. Indians led their lives like before in less accessible areas, away from the pressures of progress.

A bigger contrast in nature could hardly be imagined: the Atacama desert forms the coastal region of the Andes with the exemption of its very north and south. The jungle spreads past its peaks from the east into the Amazon basin. In the west there is no rain, in the east wet tropics feed the Amazon.

In the middle of the "altiplano" (high plateau) between mountain peaks lies hidden the ancient Inca centre of Cusco. The endurance of Inca workmanship can still be seen today in massive and accurate wall constructions as well as in the nearby ruins of Machu Picchu. The Incas came from Asia in the $12^{th}$ Century assimilating with the indigenous population. The only two areas where the ancient Inca cultures could escape as nomadic people were the "Sierra Nortena" and "Lago Titicaca". Today the ancient Inca culture is absorbed by development changes; another distinct identity has been sacrificed in the name of global progress. Identity was the password for a cultural survival. If a civilisation's identity is taken away in a survival process, their culture goes missing.

Our tour brought us back to the civilization centre of Peru-Lima. The day we entered the capital Lima—on November 2, 1977—it seemed we had picked the wrong time: garbage lay around everywhere, piled up on both sides of the roads and sending a shocking smell into the air. If the garbage collectors were on strike, they must have been for quite a while. However, the closer we came to the wealthy city centre,there was less rubbish and less smell. In the northern part of the city, where the wealthy people mainly lived, this disturbing image was virtually non-existant. What a situation!

Nine churches competed with 14 museums for attention. The museums displayed what was left after the brutal destruction of the Inca culture. A lot of the Inca gold helped to build the churches. Visitors today hopefully give the Inca culture the respect it deserves—this is all that is left for us to do.

On our tour through Peru, several times we experienced at petrol stations in unpopulated areas something that could only happen in Peru. Petrol was very cheap. The service attendant would often leave the petrol nozzle in the tank and walk away. The result was that the tank overflowed—this was probably to cash in on a couple more "Solos" (Peruvian currency).

The ground soaked with petrol could have easily spelled disaster if somebody had arrived with a cigarette. Luckily we didn't experience any place going up in flames.

On one occasion while we were driving inland we couldn't find a petrol station. Locals could give us only the private address of somebody who sold petrol.

Driving around for a while, we finally found the address—a lonely hut in a difficult-to-access area. At first I thought, this can't be it. However our request for petrol proved that we were in the right place. Inside the hut were 200-litre drums stored with mattresses on top of them. One of the family members had to be disturbed and get off the mattresses to give petrol to us from out of the drums. They asked double the price—but that was still very cheap. Their winning margin compensated them for the smell of petrol in the hut. Some people here liked to sleep on their merchandise, even if it was petrol. Dangers they didn't know, didn't concern them.

Coming closer to the border of Ecuador, tropical vegetation took the place of Peru's coastal desert. We stopped in Chiclayo—a typical Spanish-styled town—where influential locals gathered around an open central area that was surrounded by their stylish houses. The whole town population flocked around our parked car. Our German shepherd inside the car with our four children became centrepoint of their interest. Our dog finally settled down, while all the people rubbed their noses on the car windows to gain a glimpse. We could hardly get out of the car and move through the crowd towards a restaurant and surrounding shops. We gave a tip to an older man to keep an eye on our car. The deal worked and the crowd moved away from the car and followed us. It was good thinking to restore our energy with a big fish meal and to top up our food before continuing.

The closer we came to the border, the worse the road became—at some places it hardly existed. We had to find our way through dry bushland. A bridge over a dry riverbed had to be first thoroughly examined before we could take the risk of driving over it. A number of timber planks had to be put back in place. For hours wild donkeys were our only company in this wilderness. At regular distances of approximately 10 kilometres, checkpoints were established. There were eight of them before the Ecuador border.

After all these hindrances, including interrogations and inspections, we finally crossed into Ecuador by crossing a river bridge. Here we could experience how tense relations were between Peru and Ecuador. One main trigger was the disputed land claims in the Amazon where large oil and gas deposits had been found only recently. Another reason was the trafficking of narcotics, mainly cocaine, which was widely in use amongst the population to control the side-effects of living in the high altitudes of the Andes. Red Indians used to chew green coca leaves in order to boost their blood pressure and to overcome tiredness from a lack of oxygen. This cultural use of narcotics has been ambushed by other societies, misinterpreting and misusing the drugs for purposes other than medicinal. Peru obviously didn't allow narcotics to cross its borders, hence the reason for the tight border controls. Did they want to keep the profit in their country? The use of natural cocaine became so evident during that time that one only had to buy an "Inca Cola" to experience the stimulating effects of cocaine.

## Ecuador

In Ecuador we entered a different world again. Leaving the desert behind, we welcomed succulent forests—the transition from dry country to tropical rainforest. Forests of "Boab trees" with their bottle-like trunks created a striking appearance in mountain areas.

The existence of Boab trees represented a pre-historic fact that the world's continents were once in close proximity. South-East Africa with Madagascar, the Kimberley region in the north of Aus-tralia and Ecuador all have their ancient Boab trees!

*Towards border of Ecuador.*

The further we drove into Ecuador, the more tropical rainforests we saw. Water cascades appeared on mountain slopes everywhere. Going to the coastal town of Guyaquil, we passed the small town of Pinas where a car race was on its way. The whole population lined the roads on both sides to watch their heroes race like mad through the narrow dusty streets. All traffic had to stop and wait until the race came to an end.

People were so tightly packed along the streets that one wonders, what tragedy would have occurred, if a race car skidded off the road.

While we watched from a safe distance, a shop owner encouraged us to buy food from his shop. He introduced us to a fruit that gave the coastal town of Guyaquil its name. The guya only grew in this region, like cacao in Ecuador. Guya is similar to lychee fruit, only it is much larger and looks like a big green bean. Inside it is white and tastes sweet like a lychee. There are also black seeds inside. It was definitely a new taste for us. Locals praised the guya fruit as a gift from heaven.

The car race took nearly all day and this gave us a great opportunity to connect with the locals and share their enthusiasm. They would have liked us to stay in town (and buy their wares). Even here money started to drive their isolated world.

By afternoon we were finally able to continue our tour to Guyaquil. I remember reading that Guyaquil was one of the most contagious-disease places on earth. As we came down from the Andes to the coast, swarms of insects were so persistent that it was better to stay inside the car. Being at the equator, the air was extremely hot and humid, because it was blocked by the mountains.

Bananas were the beneficiaries of this climate. In banana plantations along the coast, the fruit grew to sizes we had never seen before. Red bananas could be found here as well. The huts in this region were high up on timber stumps, but didn't have any windows—it was the only way to beat the heat.

We found Ecuador to be the most beautiful country so far. Everything is close together: tropical rainforests, succulent forests and pine forests. The altitude range of the Andes makes for many climatic conditions. If you wanted it cooler and drier, you just had to go higher up. Exuberant vegetation was everywhere. From 5000 metres altitude the vegetation ceases to exist and the eternal snow starts to take over. Majestic formations of volcanoes crown the rich variety of landscapes.

Back on the "Altiplano" (highlands), we passed through Riobamba, a typical remote Indian township at a height of 2800 metres. Our car's carburettor started to play up again because of the lack of oxygen. Previous tricks of reducing petrol intake and taking off the air filter didn't work and we ended up stranded on the roadside on the outskirts of the town of Riobamba.

*Incas on the Altoplano, Ecuador.*

Indians going to the market with their piglets walked past us and didn't take any notice. However, our presence was noticed by the villagers, because soon a driver arrived and offered to help us. Jose was the mechanic at the nearby military post, where non-Indians were also posted. When Jose couldn't get our car started, he offered to tow our car to his home. He introduced us to his family, who lived in a modest flat in a large house block. While the children enjoyed each other's company in the sparsely-furnished living room, Jose towed me to the army workshop assuring me he could fix the problem. As this happened on a Sunday, nobody was on duty. With patience and time our car ran again. In return for Jose's efforts, I went to the local restaurant looking for food to take to his home. There was no food, so I bought a bottle of red wine. The restaurant, a central meeting point, was filled with locals. Everybody wanted to know where I was from—they had never met someone from so far away. I rejected offers of heavy alcoholic drinks, because this would have become a drinking bonanza. There was no need to get drunk entertaining ourselves. Jose and I preferred to spend the rest of the day at his house with our families.

*Riobamba, Ecuador; Jose's family and ours.*

Even with his qualified military job, Jose had very few possessions, but he was a visibly happy family man. The children entertained themselves with only a few self-made toys, while the adults shared the bottle of wine with spaghetti. We also put food on their table.

Our hosts understood quite well, why we didn't want our car to stay overnight on the road. They invited us to sleep in their station wagon while the children and Mars slept in our car.

The night passed quietly and without any incident. In the early morning hours, Indians walked barefoot with their little steps past our car. A colourful poncho of llama wool protected them from the night's cold. None of them came close to the car and looked through the window. They showed again surprisingly little curiosity. Was this because, having so few possessions and trapped in poverty, they could not compare themselves with others?

A hot cup of good Ecuadorian highland coffee with our hosts got everybody's day started. Jose went to the army workshop—we continued our tour through South America with a working car.

The higher region of Ecuador is of particular beauty: two majestic volcanoes stand out here—to the east is Cotopaxi rising to 5980 metres, to the west Chimborazo standing 6276 metres. Both are eternally covered with snow and are still considered active volcanoes. Small pockets of fir forests battle in these heights for their existence.

The capital, Quito, welcomed us with a green belt of vegetation climbing up the surrounding lower hillsides, giving this city a fresh, clean appearance. Churches and museums also compete here for attention. The Spanish-Islamic cultural influence has mainly driven the Inca culture out of the capital. Museums try to re-establish what is left of Inca culture.

A visit to the Volkswagen branch brought us in contact with the German manager of the workshop. I asked him to do a thorough check-up of our car.

While this happened, we toured the city and did some shopping at a modern supermarket. Cocoa goes back to Inca times. They harvested the cucumber-like fruit from the cacao tree. Ecuador is considered the country of its origin. For this reason, we wanted to also buy chocolate from Ecuador. But we tried in vain to find it. The chocolate we found instead was all Swiss chocolate for Swiss prices. What this meant was that while the cacao came from Ecuador, the chocolate was made in Switzerland and sent back to Ecuador in its new form of a chocolate.

In the shopping centre we also met the wife and children of the German workshop manager. Until our car was ready towards the end of the day, we were guests of this young German couple. They had enjoyed a couple of good years in this country but expressed a natural homesickness like most people develop in a foreign country after a while.

During this contact we learned some quite useful information about Ecuador: the tomato originates from Ecuador. After its discovery in the 16th Century, it was regarded as mainly a poisonous ornamental plant. Only in the 19th Century did it gain today's reputation of being a useful nutritious plant.

The potato is another specimen originating from the Incas in Peru and Ecuador. Eighty different varieties are cultivated here! The most common is the sweet potato. The Incas were the masters in "co-planting culture", which means they knew exactly what crops to plant together for their own support and protection. For regeneration purposes they also knew what to plant after a crop. In some areas we saw such dense crop cultivation of maize, potatoes, tomatoes, garlic, rye, cucumber and beans all planted together in one spot.

We have today "successfully" moved away from such practice—we mono-cultivate areas as large as possible and ignore the negative fallouts from it.

Another note of interest was the Inca camels—the llamas, alpacas, guanaco and vicuna. They were in their millions around during Inca ruling-times, domestic and in the wild. Today not many are left, especially the vicunas, the smallest of its kind. The alpaca, the more compact "sheep-camel-giraffe" of the Andes is more commonly found today than the graceful taller llama. Their wool in white and brown shading is renowned for its superior quality to sheep wool.

The male llama was still used as a reliable carrier of light loads across the difficult terrain of the Andes. Guanacos and vicunas are hardly seen any more, especially since the vicunas were pursued for their fine wool and skin. They have since retreated to the eternal snowfields.

The language of today's Inca descendants is "Quechua", which was mainly handed down verbally. Here are a few Quechua words for interest: machu = big, picchu = mountain, papa = potato, runa =

people, pacha = country, cori = gold. The musical instruments "sicuri", "quena" and "charango" can be seen as a cultural connection to the Incas. The "sicuri" is a multiple bamboo flute; the "quena" is a single straight flute while the charango is like a mandolin with five double strings working with a five-tone system.

Like the Quechua language, the music of Inca instruments was never written down, only handed down from generation to generation.

Coming finally to the food consumed in the Andes; the lack of protein from meat, milk and eggs was the cause of past generations of the Inca Indians to grow only to a small height. Today this has changed with an international exchange of goods.

This however doesn't reach a majority of the Indians, their stable diet is still maize, vegetables, potatoes, mandioca (cassava).

In higher regions of the Andes, hygiene is generally speaking not so much of a problem. In tropical areas on the coast and in the Amazon, food has to be seen in relation to hygienic risks.

Our conversation with the young German wife lasted for a while, so it was natural to accept an invitation to their home in the city. The mechanic's family lived in their own house that showed how they had adjusted to the country's culture in their living style. It was tempting to consider making Ecuador our new residence.

The Galapagos Islands in the Pacific belong also to Ecuador. They are known for their prehistoric wildlife of lizards, turtles, birds—everything living here is protected by the isolation. Darwin developed his theories of evolution by observing the Galapagos Islands and researching information of the Northern Territory in Australia. What inspired Darwin in those two areas was that the many wildlife creatures were pure descendants of ancient living forms that had been isolated for centuries. In reports from Australia, where Darwin never had set foot, nature's capacity of resisting changes through fire, flood, drought and even sea water, preoccupied his interest.

Our time in Ecuador came to an end and we had to keep travelling to the next country of Colombia, a largely unknown risk for any traveller.

*Equator (Linea Equinoccial), volcano Cayambe 5843 metres.*

*Equator, Ecuador—our family.*

Not far from Quito we came upon a sign in big letters, "Linea Equinoctial" (Equator). High up in the Andes on a tropical tree-boundary was a big stone-globe with a map of the equator and the point's location. Standing on the Equator was a must-have photo.

Further north, the road branched off into a field of boulders on a mountain slope. How such masses of boulders came here, was a good question. Above this rock field was a track away from the main road. We pulled in here to tidy up and rearrange our car and trailer. Not far from us worked a number of men in the rock field below. It was hard to imagine how somebody could possibly work with these monstrous granite boulders. We decided to abandon some items and gave these to the workers. They were thankful recipients—people who work on hard rock, welcome anything.

That night we preferred to stay away from the border to Colombia and have a good night's sleep in Ibarra.

The next morning we arrived at the border control of Ecuador and were told to go back to Tulcan for a departure permit. Here, all sorts of authorities had to have their say with a pile of paper. Their signatures allowed us to leave the country. As one could anticipate, there was no rush about this paperwork. Lunchtime was important, followed by a two-hour siesta. It was a clear message: don't bring rush into South America. We played by the rules and waited. At least on the same day we had the final stamps and signatures on our papers, allowing us to drive back to the border. The border crossing was then a reasonably quick process.

## Colombia

The next hurdle was the border crossing into Colombia. Nobody else was there trying to cross into Colombia. We were told that "nobody had passed through Colombia on the road before". We could not believe this. We were given clearance but our passports were given two temporary visas—one for us and one for the car. Thirty days for us, only five days for the car. No explanation was given. It appeared that they were after our car. Such directions not being enough, we were forced to take into our car a policeman, who should stay with us all the time. With luck on our side, the policeman got frightened by the presence of our German shepherd. A "solid tip" helped him in his decision to leave us alone.

One problem solved, the next one waited for us on a steep descending dirt road. It was already late in the day—the last sunbeams reached us from across the mountain silhouette. Despite the poor road condition, I was driving fairly fast. There were no other cars on the road, when suddenly two men appeared.

One man moved towards the car, but didn't make the distance in time, throwing a big board with nails sticking out at the car. As I had closely watched him, I suddenly accelerated the car to avoid the board. It actually passed between the car and the trailer. The message was clear, crime waited for us.

We continued the rest of our crossing through Columbia with great care. Some 2500 kilometres laid in front of us through one of the highest mountain areas in the world. Three times we had to climb from sea-level up to over 5000 metres on poor roads. We had one only thing on our minds—we had to make this passage in five days. Sightseeing was definitely not an issue.

We recalled stories from Brazil, where people told us: "There is no record that a foreigner has made the passage through Colombia". Well we took the challenge, because we had no other option.

As soon as we left the coast in Cali and turned inland, bad weather moved in. In a passage,where the road was cut into vertical rockwalls, water from the rain ran across the road in masses, carrying mud and stones. People in two cars behind us had stopped

to watch this mud current. A truck just in front of us continued its run slowly. Its big tyres pushed the mud and water off the tracks for just a moment. Watching this, I followed straight behind the truck, before the mud had its chance to close in on the road. My car spun its wheels for a few seconds, but then gained contact with the road so we could follow the truck.

The two cars waiting behind us did the same and followed behind us. It did not escape my attention that the wall on the side of the road was unstable. There was no time to think about anything; just keep moving ahead. I then watched in horror through my rear-vision mirror as the whole mountain behind us crushed over the road, taking everything in its path down the abyss on the other side of the road, probably another 2000 metres.

Never before nor after this incident I felt so shaken in my life. I had to stop and try to get over what we just experienced.

The two cars behind us didn't make it. I saw them thrown into the air from the rushing mountain masses. If we had stopped before, we would have been cut off completely. In such remote area, any help would have come too late.

Masses of water from the recent storm must have washed out cavities behind the rockwalls, filled them up and pushed everything in front of it across the road into a deep valley underneath. This was a moment we will never forget how lucky we were.

Our children fortunately didn't realise the full extent of the danger we had just escaped. I also knew that if our car had got bogged, there was no way we could have walked out alive.

I parked some distance up at a safe water cascade. Even after one hour of a rest, my legs still felt weak. It was impossible to think what had happened to the people in the two cars behind us. They were caught by bad luck here and could have vanished for ever.

A climb to Armenia at a height of 5270 metres directed us towards the capital Bogota. Men brandishing bush knifes in the middle of the road, made us slow down. They all looked through the windows of our car. When I asked: "How far is Bogota?" They answered: "Twenty-one hours with the car". I had to ask again: "Are you sure?" They reluctantly returned: "That's it."

Looking at the map, I could not believe it could take that long, because the map showed only a short distance. As we found out, they were dead right. It took us 21 hours to reach the capital Bogota.

Descending to the valley of Rio Magdalene we were not spared witnessing a bus in front of us skid off the road and plunge down a mountain slope of over 1000 metres. I stopped on the other side of the road in a safe spot and saw the bus way down on the bottom. There was nothing we could have done here without risking our situation. When something like this happened, it was no surprise that nobody took notice of it. No other car came past for a while, therefore our program was continued. We could not afford to go beyond our precious time limit.

From Rio Magdalene, the road climbed up again into the Andes. It was raining as we arrived in Bogota through a system of road tunnels. We were well on target for our five-day passage limit.

The Colombia we met on this tour was typical all the way: rainforests covering the lower levels of the mountains, changing into a different vegetation the higher we came.

Somewhere in the centre of Bogota we asked for directions, as the rain intensified into the night. A young man of a student-appearance looked into our car from the footpath and burst out: "If you value your life, you better get out of here as soon as you can; you are in the black-quarter of Bogota".

We certainly took his advice and continued our drive until we reached the northern suburbs of the city. The dark, heavy rain obscured our vision. We parked our car in front of a restaurant where horses stood. Despite the heavy rain, a couple of youngsters noticed us, but our dog's presence kept them curious from a distance. Meanwhile we introduced ourselves in the restaurant, and the proprietor assigned us to a table. A lot of men were around in the restaurant at the time. When ordering dinner for my family, I asked the waiter whether I could pay in American dollars. He went to see the boss and returned with him.

I was asked for identification and showed my passport. Afterwards the boss looked at us passing his flat hand in front of his throat. I was not waiting to answer his symbolic gesture, but pointed my forefinger towards him. No further questions were asked, the message was clear.

After dinner, we paid in US Dollars and received change in Colombian Pesos which we urgently needed to continue with our scheduled passage through the country. We had arrived too late in Bogota to see a bank for a money exchange.

Most South American countries had their currency in "Peso", Brazil had the "Cruzeiro", Ecuador the "Sucre", Venezuela the "Bolivar".

When we left the restaurant, the night had already advanced and the rain had not eased at all. Because of poor visibility we had to stop and rest for a couple of hours until first daylight better revealed the road conditions.

Sparsely populated areas lay ahead, a tropical "green hell"—the drug lords' territory.

As I mentioned before, the Inca Cola contained natural cocaine. From time to time during this trip, I drank the cola and the result was astonishing. Despite driving without a break, I didn't feel tired at all. If I continued like that, we could make the border of Venezuela in three days. The only car we met on this last section was stuck on a mountain pass. A couple of men were hanging on to the car to prevent it from going any further down the mountain slope. We drove past and didn't offer any help. We were not sure of the outcome, the men may have wanted to "swap" their car with ours. Trouble can make people inventive and many people here endured widespread poverty.

It was understandable then, why young boys turned up on the side of the road, occasionally with big stones in their hands that they used to smash the car windows of travellers. If this had happened in a wrong spot, it could have spelled disaster. When one lad turned up with a big stone, I had no choice but to threaten him—this worked in our favour. Further north, a long way from Bogota, we drove through valleys in the middle of dense jungle. Each valley meant going down from the Andes and climbing up to heights of 5000 metres again. In two cases we drove above the tree boundary at 5000 metres.

As we came closer to the border of Venezuela, the road cut through low land. We finally arrived in Cucuta, almost at the Venezuelan border, on the night of our third day. We wanted to celebrate but it was too hot. We found ourselves in one of the most uncomfortable climatic zones on earth. In the morning hours Cucuta hit 42 degrees Celsius, 100% humidity and no breeze. We parked near a police station thinking this would give us some security during our short break. The police were constantly chewing green coca-leaves to survive the incredible heat. Our presence raised the police officers' inquisitiveness and they even requested our passports. We quickly decided to move on because they started already to look into our travel set-up.

Three days of non-stop driving and the change from the heights of the Andes to this climate took its toll, especially on me. But we didn't even think to rest anymore in such a " hell ". Our assumption proved correct—as we reached the mountains again our wellbeing improved immediately. We passed through the Colombian border control in the middle of the night. It passed reasonably quickly because I stood my ground decisively, stopping the border guards from conducting further investigations.

## Venezuela

After crossing the border in Colombia, we were so euphoric that we missed the border crossing into Venezuela. After a short time driving, we realised our oversight and turned back to find the border crossing. The guards were asleep in their hut and had left the toll-bar open. Our caution to call upon their attention paid off with a quick clearance, so we could continue our tour into Venezuela with no worries. The road rose constantly uphill again leaving behind the area around

Lago Maracaibo, a heat-basin enclosed by mountains. Further inland rises Pico Bolivar to 5270 metres height—the highest mountain of Venezuela. Its name refers to Simon Bolivar, the liberator of northern South America from Spanish colonial rule. Dense rainforest covered the mountain slopes. As we travelled at night, we didn't continue for long. A path branching off into the jungle became our resting place for our first night in Venezuela. Having a real good night's sleep was easy after this tour of torment through Colombia.

An option to follow through Panama was abandoned, because the road through the tropical swamp areas never was finished. This was due to incompetence and differences between Colombia and Panama. The area was infested by tropical diseases. High up on the slopes of Pico Bolivar the night became rather cold. We managed to sleep even into daylight as the jungle stopped the first rays of the sun from reaching us. We were woken by a knock on our car window and our dog barking. A smiling face welcomed us. As it turned out, not far from us lived a family in a log cabin in the middle of the rainforest. Our children again received most of the attention. The family lived off cattle skin preparation—scraping the skins clean, disinfecting them with salt and drying them in a specially built shed. The skins had a variety of colours.

We were also invited to use their "bathroom facility" which was a hanging shower-bag made out of skin. At a joint breakfast, we received interesting information about the area. The family told us that Lago Maracaibo supplied wealth to the country through its oil wells. The oil pressure under the seabed was so great that oil was everywhere, even to the highest levels of Pico Bolivar. "Have a look for yourself, how easily we can make a bitumen road here. The road you entered last night that leads to our house has only had the top cleaned and a steamroller used to compact the surface. This allows the bitumen from within the soil to close it completely. We are living here at 3000 metres altitude," the family said.

The lost human contacts of Colombia were re-established upon our first arrival in Venezuela. The contact with people was open, friendly and by no means of any curious nature. They looked at us not as a "travelling piece of news" but as another natural addition to the country.

As soon as the road left the high regions, a steamy hot climate welcomed us again. One of the many rivers coming from the mountains proved a good place for a break with some necessary caution to be observed. Rainforest rivers carry unknown natural elements, which was better to respect. The spot we had chosen was flowing over a stone bed and was not stagnate. The cooler river water gave us the refreshment we needed. Despite our precautions, we realised later that the children had picked up a bug from the water, causing terrible itching on the legs.

Only high up in the Andes mountains could you safely take water out of natural courses—but from nowhere else, as we obeyed.

The main roads in Venezuela were quite good, with very little traffic. The few towns on our way were all located off the road, looking like a well-planned future. Next to Barquisimeto we left the road and visited a local supermarket. As a country town, Barquisimeto reflected a very modern image. Everything was available in the supermarket. What surprised us was the fact that nobody was interested in foreign currency—so far the only country in South America. This caused a slight problem as we first had to find an open bank to change our money into Venezuelan "Bolivars".

In the supermarket were a variety of goods, many of which we hadn't seen for quite a while. Basic food like milk, cold meats and many others helped to diversify our menu again.

Halfway before the capital, Caracas, the road led on to a high-plateau, stepping down sharply again near the coast. There was a steady increase in traffic towards its capital of 2 million inhabitants. The road had run-off tracks on the side to safely slow vehicles, if they had to stop due to brake failure.

Slums on the outskirts signaled the start of the city which followed a high valley through the coastal mountain ranges. An elevated air-highway in the centre of the valley directed the traffic to the city, leaving the slums behind. This central traffic arterial above the city was a fantastic solution! Even foreigners could find their way around easily. Everybody drove fast on this four-lane arterial that had a number of exit ramps to various parts of the city.

When we arrived in the city centre, it was late on a Sunday afternoon. The valley allows the city to stretch out with many parks, where we saw a great number of people spending their Sunday. Large trees spread their shade over a park, which started in front of the Presidential Palace. Police made their presence known in the crowd which boasted a great number of children. It appeared that people didn't need much to entertain themselves and be happy.

Later in the night, when everybody had disappeared from the park, we decided that this was a good place to sleep overnight—particularly as the Presidential Palace had dressed guards in front of it. Two of the guards approached us asking for identification.

They said they were prepared to bend the rules and allow us to stay, if we parked a described distance from the palace entrance and leave before six o'clock the following morning. We knew then that here would be safe and quiet.

The next morning the special guards didn't fail to remind us to be out of the area before six o'clock, when the President's day started. A tour of Caracas was on our agenda since our South American tour ended here. We had planned to board a ship from Venezuela across to America and continue on the west coast to Vancouver in Canada, where our Finnish friends from South Africa were living. Visas were already in our possession, but a ship passage had to be organized.

A parking spot near a mechanical garage with a display of luxury sport cars became a central point for our operations in the city centre. Walking past a pharmacy, a gentleman addressed us pointing to the legs of our children: "The children need something for their leg—rash, I'll be back in a minute with the right ointment, if you wait." Returning from the pharmacy, he demonstrated how to apply the special ointment, adding: "This how it's done, it will help very quickly, you must have picked it up from a rainforest river." He refused any payment explaining: "I am a doctor, I want you and your children to have a happy stay in our country". What a great gesture!

Not long after, an elderly man from the mechanical garage joined us at our parked car. He must have heard that travellers were in town. He asked: "Where are you from?" I answered: "We are at the end of our South America tour from Brazil." He said: "But you are not from Brazil!" When the gentleman heard, we also came from Germany, he introduced himself: "I am Carragiola, the driver of the famous Mercedes "Silberpfeil" racing car. You must have heard my name. I have retired here in Caracas and I am running a workshop for my car collection and those of other collectors in the country. Venezuela has enough people with money, who want their special cars properly serviced. This way I keep better in touch with the outside world and also have plenty friends. You are more than welcome in Venezuela. We need people like you, come into my office and we can have a coffee together."

He continued to tell us more about Venezuela: "Our country is immensely rich, we not only have oil—everything else is in abundance. Venezuela is also a big country with only 15 million people. We need specially-qualified technical people. The country is beautiful all year around with blossoms of the "apamate tree", acacias, bougainvilleas and our national "araguaney-tree". We also have eternal snow on our high mountains around the Lago Maracaibo and Merida districts. In 1800 your Alexander V. Humboldt had fallen in love with our country describing it in great details in his 36 volumes of "Voyage into Equatorial regions of the New World". Others like Appun, Russell and Depone followed in his footsteps".

Carragiola gave us the addresses of both the Finnish and German embassies as well as lots of other useful information. The reason we wanted to see the embassies was to get information on shipping lines from Venezuela. I first went to the German Embassy, while my family remained in the good hands of Carragiola. I still had the door handle in my hand at the German Embassy, when I was welcomed with: "Another f** globetrotter. We are closing, we have no time." Making the officer aware that I demanded as a German citizen my right to be heard at the Embassy, he said: "Sorry, we can't help you with your enquiry". Well this was one way of keeping out anything that looked like work for them!

Returning to our stay, we decided to give the Finnish Embassy a try. The car could be left with Carragiola, he reassured us. At the Finnish Embassy, my wife had to find her Finnish tongue again. We didn't speak much Finnish at home and my wife had lost a bit of her fluency. The Finnish Embassy staff had no problem to overcome our first introduction hurdles: "Have a seat first and we will prepare you a cup of coffee, would the kids like a soft drink? When you have settled, we will talk again."

The initial lack of Finnish was this way quickly overcome. Nostalgic feelings came rushing back here, in this little bit of Finnish territory. For years Arja had spoken only German, Afrikaans, English and Portuguese. This can only be experienced in life situations.

During the next two hours the Finnish Embassy organized a shipping passage in the next three days for our car to Germany. We had to abandon our plans to sail to North America. No ships were going at the present time to America because of a dispute with the Transport Union in the United States. The "die was cast". We would travel to Germany first, with our dog Mars. The car could be transported by ship. For ourselves, we could book a flight to Frankfurt from the Finnish Embassy. Regulations for freighters didn't allow children under seven on board, therefore we had to choose a flight. Before leaving the

Embassy, we thanked their staff with little souvenirs we had picked up on our South America tour.

Our next destination was the harbour city of La Guaira, where all goods entering and leaving the country went through. A short drive out of Caracas brought us to the remaining descent down to the coast. What a climate difference waited here for us! Colombian-Cucuta conditions in Venezuela—not a real holiday atmosphere. It was too humid and hot for most people. The small population of Africans in Venezuela lived on this coast. Nobody would think much about work here! The majority of the population across Venezuela is mixed. A large percentage is "mestizo", a mixture of Red Indians and Europeans. The majority of the country's wealth is, however, controlled by the minority of European descendants.

Until our departure from Venezuela, we booked into a hotel, mainly to enjoy an air-conditioned room. The trailer of our car remained in Venezuela paying for the accommodation and meals. Luxury rounded off our 18,000 kilometre expedition through South America.

The only two countries we didn't visit were Paraguay and Bolivia. With our mixed "crew" we couldn't include everything.

On one of the next days our car went on to a ship, destined for Bremerhafen in Germany. I stood at the dock witnessing the departure of the ship with our car; nobody wants to pay for something, which doesn't arrive.

Our day of departure by air arrived. Before leaving Venezuela, we sent a telegram to Germany to my step-parents announcing our arrival. This proved to be a fruitless exercise as the telegram never arrived. Our exodus from South America began with quite a scare, when our plane started on the runway with the back door still open! Just on take-off, a pilot rushed out of the cockpit and shut the door with its big red leaver, most likely in time. Some heavy arguments passed between the crew.

# Germany

Landing in Frankfurt early in the morning of November 18, 1977 brought us back into new realities. On departure in La Guaira, the temperature was 42 degrees Celsius, in Frankfurt the reading was at freezing point. This alone was enough of a reminder of colder conditions. A telephone call to my step-parents supplied our first "cold shower": "We have visitors, you can't come now". They hadn't received our telegram and so we had arrived out of the blue.

The next call to Finland was different: "When are you coming, we are waiting for you?" The answer was straight away. It was decided that my wife and children would leave for Finland in two days time.

On a second call to my home town, my step-parents had a change of heart: "Come and we see what we can do". Still in Frankfurt, our children tested our flexibility when our little girl, Mirja, disappeared at the train station. While searching for her, we had to put up with piles of rubbish throughout the entire Central Station area; to what kind of Germany we had returned?

Nevertheless, the police turned up with Mirja, who had started to explore this new world with its crowds of people and eventually played hide-and-seek with us. All this was just typical for children, sometimes parents have to follow them.

Germany also showed its international image. People from all over the world rushed about this major European transit station. We couldn't even escape from accommodation offers. I followed one up just for interest to find out what the prices were. Our German shepherd represented the biggest obstacle in obtaining accommodation in the city. We already had one, too many children for a standard room. We abandoned very quickly such an enquiry, preferring to take the train to the south, where my step-parents lived. Visitors from other family branches helped to overcome the first surprises of our unexpected visit.

Some convincing had to be done to allow the dog to stay with us in the cellar of my step-parents' house. Our dog showed better manners than the children, he was the best family-member we ever had. For him it didn't matter where he was, the main thing was that he could be with our family. Nobody thought any more about the presence of a dog in the house, until my step-father too confidently entered the cellar. The dog challenged him like an intruder in his own house. The result was that the dog had to leave the house immediately. A lot of other things had to be tackled all of a sudden: my wife and the children travelled by train and ship to Finland, where they would stay with her family until I had organized work and accommodation for a trial stay in Germany.

The dog was put into a kennel, where I tried to visit him daily. From this moment, he started to hate other dogs, when they barked either out of curiosity or boredom.

When Arja left for Finland, my family finally realised that she was speaking German—this should be regarded as a slight under-statement after 10 years of marriage. It rather proved how little attention she had received. There are people, that cannot get out of their "own shadow"!

Through an international technical magazine, I had already made contacts from Brazil with employers in Germany in case we ended up there again.

As soon as our Chevrolet stationwagon arrived from Venezuela, I went straight to pick it up from the port of Bremerhafen. I was lucky in that I gained still access to the car just before the weekend and so did not have to wait unnecessarily until Monday for the car's release. The harbour personnel were very helpful—this is not always the rule in Germany. During shipping, petrol had been removed from the tank and filled with water for safety reasons. Having the car back in a good condition, I could now move more freely. I replaced the water in the tank with petrol and the car started immediately; a German car wouldn't have started like this again! In Brazil, bigger engines were designed to run up to 10% water through the carburettor in order to save petrol. Brazilian people were very innovative when it came to saving money. One of the many tricks that only Brazilians could "invent" was a compression-checking method of motor cylinders: take the spark plug out, plug the hole with a paper ball, give the engine a short start, mark the end-point, where the paper ball has ended then by comparing the end-points of all the cylinders you will learn a lot about the condition of the cylinders.

But now we were in Germany, let me continue there. My wife and children arrived well in Finland with winter in full swing.

My first visit to a company near Nuremberg, which supplied drawing instruments offered me employment, but no immediate accommodation. My next visit was Stuttgart, the manufacturing powerhouse of Germany. All the big names like Mercedes, Audi, Porsche, Bosch, Festo, IBM etc. were there. A small family-business in this area expressed their interest in my application. One family member negotiated a deal with me,which included housing for the family from the beginning of the New Year. I started immediately with this appointment and stayed overnight in a nearby motel up on the hills of a valley where the Fils river joins river Neckar. I had our German shepherd, Mars, with me. During the day the dog stayed in my car and at night slept absolutely quietly next to my bed with his head resting on it. The motel owner at first refused to allow the dog inside. But when he saw our Mars, he was impressed with his good behaviour: "Under the condition the dog stays clean and quiet, he can stay with you." Mars must have understood these directions. I didn't even need an alarm clock. Mars snubbed my face with his nose exactly on time so we could first have a morning walk outside together before I started work. During the day I looked in on him a couple of times in our parked stationwagon. The dog's cooperation couldn't have been better, he understood every single word. It looked like the dog understood everything, do we understand them?

My co-workers at the company tested me with the welcome: "The banana bender from South America has arrived to teach us." Their expression of a freedom was displayed in many places in the workplace by pornographic illustrations. I personally found it absurd and in the wrong place. Calling everybody to a meeting, I raised the question:"One third of our life we are at work, should we make this time so different from what we are like at home? Our work environment should be in a way that we can show it with pride to our families. Please take these posters off, here is no place for them." The next day I came to work, the posters had disappeared.

With the initial first barriers overcome, the team approach started to gain a foothold in the company. Some individual performers tried to maintain their exclusive positions until they gave up their resistance and joined in the team approach. The company was headed by two brothers and one sister. One of the brothers employed me with the technical responsibility task. He had been in America for some time and wanted new blood in the company. The other brother and sister were on the administration side of the company with a more conservative approach.

The end of the year arrived and I headed to Finland by train and ship for Christmas. A cold and white winter introduced tranquility into this northern part of Europe. Our children were busy familiarizing themselves with the snow for the first time in their lives. It came as no surprise that the eldest son broke his arm on a slippery rock. Christmas 1977 became a heartfelt event in Finland for the whole family after five years in overseas.

Santa Claus lives in the north of Finland in his workshop of Rovaniemi. He is all year around busy answering children's letters from around the world. On Xmas Eve he visits the well-behaved children, fulfilling some of their wishes and encouraging them to stay on that good track. A Santa Claus came to our Christmas Eve in his full winter outfit leaving lovely memories behind.

Before children become adults, they need good "deposits" of fantasies to make it through a real life.

Once we were in Finland, we could not escape from a Finnish sauna, which became a bonus in a cold winter. On the first days of January I had to be back at work in Germany and this time my family also came with me. We didn't miss the opportunity to visit our friends, Pirkko and Kalevi, in Helsinki,whom we met only from time to time, but that was enough to keep up a lasting friendship.

Our ship left from Helsinki to Travemunde, Germany. A journey is always exciting and so was this one. The ship "Finlandia" travelled at an impressive speed through the icy Baltic Sea offering great comfort on her decks.

Arriving in Germany, my wife experienced an exceptional stay with the parent-in-laws until we could move into our new accommodation near my workplace. Our German shepherd had to struggle putting up with noisy dogs in a suburban kennel. When we came to see him, each time he displayed his happiness by jumping up on everybody and giving his special kiss. But when leaving him, he became the saddest dog on earth with his head down, his eyes still trying to catch us. One weekend, when I came from Stuttgart to join everybody in my step-parents place, I made a mistake by bringing Mars from the kennel with me in the car. The dog caused an upset to my step-parents, they demanded: "If you keep the dog, we don't help you". Our answer was clear: the dog belonged to our family. The eldest of our children received daily school lessons from my step-father behind closed doors with an emphasis on "that you become a good educated man one day". The young boy had difficulties understanding such measures and didn't follow the studies with much interest. This wasn't well received by my step-father.

## Life around Stuttgart

To the relief of everybody, the time had arrived, when we could move into our new accommodation with our dog Mars. Until our container arrived from Brazil, we had to improvise in our living area. When the container did arrive in front of the house, the curiosity of surrounding neighbours reached its climax. They had no trouble standing behind their window curtains all day watching, what was carried out of the container. Once everything had its place, the neighbours must have had their opinion about finalized. They probably knew more about us by now, than we did.

At school our two older children were set back by one year in their progress with the explanation: "Coming from Brazil, you have more to learn first". What an arrogant judgement! For the next two years, at least, our children were completely bored at school, they had learned all this in Brazil before. With discipline in place, Brazil could achieve higher standards in their education. Germany had not yet finished with its education experiments.

I experienced one day a good example of this, when I went to see our eldest son's class teacher to find out about his personal progress. Standing in front of the closed classroom door, I heard much noise from the room and thought the teacher had not yet arrived. After a while, I opened the door and tried to catch a glimpse into the classroom. All students, boys and girls were up and around in the room with the noise still going on. I asked one of the nearest students: "Is your teacher coming today?" The answer was unexpected: "Our teacher is with us here in the class." The teacher then appeared in front of me, suggesting: "We better remain outside that we can talk. My students have their romping time, which is a main subject in the Primary School."

Since when the world has a romping time? No wonder this generation might face problems, when they have to stand up to the later demands of life. Nobody will give you romping hours later on!

The female teacher was still young, expressing very progressive teaching methods, as if she were looking for excuses for the mess.

Not jeopardizing the progress of our children at school, I listened to her without adding any comments. The result of such educational experiments with a lack of discipline eventually became a task for the parents to sort out. This is not really demonstrating a good cooperation between school and parents. Our two children visiting the school at that time spoke quite fluently German, English, Portuguese and Finnish—an achievement not recognised at the time. How many of the teachers could claim such knowledge?

On the contrary, most other children couldn't understand any horizon outside of their small town. Listening to our children's reports of life in Brazil and South Africa, the students couldn't believe a word. "When it rained in Brazil, we ran out of our house in shorts, had a good warm shower and lots of fun." Our kids were labelled as liars. One day Risto came home in tears: "Mum, at school they don't believe that we have a bird-spider from Brazil, they called me a liar again." On the next day my wife decided to rectify this incident. She went to school with Risto and took the bird-spider along. "Vow, what a monster of a spider!" everybody exclaimed.

This incident was prompted by what had happened in Risto's lessons the day before. When the teacher wrote on the blackboard the words 'bird' and 'spider', Risto jumped up and said: "We have a Brazilian bird-spider at home!" This became too much for the rest of the class and they shouted: "You are liar, nobody has got a bird-spider!" So, after having been face to face with a real bird-spider, the mood of the class turned completely and everybody wanted to be best friends with Risto.

Now they started to also believe about the rain-showers and possibly much more of the children's African and Brazilian stories. A major step in a necessary association with the local children succeeded. Even our German shepherd became a centrepoint of attention. When the dog had his walk with us, all the children in the neighbourhood wanted to pat him. He was exceptionally big, strong, beautiful and good natured—as long as no other dog crossed his path. We had to keep a close eye on this, since Mars had been in a kennel with other dogs.

This improved image in our new neighbourhood wasn't without some detractors. An elderly woman was worried about her peace and quiet, when we moved into the house with the four children. She made her point clear from the beginning, calling on the phone, knocking on the ceiling or wall—all for nothing. When other children visited our children from school, she turned them away from the house with a broom like a witch. At least one trouble-maker had to be in the place, otherwise the world wouldn't work? Her words were often of a very rough nature. Could a soft core be found behind a hard shell? One small consolation emerged with time as we realised,we were not the only ones treated harshly by this "special person". She was one of those,who kept watch all day about what was happening around her. If there was something she disagreed with, she didn't fail to make her point loudly, followed often by strong swear words. A neighbour, who parked her Mercedes in front of the house received the blunt message from this woman's kitchen window: "You f**bitch park your shit-box somewhere else and piss off."

As this woman was not yet of pension-age, I suggested on one occasion to her, as she leaned at the window checking the world outside: "You are still young enough to go to work instead of staying at home growing old and insane." This set off alarm bells. She yelled: "I am not that stupid, I do not have to work like you idiot!" Ultimately she became probably the best known person in town, even though through her negative attitude. Life had to continue: "an old dog wouldn't learn new tricks."

## Transylvania

Summer was usually the time when people took holidays. In June 1978 we finally made the decision to pay a visit to Transylvania, where my biological father's family still lived. It was in South Africa that the father's letter reached me after more than 30 years of searching. The moment had arrived, when our Brazilian car took us all south towards former Yugoslavia to enter Romania from there. Upon our departure the woman next door didn't miss in giving us a special farewell: "Bunch of sows, don't come back!" We replied: "In the meantime you can look after the house and have a good time!" "She replied: "Shut your trap and get lost!"

We became part of the holiday rush to the south. Everybody must have thought that they would avoid the traffic congestion, if they left early. In former Yugoslavia the traffic sometimes slowed to a halt. Businesses popped up like mushrooms on the roadsides with traders making all sorts of efforts to get the holiday travellers' money—whether it was for petrol, food or breakdowns.

Such mass movements were new, people rushed for a holiday freedom, but got caught up before gaining it. One could sometimes get the impression that during such a rush we had unwillingly caught up with the people we tried to leave behind. When traffic on the Autobahn to Beograd didn't move, some people came out with their spoiled expectations, reminding me of our neighbourhood. Fortunately the main traffic rush was not our way, so we gained our freedom after the capital Beograd. The capital, itself under a communist rule, had the usual pompous centre with its wide roads and big buildings that didn't impress us. The city lost its image the further out we went. The border to Romania lay to the north before the town of Timisoara. On the way we passed through typical Balkan rural villages with their wide dirt roads and farmhouses on both sides. Big winged-gates closed the interior of the farm from the road. Fat, white geese, chooks, sometimes pigs asked for the right-of-way. Hardly any traffic could be seen here.

Agricultural wagons pulled by cattle or horses outnumbered tractors on the road. Outside the villages, vast fields of wheat and maize continued on both sides of the road. The crossing of Europe's biggest river, the Danube, was long behind us when we arrived at the Romanian border. Both countries with their communist rule, surprised us with their strict border-control. Former Yugoslavia was, however, more open to the West. For that reason, the communist country of Romania had to "protect" its citizens more thoroughly from "getting lost" in the neighbouring country.

After having passed the formalities at each border, we could continue with our tour into Romania, heading for its northern part of Transylvania, famous for its Dracula character.

Where did this image of a Dracula come from? Transylvania is surrounded in its south by the mountain-belt of the Carpathians. Over 800 years ago, early settlers from the area of today's Luxemburg came here into a wilderness of forests and started a long tradition of farming, while maintaining their "Saxon" dialect across their entire history. The first settlers shared this isolated wilderness with mainly bears and wolves. A later migration from Austria brought Protestant refugees from the rule of Empress Maria Theresa. Their Protestant beliefs became a strong support for this society. Over the centuries they successfully fought intruders with their church-castles that can only be found in Transylvania. The mainly farming community had built their churches as fortified castles, where they kept whole harvests and livestock in case they had to retreat and defend themselves. Against the background of this wild natural country with its strong farming culture emerged the myth of a person with the Dracula image roaming in the mountains and forests in the company with wolves and bears.

Dracula-country is more commonly known than the names of Transylvania or Siebenbuergen. Dracula owes his name to an incident that occurred to Englishman Jonathan Harker during his voyage from England to Transylvania. On the last leg of his journey he arrived in the middle of the night on the mail coach through the mountainous Borgo pass. In complete darkness, he came face to face for the first time with his business counterpart. All he could see was the pale white face of a meagre man with a sharply hooked nose and reddish eyes. The man in front of him was the Earl of Dracula who wanted to buy, with the assistance of Jonathan Harker, some real estate in London. Harker's notes of this journey gave rise to the fantastic illustrations by English writer Bram Stoker in his book "Black Earl". It was Stoker who developed this image of the blood-sucking vampire Dracula—even though he had never visited Dracula country. This fantasy surrounding the Earl of Dracula conquered the world and forever changed people's perceptions of the country.

I was born there in 1941, taken out of the country in 1944 and returned now in summer 1978 for the first time to see my father, who had searched for me for all those years. First impressions of the countryside resembled very much the countryside in parts of Southern Germany with its lush green pastures, high-standing crop fields with islands of beech and oak trees. In summer it gets fairly hot. However, in winter Russian winter conditions take over.

The first city we visited was Sibiu (formerly Herrmannstadt). In the marketplace in the city centre we asked people for directions. They responded openly and friendly in German, not in their traditional "Saxon" dialect, which is different from written German.

Most people in Transylvania spoke Saxon, German, Romanian and often Hungarian. They have lived here for centuries with other nationalities, which have pushed into Romania in the past. Therefore the make-up of the population in Transylvania became quite complex throughout history: in the west was the Hungarian part, while in the east was the Saxon-German part, where I came from.

Not far north from Sibiu lay the farming village of Seica-Mica (Kleinschelken), where we were heading on a busy road.

Seica-Mica was my birthplace, which I had not consciously seen since. On our way we came past goldmine fields near Medias (Mediasch). We had only seen such goldmines in South Africa.

Romania, as a whole, can be regarded as a rich country with resources of almost everything, in particular oil. It remains to be seen whether the democracy in the country of today can bring wealth also to its people and not disappear in widespread corruption.

When I write the names of places in two languages, this reflects also the multicultural fabric of Romanian society. Transylvania has lived together with other ethnic groups, but always strongly maintained its religious, cultural and language traditions in a partly self-inflicted isolation. The Second World War had changed all this with a previously unmatched destruction. The symbolic seven fortresses in Transylvania, which are shown in their heraldic flag and are the origin of the country's name "Siebenbuergen" (Seven Castles), could not withstand the mighty Russian military power. Some of these unique church-fortresses are still today in a surprisingly good condition, despite most of its population having fled the country, mainly to Germany.

At the time of our visit, Romania had been under the communist rule of Ceausescu. The first address we had of my brother was in the neighbourhood of my birthplace. A dirt road slowed us down as recent rain had filled the holes in the road with water. For the small population of Eibesdorf, the road condition didn't matter as hardly anybody owned a car.

Arriving in the main road of the village with farm houses continuing on both sides, we met first a few old women sitting alone on the doorsteps of their houses and watching the events in the place. A car in the village was something new, which they related to a visitor from the "West".

Everybody knew everybody in this place, so it came as no surprise that we were directed straight away to the address of my brother. Brother Hans was younger than me, for that reason we had never met before. The welcome, however, was so heartfelt as brothers only can experience. Despite communist rule, he lived with his family in a house on which he had worked hard to become more independent. Building materials were not readily available so everything had to be improvised. Even when people didn't have much of their own, a guest received all the attention they could possibly bring forward. Food came on the table with excellent local wine. Wine was cultivated in Transylvania throughout the centuries to perfection under a favourable climate with hot summers and very cold winters. The wide limestone of the Carpathian mountains created a fertile soil which supplied rich crops of nearly everything.

The brother's father-in-law was the police officer of the village. Only this fact made it possible for me and my family to stay overnight in a relative's place. Guests had to be accommodated in the few dedicated hotels in the country. The police officer in the family had the power to make the exemption for us: "When somebody from the family comes from that far, he stays in my house. Nobody can change this!"

Television in a house was something special at the time. During our stay we could follow Germany in the soccer finals against Argentina.

After the first two days with brother Hans it was time for us to move on into the neighbouring village of Seica-Mica (Klein-schelken) where father Michael didn't yet know about the presence of his stolen son. The church-fortress occupied the centre of the village.

The road, with farm houses on both sides, followed the course of the river Kockel. The parents' house, where I was born in 1941 had a big two-wing door to the inner-yard. Father Michael had married the sister of my mother after she passed away. They lived all their lives with four more children in this house. Wife Elisabeth welcomed us like my own mother with tears of joy in her eyes. Father Michael was still working outside the village in a field. As we had sunny weather, I decided to walk into the direction of the field while my family settled into the house.

I did not have to walk far to get out of the village on to a hillside with fields of barley and maize. On the path appeared a man with a stick of a hoe over his shoulder. The slim-built man resembled me so much, or vice-versa, that we recognized each other immediately—even from that distance. Father Michael put down his hoe on the field-path and embraced me for a long time, as if he didn't want to let me go away any more. The old man broke into tears: "I found my lost son". Thirty-five years had to pass to make this happen.

Back in the village he opened the two big door-wings of the house front to allow our car to be moved off the road. Each one of our children he embraced whole-heartedly. No words could explain this reunion.

*My birth-family, Transylvania: Alfred, Hans, Georg, Elisabeth, Martin, Michael—Elisabeth, Michael.*

*Kleinschelken, Elisabeth, Martin, Michael.*

*Kleinschelken, 2 village-girls.*

A sip of his own plum schnapps helped to gulp down the past. Everybody had his life story to tell. Here in post-war Transylvania life had changed neither for the worse nor for the good. A communist regime had established its power in Romania when everybody after the war was "more dead than alive".

Not many people could work their way up by owning their property again like my father. A lack of basic building materials had not allowed him to improve on the house as he would have liked.

Grudges by other ethnic groups stopped progress for everyone who tried to escape out of this power grip into a better life. Such people were declared enemies of the State. Everybody was forced to play his humble role and not emerge too strong. This situation in the countryside was generally better than in cities.

People in the city were not often forced out of their own houses. A much less ethical method was used by randomly selecting people in big numbers and putting them into their houses with the result that this majority brought their own rules. Intellectual people especially copped these conditions, if they were spared the concentration camps in Siberia that was the fate of many Transylvanians.

The brutal forces of communism were the only power that could break the traditional defence of the Transylvanian farmers' society.

The journalist Paul Schuster described Transylvania with its surrounding belt of mountains as a gigantic amphitheatre. Constantly infiltrated battles took place in this "arena". Foreign warriors came and went, but the "spectators" remained.

No war was ever started in Transylvania. The shepherds and the farmers of the "Dakers "dating back to Imperial Roman times have succeeded into present times, leaving the Roman history to survive only in books. The shepherds and farmers of Transylvania can be regarded as the longest surviving culture in living memory. Shepherds still wear the cap, jacket and pair of trousers that the "Dakers" used to wear also during Roman Imperialism. The historic Trojan-column is displayed on contemporary reliefs in commemoration of a victory that the Romans ultimately did not survive. But the descendants of the Dakers, the shepherds and farmers of Transylvania did survive.

Going back to our reunion with my father. I also met my only whole brother, four three-quarter brothers and one sister, plus my step—mother, the sister of my biological mother. We all had a couple of days together in the parents' farmhouse.

Underneath the house was the wine cellar, where big wooden wine barrels were stored. The wine came from a small vineyard, which climbed up on a hillside behind the house. Communist Romania gave concessions in the form of small properties to people in the countryside, so that the crops from "kolkhoz" property became channelled only into government resources. Every farmer did his bit on a "kolkhoz property" but only as much as he had to, keeping time and energy for his own block of land.

Father Michael had planted between the vines all the vegetables being used in the kitchen. Production on the small personal properties exceeded the "kolkhoz" output by miles.

In father's wine cellar were stored different wines which hailed from the same vineyard. "This is the wine for the cityfolk and here is the wine for our family and friends," I was told. Only on important missions did father take the family wine out of his cellar, like everybody else.

A couple of wooden barrels with schnapps and liquor from plums, peaches and cherries waited to improve on age.

Farmers didn't use toothpaste to clean their teeth, a sip of schnapps did the job for them. The eating habits of the farmers were limited to what was available and they could provide themselves. Their eating habits were rather heavy and fat, therefore the schnapps played an important role in maintaining their health.

We are all subjected to our habits to a certain degree. Education can change it to the better with time. Our nine-year-old son, Risto, demonstrated his fondness of alcohol, when he emptied the schnapps and wine glasses left on the table after we all went outside. Mixed drinking made him very sick for the first time, but not the last.

As time drew closer for us to leave again, we had still to squeeze in a couple of visits. One of them led us to Cisnadie (Heltau) on the foothills of the mighty steep Carpathian mountains. A circle of events dating back 35 years began to unfold at the table of my sister-in-laws' relative, who was a kindergarten teacher during World War II in 1943. She openly admitted having received money from my step-parents to take me away from the kindergarten without authorization. Here I had the confirmation that I was simply stolen. For the kindergarten teacher the chapter was closed, so it was for me also. Going back wouldn't make sense any more, looking ahead in life became my password.

During our stay in the family farmhouse we made a secret plan to take with us to the "West "my youngest brother, so that his family could follow later. As it turned out later, we were not secretive enough. One member in the wider family reported us to the Secret Police Service, and so our plan failed later at the border to former Yugoslavia. One incident must have triggered this behaviour. We had played soccer on a weekend near the village on a meadow. One family member claimed to have suffered an injury and obviously didn't think we had paid enough attention to him. For personal revenge he managed to prevent the brother from leaving the country with us. The consequences could have been dramatic for us, but we were lucky. The day of our departure arrived. It wouldn't have been realistic for us to settle with my family in Transylvania. A conflict appeared between the choice of where our hearts belonged to and where our life was to continue. The latter received strong support from the fact that most people, especially the younger generation, wanted to get out of the country and settle somewhere else for a better economical future.

My youngest brother took an extra seat in our car. The golden necklace I gave to the mother found its place on a hook on a wall in our room. I could not understand why. My brother explained saying:

"In Romania nobody is allowed to own gold, all gold is the exclusive property of the communist government. Possessing gold is regarded as a theft from the government. The mother didn't want to offend us by returning the present. She hung it instead up on the wall, creating the impression that we had forgotten it." How intricate our world can be!

Stopping in the centre of Timisoara, not far from the border, must have caught the attention of the Secret Police. An officer approached us asking all sort of questions including the presence of my brother, as he was the only one speaking Romanian. Even for us the whole situation appeared suspicious, no matter from what angle one was looking at it. I doubted already the success of our plan, but the brother insisted that we carry on. We must have been out of our minds continuing our trip together to the border in front of the Secret Police. On the way another possible mistake was made when we stopped on the side of the road not far from the border-control to hide my brother in the car. The radar system might have picked us up already. We had agreed, however, that in the event our plan didn't work, we would both tell only the truth—the best way to avoid contradiction.

At the border there was a queue of cars in front of us. We just had to join and wait. Occasionally border guards passed next to the cars, keeping their eyes on the scene. When our turn came to drive to the first toll-bar, a guard appeared in front of our car stopping us. This was not a good sign! He ordered the first toll-bar to be closed, while other guards approached us and demanded that we get out of the car. I knew then, our case was lost.

As if the guards knew, they looked straight under the back seat, where my brother was hiding. He became the first one to be escorted into a nearby building. We knew also that our situation had turned serious. We could have faced lengthy prison terms for kidnapping a Romanian citizen. Communist Romania did not accept a person's choice of freedom—even in a case of family connections. The only thing that mattered now was salvaging the best possible outcome from a difficult situation. Calm was the order of the moment.

We didn't see my brother any more. We only hoped that he wouldn't face harsh punishment. We were locked in a room at the border station for hours. Our passports were confiscated and a waiting game started for us. Interrogations became very difficult as I could only answer in French.

Later in the day a new move happened: we were told to go back in to our car with a border-guard as driver. We were taken back to Timisoara, exactly to the spot we had stopped earlier. The only hotel in the place was in front of us. It was here that the guard booked us in at our expense. An elegant imprisonment arrangement!

The very first thing we organized from the hotel was a phone connection to the German Embassy in Bucharest. I was lucky that the Ambassador answered my call and I explained what had happened. He was actually very forthcoming and promised to help our case. We all were locked into the five-star hotel-prison without our car and belongings. The next day the police picked just me up and brought me to the Police Headquarters to appear in front of the magistrate. I was asked whether I could answer in French, which I did. The Magistrate spoke fluently French so I could bring our case better to his attention. My remorse in doing the wrong thing to the communist country of Romania found acceptance. I was even assured that my brother had not received the punishment, which was the rule in those days. The verdict was that we had to leave the country the next day with a policeman driving us back to the border. The gentle closing of our case was most certainly owed to the mediation behind the scenes by the German Ambassador. We had a bitter pill to swallow, however, as we were not allowed to enter Romania for the next 10 years. This put a real question mark on our plan to help my brother to get out of the country. Romania officials didn't lose their face in this process as they gave us a chance with a reminder attached.

The clearance at the border went quickly this time. Only after the second toll-bar did the police officer leave our car, allowing us to proceed to the former Yugoslavian border.

From now on we could move freely again, even in former Yugoslavia. It was a big relief for all of us. It was time to head home as my leave had come to an end. The restrictions in the life of a communist country taught us a lasting lesson.

Rolling into our home town, we could not have expected a different reception from this one: "The rabble is back, I didn't miss you", shouted the neighbourhood woman. We returned: "Nice to see you again", which prompted her to close her window with a bang, shouting: "Shut up!"

Life returned quickly to its normal course. From Transylvania we received by mail confirmation that my brother returned to his home unharmed.

The children went to school again and my wife was holding the fort at home with the support of the quiet German shepherd Mars. I ran the show at work. Locals, however, couldn't stop giving their opinion about the size of our family—even a doctor joined in the comments during my wife's routine visit, saying: "In Germany one child is good, the second one is still just okay, three children you are antisocial, more than three you are a criminal." Did the doctor forget that we looked after our children and not he? At least we knew our position in Germany from now on.

Ignoring this, we still developed a new hobby outside the daily demands of work. In the Swab Alps lies a place called Holzmaden. In ancient layers of oil slate, prehistoric fossils could be found imbedded: Ichtosaurs (fish lizards), Steneosaurs (small ocean crocodiles), Ammonites and Sea Lilies—all about 180 million years old. The place was not far from us, so we could go there quite often and collect our own samples in permitted areas. With an elderly couple we undertook many excursions on foot. They knew the Swab Alps like their own pockets.

Its limestone formations do not hold rainwater and as a consequence, not much natural forest could be found. In winter the area often had snow with its harsh cold climate perfect for winter sports.

Our children gained an interest in gemstones we had collected in Africa and South America. The elderly couple supported this interest with their own collection. Special exhibitions in the area during the year helped to build up a special knowledge of sample names, their origin and geological age. Our eldest son, Risto, always won the knowledge quiz. Would he later become a geologist?

On Christmas Eve we gave my step-parents the honour of celebrating together with personal gifts under a bright and colourful tree. Another year, 1979, came around in a blink of a moment. Still in winter, in the beginning of February, carnival season took over many parts of Germany. It is said: "If we don't turn crazy at least once a year, we are all year around crazy." During carnival time, many people tried to follow that "rule".

A place further south from us called Rothweil followed an old tradition with its carnival festivities. Together with acquaintances we all headed there for one day, called Rose Monday, to watch the local population in their costumes as they promenaded through the town dressed as witches, knights, kings, soldiers, fools, citizens, red-Indians and cowboys. The highlight of the promenade was when the witches jumped across their brooms—an ancient local custom designed to rally on the carnival and banish the evil forces for the rest of the year.

The winter was so cold that we constantly had to seek refuge in heated pubs of the town. It was not that long ago that we had lived in Brazil so we still had problems adjusting to the colder climate in Germany. Our children sometimes sparked controversy at school by still wearing warm clothes while others had put their shorts on.

After another winter in Germany, we moved again like many others during summer holidays southwards to warmer fields. A move on such a scale could be regarded as modern migration. In fact, it was the economical consideration of holiday-pay loading,which enabled people to take their holidays away from home and help spread their currency in other countries—thus giving a certain buying power to the country where the money was spent. Everything goes in circles and so does money.

Measures like these were new and this required careful economical-social considerations working with the theory that extra money out of an efficient economy creates consumer demand. In other words, only good economical times could supply extra benefits.

## Greece

Four weeks leave seemed to be enough for a holiday in Greece. Family friends wanted their daughter to join us because nobody in their family had been outside of Germany. They thought we were experienced enough with other countries. As we left home, our curious neighbours were again out to see where we were going. We just waved our hands and they soon disappeared behind curtains saying: "We are not going away". This was actually good that not everybody went away for a holiday.

On our first leg to the south, we ran into traffic congestion again—it was as if everybody was on the move. Along the Adriatic coastline of former Yugoslavia we found the summer we were looking for. South of Trieste, dry barren rocky country climbed up towards the inland continuing until Dubrovnik. A small market-place past the modern city of Split surprised us with its residents speaking Italian—an indication of a close relationship between this coastal part and neighbouring Italy.

The historic setting of Dubrovnik against steep mountains invites everybody for a closer inspection. The town has narrow streets within a fortress that has protected the town from the sea for centuries.

In Herzegovina a small ocean arm leads inland flanked by steep mountains all around. A ferry boat cuts across here to the other side.

When lining up for the ferry, we experienced an unfortunate incident. A local car behind us bumped into our car with the result that the bumper came off his Volkswagen Passat. A big drama unfolded: the police were called in and we were blamed for the damage on the Passat. The owner surprisingly spoke some German, which suggested that he must have worked in Germany but did not have good memories of his stay. We became the scapegoat for his anger. He demanded compensation, but I bluntly refused. Demanding is one thing, giving in, another. As time dragged on, the inconvenience of this incident grew out of proportion. I was not prepared to waste any more time and gave some compensation, meeting the demand halfway just to get away.

We had lost our position in the queue in front of the ferry and had to go right back to the end of the queue. We refused to do so. Despite having purchased the ticket, we decided to drive around the sea arm. This was a good decision as we realised what beautiful views we would have missed by taking the ferryboat. The passage around didn't take that long and so really didn't justify the shortcut across on the ferry. Nature compensated us for human shortcomings.

Montenegro and Kosovo occupy large areas of high mountains. On our way we saw forest pockets, fig and olive groves and beautiful blossoming cacti spread in the lower region. Minarets appeared in hamlets pointing towards the ethnic diversity of the population, which had managed to live together in harmony until politics turned everything upside down in 1990.

In the valley of the river Moraca the road was completely cut into vertical rockwalls in a giddy height above the narrow valley. This was a particularly interesting part of our journey.

Around Skopje, the houses were built like in the Swiss Alps: stone was set from the ground, timber construction further up with steep shingle roofs, which allowed the snow to slide off in winter. A veranda with tall flower arrangements highlighted the beauty of this area. People were also very obliging, regardless of whether they were Orthodox,

Muslims or Catholics. When we were buying items, we pointed at the goods with our fingers. In return we received the local name, repeated it as good as we could, and got big smiles.

It is hard to comprehend, how these kind people could have turned against each other with atrocities beyond belief—the result of a political incapacity.

Our destination of Greece came closer. Oleanders in different colours along the centre of the road welcomed a large number of travellers. Most of them had taken the inland road through the capital Beograd. Our route along the coast rewarded us with its beauty. The Greek controls didn't stop the traffic entering the country for long.

The summer heat had already dried out the country, leaving wide areas burnt brown. Closer to the Mediterranean and on the foothills of Greece's highest mountain Olympus, green vegetation appeared in lower areas due to the irrigation of crop fields, whereas the higher areas were covered with bush and pine forests.

Olive groves showed up everywhere as well as citrus plantations from time to time. Even in summer, Mount Olympus had snow on its summit. Before reaching Athens, a road branched out here to the nearest coast, inviting us to follow it. Away from the tourist road, the small village of Martinon supplied a pure impression of Greece and how its people lived. At that time, most of the houses on the coast were built in block form with a flat roof and everything painted white to reflect the summer heat. In summer, the door was a row of string lines attached with sea shells, allowing air circulation through the house.

Hardly anybody was in the streets. Everybody kept inside in the cooler shades of the house. Life was not rushed. When I asked at a petrol station for petrol, I received, besides Greek sentences, clear hand signs from the owner saying, no petrol left, further down the road might be some.

Water ("hepo" pronounced "nero") we had to buy in plastic bottles—which indicated a shortage in supply. Our first beach visit was spoiled by a neighbouring steel plant. The water was at least warm enough for a swim. When we looked away from this industrial site as night approached, we saw the moon rising in a dark clear sky. With a bottle of Greek "Amalia" wine we started to build on the image of a Greek summer night. The wine, however, was a disappointment. Greek wines were cultivated by an old tradition in casks, found equally in Spain. The wine received a resinous taste from its storage in the cask—new vintages were stored in these barrels. Pine resin covered the inside walls of the barrels to control bacterial growth. The resin's application process is a well-kept secret.

I wonder whether somebody from outside the trade has ever seen this process. From contacts with wine growers in Spain, I learnt there were two methods applied: in one, the barrel is heated from outside over a smoke fire with the resin clinging to the inside wall, while the barrel is slowly rotated. In the other method, a flare is introduced into the barrel, heating the resin and burning it into the timber. The unusual taste of the wine was not to everybody's liking. Locals told me, it was just a matter of getting used to it. People like us, who were used to the straight wine taste, had difficulties adjusting to resin wine. Only later we found out that some wine bottles carried an indication whether they were resined. Non-resined Greek wines tasted excellent, as we soon found out.

With our first Greek wine experience behind us, we headed the next morning to Athens. Ancient culture lived here and in the whole country together with modern civilization. Greek ancient culture is the oldest in Europe, long before Christian cultural expressions had introduced their influence. To describe all the historical sights of interest, is not a task of this book. I believe in a certain importance of how we meet with other parts of the world and create a new time-document for others.

Along the road we discovered, from time to time, miniature Orthodox church models on a pedestal with relics behind small glass faces: faded pictures, small bottles, dried flowers, written papers, coloured pieces of glass. Were these places of worship, signs for a direction or obituaries? We couldn't find out even though they were quite plentiful and obvious.

The metropolis of Athens is overlooked from its north by the rocky elevation of the Acropolis with the uncompleted "Pro-pylaea" on its west and "Parthenon Temple" to the east. The Acropolis can be seen from everywhere in the city with its white temple ruins against an azure-blue sky. Before heading to it and meeting tourists from around the world, we parked in the city centre next to a café. Instead of driving around in the city's traffic, one party remained with the car in front of the café relaxing at an outside table under the shade of large elm trees. The other party took a taxi to different parts in the city, avoiding parking problems. The first taxi had problems getting started as its meter went on strike. Knowing how to hit and shake the meter, the driver got it working again and our tour began. Banking and shopping was on our agenda before leaving the city again. The taxi service turned out quite cheap at that time. Until the peak of the daily heat dropped again in the afternoon, we waited in the street café under the shade of elm trees. Later in the afternoon we decided to visit the Acropolis. Sitting on its rocky elevation between ancient temples, our minds wandered back to its time and we tried to comprehend, how life was then. The idea of democracy was born here well before our time-count.

Early Greek philosophers documented the beginnings of our consciousness towards justice in all areas of a society. Socrates spoke in "polis'" (town) about the interaction of people's ethical behaviour. His student, Plato, became inspired and wrote "About the State", which again gave rise to Aristotles, who defined the terms of democracy. The power systems of "Monarchy" (single ruler), "Hierarchy" (multiple ruling), he opposed with "Demos" (people) "Kratein" (power). Since then we have, in my view, constantly "fiddled" with democracy with very little success since Aristotles.

How revolutionary these ideas were at that time, demonstrates the case of Socrates: he escaped first from his death sentence imposed because of his "infidelity", but instead had to take the "Schering's cup"—a cup of poison.

Another Greek historical institution was the "Oracle of Delphi", a continuation from Egyptian culture to ask a natural phenomenon for answers in uncertain situations. Observations by "Auguren", for instance, were not only used to predict weather patterns but to exercise power through a free interpretation.

This was the forerunner in an evolution of our minds leading to religion and now to science—the superimposed direction escaped into a tradition.

Returning to the Acropolis (Acro=upper, polis=town), it is still admired today by how much time has left for us to view and how these temple columns were made and put in place. Sacrifices were always the strongest indicators for cultural expressions.

"To carry owls to Athens" is an old saying dating back to the goddess Athena, the tutelary god of Athens. Owls were widespread in ancient times because they enjoyed a special status. Their fixed eyes could see and keep vigilance even at night, giving them the reputation of the guardians of science as well.

"To carry owls to Athens" today means doing something that is unnecessary. In ancient times many owls were in Athens, there was no need to bring more owls.

Looking down from the Acropolis to Athens with its vast ocean of houses in front of the Mediterranean begs the question, what have we achieved in cultural terms today?

We wanted to leave the city before nightfall, driving west, back into the country. The harbour town of Piraeus continued straight after the city. Greek shipping was connected strongly to the name of Onassis, one of the most successful entrepreneurs of international shipping. The name 'Piraeus' connects to the actress and singer, Melina Mercouri, whose famous song said: "Never on Sundays, I am a girl from Piraeus and love the ships, the harbour and the sea …". She put the town on to the world map.

Isthmian Corinth is the land bridge between the mainland and the southern Peloponnesus. The Roman Emperor, Nero, had first ordered work to start on a passage between the two gulfs of the Mediterranean. The passage of today was first finished in 1893 with a road and a separate railway bridge over the Isthmus. We stopped briefly to watch a ship being piloted by a small boat through the deep-cut channel. Busloads of people crowded its shore with shopping and hotel facilities next to it. This was not a place for us to stay overnight. A good road to Patras asked for a couple of toll-payments. The area had changed from a dry image to well-established olive groves, where the soil was only recently clean ploughed. The mountains of the Peloponnesus had on their foothills cypress and pine forests. The green colours returned here to the land. We reached Patras, the western end of the Gulf of Corinth before darkness.

When making our enquiry about a ship passage from here to Italy, a young woman gave us the information in German: "I have lived here a number of years already. I am happy, life is so much easier here than at home in Germany. As a woman I receive much more respect, the Greeks are gentlemen. I won't go back." This was certainly something to think about—quality of life is not measured only in terms of progress and money. The lady received our bookings to go in 10 days by ship from Patras to Brindisi, Italy.

We didn't want to return home the same way as we came.

From now on we had 10 days of holidays on the Peloponnesus.

Fresh provisions from shops got us on the way with the advancing night. Crop fields, the ever-present olive groves, sudden bamboo fields and vineyards appeared in the floodlights of our car. Once the traffic from Patras was left behind, a dirt road towards the coast became our new direction.

Not long after, we established our night quarters near a farm with fruit trees. The day's heat still remained in the dark air of the night. Bright moonshine lightened up the area so we did not need lights.

Only crickets broke the silence. With a good feast at the end of a day, life could not have been better.

Next morning, daylight revealed that we were not far from the beach. A footpath led down to the shelving coast. The following two days were dedicated to this place camping on the upper side of the sandy beach, above the spill-line of the sea water. What do people do best on a beach was no question for us: relaxing, swimming, wandering, playing, reading and planning ahead. The house of a local fisherman provided tables and benches under a bamboo roof where people could eat fresh fish. The fisherman told us, though, that fish had become scarce—the sea was already over-fished. Only on the next day he was able to serve us with fish he caught overnight. Dinner was served in typical Greek fashion: fish, lots of vegetables, olives, ewe cheese, non-resined red wine called "Alegre" and the ever-present Coke for the children.

Back on the beach, a young shepherd boy paid our children a visit, leaving his flock of sheep and his dog behind on the higher land behind the beach. It was interesting to watch how children communicate without knowing each other's language. A sketch-book and colouring pencils was all they needed. Only when the shepherd's dog came to join us, this harmony disappeared all of a sudden, because our dog didn't allow the other dog's presence. The boy retreated with his dog, but not before our children had left him a couple of their colouring pencils, which he gratefully accepted. He remained at a distance for a while waving his hand joyfully before slowly disappearing.

Leaving the beach the next morning, we caught up further inland with the shepherd boy, his flock of sheep and the dog. The boy appeared to be contemplating something, when we fare welled him again. What had crossed his mind,when he met us? How come that he was stuck in one place, while others could move about as they wanted? What was better?

On the way to the next destination, Olympia, we passed Pygros. In the southern part of the Peloponnesus the humidity added to the daily heat. Black clouds above the mountains towards the inland announced an afternoon storm, which we experienced just before Olympia. Traces of red soil and the humidity explained, why tropical vegetation could be found here: bananas and loquats. The opposite location to Africa made its influence over the climate. This small pocket of Greece became a tropical oasis in summer. Vineyards of the small currants were also found here. Vine branches were loaded with large bunches of grapes, promising a rich harvest. There were so many around in the area, it didn't really matter, if we picked some for our own use. These fully-ripened currants tasted sweet and aromatic, as currants only do.

In the hillside region, away from the coast, Olympia waited for us first with a dust-clearing thunderstorm and then with crowds of tourists. Where did they all come from? Not from where we had come. Numerous souvenir shops mainly made up the settlement of Olympia before we reached the historic complex, which was surrounded by old grown pines. Nearby were the Hera temple ruins, which included a 192-metre-long arena built in 776BC were the site of the Olympic Games every four years.

"Ekechiria" ruled then the peacetime of the games and stopped all hostilities. Only men competed at that time, women were not only prohibited from participating, but also watching. Sport winners (Olympionics) received a head crown of wild olive branches. Many "Olympionics" received the highest honours by having their likeness immortalized in a sculpture. These sculptures were kept in the great acoustic Zeus temple. Today they can be found in museums around the world. The Olympic Games stopped being staged after the Antiquity. The French Baron Pierre de Coubertin organized the Olympic Games again in 1896 in Athens. From that time they were held almost regularly every four years—and with the participation of women.

The heat rather increased during the day away from the sea, so we decided to drive back to the cooler breeze of a beach. Before Kyparissia we stopped along a bay. The railway line stopped us first from reaching the beach. Only one crossing allowed us finally to get there. Our tent, a shade tarpaulin, went up, raised with branches on the upper part of the beach. Everything was ready for a beach life. Being on our own on this beach we found out the next day that most tourists had gathered in the nearby village of Kyparissia. Tourists in their numbers did not always respect and preserve the peculiarities of a foreign place. It didn't take long for curious people to turn up at our place, which we thought was far away from the tourist congestion. Two women out of a group of people approached us with their catch of sea urchins explaining to us the nature of them: "The grey-red shell is a young sea urchin, they only are good to eat as long as the spines around the shell are still moving, which indicates that the shell is still alive". One woman opened the shell around its centre with a knife, exposing a dark jelly-mass inside. She asked us to have a taste. Only two of us ate it cautiously and only part of the jelly. The salty seedy taste did not impress, so we abandoned the idea of buying their catch.

What made me worry only afterwards, was the fact that the women didn't have a taste first. Not long after we suffered stomach congestions with nausea. There was only one thing to do: drink milk and empty our stomachs. Luckily we had taken only a small taste. Openly speaking, we were stupid to follow the directions of the two women. They spoke French very well, which gave us the only opportunity to communicate. As we found out later, they had intended to poison us. The group of people disappeared as suddenly as they came. Thanks to our fast action we overcame our predicament quickly. As I said, too many tourists can spoil an atmosphere.

On another day, we went shopping. The man at the cash register had developed his own way of making the most out of the tourists: he wrote on paper the prices of only a few items at a time, and then moved on to the next customer. This allowed the customers more time to buy more goods, which helped confuse the calculations for the final bill. Asking for wine, I was shown into a separate room with two wine casks—one holding red wine, the other white. The owner's son dropped a plastic pipe into the cask, sucked the liquid up with his mouth putting the end of the pipe into a bottle. One could only say, what a personalized service! In my case, it took me nearly one hour to get past the cash register and I had still no clue how my bill came together. It was definitely not to the disadvantage of the shop owner. "Tourists have the money, they can leave also something with me," he might have thought, because after the summer the place quite likely turned quiet again with the tourist crowds gone. Our departure early in the next morning was quite sudden because of the appearance of four strong men. Our dog announced their arrival at our camp place. They stopped just a short distance before us, making the dog defend us. No word was said, the men looked at everything we had. Our friendly gesture didn't change their demeanour. I was not sure about them, because the dog told us that something was not right. I decided to pack up and leave immediately.

Back in the mountainous area of the Peloponnesus we again found the original Greek people, who lived in their neat white houses close to each other on the mountain slopes surrounded by stone walls. In these small areas they developed their own paradise with an extensively-cultivated garden. The occasional bay of a donkey could be heard from behind the walls. The houses often had no windows, just two nice timber shutters which helped control the light intensity and air circulation. Red half-round roof tiles matched nicely with the white house walls.

Around Pilos, the area was more arid and rocky again. Only 30 kilometres further into the plains around Kalamai tropical vegetation had gained a foothold. The area was also used for the deployment of NATO's military aircrafts—their thunder frequently filled the air with one hell of a noise.

A visit to a restaurant in the narrow streets of Kalamai introduced us with colour pictures of Germany on the walls. Here we are, in Germany people "dream" of Greece and here people "dream" of Germany! As we found out, the restaurant owner had spent years in Germany saving money to come back and open his own restaurant. He was very obliging, speaking also in German to us and recalling his time in Germany.

The tour along the "middle finger" of the Peloponnesus led to Aeropolis on a shelving coast with magnificent views into small steep, rocky bays full of dark-blue sea water. They were ideal places to stay, but were impossible to access. On the other side of the Peloponnesus "finger", the picturesque village of Ytheion stood on a hillside with colourful fishing boats on the shores of the bay. The area seemed a good place to camp at the seaside, but most of these places were already occupied by other tourists.

At one bay, however, we discovered out in the sea a small rocky island rising out of the bay. This was the place we wanted to camp!

After local divers confirmed the non-existence of sharks, I swam across to the island to investigate. I returned all excited and we started preparing the rubber dinghy mainly for our children's passage. The car remained on the mainland at a visible range. Most of our belongings also went into the dinghy including my camera equipment that I had stored away in a specially-designed water-tight plastic bag. Floating this special load across to the island worked like a dream. An illusion of a "Robinson Crusoe" idyllic life away from civilization started to build in us. Nobody else was on the island, except us. In front of a rocky wall lay a small sandy beach dropping gradually into the water. This was a good place for the children to play. On the highest point of the wall there was a small niche, where we pitched our tent. The island dropped on the back slowly into the sea with heavily washed-out rock galleries.

When I went to grab my camera equipment to catch these first impressions, I received the shock of my life: the plastic bag proved not to be watertight. The camera and the film camera were swimming inside in salt water—a death sentence for this equipment. For a long time I couldn't work out what had happened. From now on we couldn't take photos any more. Isn't it equally important in life that we learn to deal also with losses?

The failure of the "special" plastic bag was very costly—a Leica and a Nizzo film camera had been lost. Claiming the loss, was a fruitless undertaking—usually the legal side emerges as the only winner, when "two fight, the third will be the winner".

The views to the mainland across the water with mountain ranges in the background, lush green growth along the coast, a summer sun out of a blue sky—all this compensated for the losses. With swimming, reading, cooking and establishing our new "home", the day passed in no time.

Our German shepherd family member swam independently with us to the island. He was a quite happy dog indicating to us that everything was fine for the time being.

Very often when something is at its best in our lives, it waits only to be challenged. We didn't become an exemption: later in the afternoon the sky began to close-in with a dark cloud-cover, sudden flocks of bats cut through the air, the crickets stopped chirping and rain set-in, starting to increase with the wind.

During night the wind developed into an all-mighty storm, which lasted for several hours and had us worrying, whether the sea will reach us on our highest island spot. I didn't dare to close even one eye during night. Instead, with the torch, I was on a close watch for the waves, which tried to leap up to us. Luckily this did not eventuate, because there would have been no escape for us.

With the returning daylight, the storm had died down, the sea around us lay calm again, as if nothing had happened. The idyllic conditions had returned, but we left the island and returned with the rubber dinghy to the mainland, not wanting to risk another night with the fury of the wind and waves coming so close to us. Our dinghy just made the return-trip before it turned into another loss by falling apart. The "Robinson Crusoe" experience turned out to be short-lived, but also included highlights.

Holidays can be seen as an escape into a life away from daily routine with eventual challenges asking for new skills and attitudes. From this point of view, we had done quite well so far on our Greek holiday. Nothing stood in the way to continue from there. Sparta, at the beginning of the Eurotas Valley, looked back at a long history. Temple ruins come from a time in 2000 B.C. when the Dorer occupied the area and founded the State of Sparta with its strict order of the dominant "Spartan class". The area's original farmers had to surrender and work for them on their own land. The Spartans were the warriors, strictly trained from the age of seven to 20 years to join the forces. A competition for leadership in the area of today's Greece between Athens and Sparta initiated the power-loss of Sparta and its one-sided established warrior-society. When two fight one another, the third will be the winner: this happened, when Rome subdued Sparta to its rule 146 A.D.

The road climbed up the mountains to Tripoli, a small town with a well-established main arterial road layout. Its centre was landscaped all along with rockwalls, containing imposing palm trees.

While resting in an open-air café, we watched the passing parade at a nearby bus station. The bus driver collected the people he wanted for his bus trip and waited until he got his full quota. By the time we had left the café, the bus driver had not reached his number of passengers and was still waiting. Nobody seemed in a rush.

I doubted if the locals had the "sickness" of a modern civilization, where money pays for our aspirations?

What goes up, usually comes down, and so did our road to Argos. On the way peasants awaited with their stands on the side of the road, offering a typical Greek variety of meat pieces grilled on a spit above glowing charcoal, white bread slices with hot garlic, ewe-cheese and a glass of red wine supported by a glass of ice-cold water, vegetables were also ready to be added from a hot cooking pot. Nobody could decline such an offer at a good price.

Many other passersby had taken this opportunity, including us. Refreshed, the tour took us to Navplion, a place on the seashore. Here we experienced for the first time what most of tourists endured. It was almost impossible to find a place amongst the many camping sites.

*Navplion, Peloponnesos, Greece.*

If we looked closer, we might even have met our "neighbours" again, squeezed together like at home—the only difference being the Greek sunshine and environment. Our presence would not have made the slightest difference to this gathering, so we could get away unnoticed.

Nauption was a fortress, standing on top of a barren rocky hillside with a second smaller fortress down along the sea. The town was packed around the foothills with its very narrow streets and not originally built for today's traffic. No passage could be found along the seaside out of the place.

Before returning from where we entered the town, we visited a Greek butcher. Our German shepherd, Mars, was on our minds as he hadn't had his daily bone for a while. How to tell the butcher, what we wanted, became the question. Our dictionary told us the Greek name of a bone: "kalispera". The butcher received the name with a smile. I showed him with my hands a size and imitated a barking sound. The butcher burst out laughing and opened a fridge door in the back, turning towards me again with a big plastic bag full of big fresh bones. "Is that enough for your dog?" Now came the task of making him understand that I needed only a small number of bones. The butcher's words came out, as if he had understood, but turned again towards the fridge door, pulling out another bag of bones: "How is that now?" It was my turn to laugh. The only way to solve this impasse, was to take a number of bones out of one bag indicating with a horizontal hand-movement that this was enough.

The butcher seemed to understand even my next hand-sign with the thumb rubbing the index finger in the air, which indicated: "how much for the bones?" The butcher waved his hands in the air, most probably saying in Greek, "this you can have for nothing". I responded to his gesture with a courtesy, putting a note on the counter, which was followed by a torrent of Greek words. I left with smiles on both sides, experiencing through bone-shopping, how obliging and friendly Greek people were. Our dog really appreciated his unexpected bone present.

Tobacco plantations were in brilliant flower on the coast opposite to Athens on the hills towards Epidaurus. Citrus and olive groves had fences built around, different from other areas of Greece, another unfortunate development from the large numbers of tourists attracted to the area.

In search of a swimming opportunity, we were prevented from entering a beach area behind an exclusive entrance. It seemed that access was only granted to French citizens. I found it strange in a foreign country! The coast was difficult to access in most areas, and when access was given, a private property or a hotel had reserved its right to keep unwanted guests out.

We had no luck finding a beach. Most places could be reached from the sea only by boat. A steep rocky coastline rose out of a blue sea, dark green old pine forests covered rolling hillsides, where plantations in flower and white houses had not taken the spaces. By all means a picturesque Greek scenery unfolded here.

Just before the Isthmus of Corinth, a ferry service offered a passage across to the mainland. Only a few cars waited for the box-like ferry, which took one car at the time. The movements of this boat were unique: a chain on each side of the boat pulled it over a winch from one side to the other of a gulf strait. The operator had to keep a close eye on the shipping traffic so that he could submerge the pulling-chains into the water to allow a ship to pass.

Ships moving in and out of Piraeus harbour appeared in the distance. Near Athens, the sea water had lost its blue colour.

Our destination was Patras where we would leave Greece by ship to travel to Italy. We spent the time until our departure near our previous beach location. We could not find the access road to the beach we had previously visited. That didn't prevent us from having a good rest on Greek soil for the last time. Here we collected our memories of this holiday: summer sun flooded Greece surrounded by the Mediterranean, mountains, plains, dry and sub-tropical countryside, cultivated groves everywhere with crops in between, ancient places, friendly Greek people living their lives in harmony in places where tourists didn't disrupt Greek life.

We can learn a lot from other countries through their population.

On our last day in Greece we had a chance to watch a whole colony of hoopoes in a field. They were already driven close to extinction. No photo opportunity was given to us by these shy creatures.

On our last shopping spree on Greek soil, we bought Greek canned peaches, discovering that the same peaches cost only a quarter of the price in Germany, yet Greece was their country of origin. What a bizarre world of so-said progress we are living in! The exchange of goods is still driven by money-factors and not by necessities.

It wasn't as easy as we thought to get on board the ship "Santa Andrea" in Patras harbour. We first had to prove that our tickets were genuine and bought from an authorized agency, of which were many around in town. Boarding a ship in an easy manner would have taken all of the excitement out of the occasion! Fees had to be paid in addition to the ticket. Many people offered help for a tip—control after control. We made sure our car was not left behind. Once we set foot on board the ship, it was left to her to do her job. The ship was crowded with passengers, as if everybody wanted to leave Greece for Italy. On the top deck was a box for our German shepherd. With plenty of boarding time, the ship left on time at night. Leaving the lights of Patras behind, the darkness of the night caught up with the ship. Life on board started to settle in: passengers occupying cabins, relaxing in seats on deck, discoveries, food from the kitchen, music everywhere from speakers as well as from individual portable radios, and the noise from the passengers' voices drowned by the ship engine's pounding. The initial excitement died down with night in progress, only the ship's engine kept going. The night sky remained calm, the air warm, the stars and the moon at the ship with their pale lights. The ship pushed her way through a calm sea.

With first daylight the island of Corfu appeared. The ship stopped for a short time to allow passengers to go off and on. The mountains of Greece continued on their islands. Against a dry brown-yellow land stood out the dark green of pine trees with the white houses of Corfu town.

The ship reached Brindisi at the heel of Italy with a delay towards the end of the day. The land here was flat—a ring-wall closed the harbour off from the sea. Before clearance was given to our ship, it was enough time to watch the town and its harbour. People to anchor the ship, probably must not have been on hand, the whole exercise took hours, while the passengers had plenty of opportunity to get a suntan. The longer the waiting took, the more people became unsettled. Our German shepherd probably was the only one staying calm, because he was happy to be reunited with us again after his time in a box of the ship.

It came as no surprise that the clearance of the passengers was not in the same sequence as their cars. Until the driver turned up for the first car to leave the ship, abusive language could be heard in different tongues. If the first driver had not appeared, not much was needed, before a brawl would have started. The situation calmed down and people clapped their hands to applaud the first car to leave the ship.

First impressions on Italian soil changed into a more pleasant experience, once we got on an "autostrada" to Bari. This pleasure was not for free, Italy charged substantial toll-fees at regular distances for the use of their good roads.

Before sunset, we realised the area of southern Italy reflected a continuation of the Greek landscape with its vineyards and orchards. The houses were constructed more with arches outside, giving shade on verandas, whereas in Greece houses were built more in a block-form, often with flat roofs.

Driving into the night, we managed to reach Ancona. At a service station, people were outside next to their car sleeping on mattresses, which encouraged us to stop and do the same. The air remained still fairly hot during the night, thus it was a good idea to sleep in the open. Our dog kept a good watch over our sleep.

With first daylight, our tour continued. We decided not to travel to Rome because the make-up of our travel party with children and a dog would have made life in such a big city anything but easy. Rome is worthy of its own destination with a well-planned tour.

Further north, clouds announced different weather in a new area. Mountains appeared inland partly-covered with forests, green meadows stretched along the coast. At Pesaro, a last try to enjoy a beach was not successful—instead of sand, we found mainly stones. Heavy rain around the industrial centre of Bologna convinced us to continue our tour. Southern France crossed our minds for another quick holiday-break on a beach, before heading home again.

At the time of our tour, the world experienced an oil-supply crisis.

In countries like Germany, Italy supplied petrol coupons for tourists wanting to visit the country. The coupons, in fact, supplied petrol to foreign customers, but the service stations introduced their own conditions to make you pay on top of the coupon. They considered it a fair price. Was it a little bit of a "Mafia" game?

Passing Bologna, we found ourselves in dense traffic where large industrial factories like Fiat dominated the area. Turning south towards the Mediterranean, an Italian masterpiece of an "autostrada" led through the Apennine mountains to Genoa. Road tunnels kept the road on a sustainable gradient, partially rising to two levels, where the heavy transport remained on ground level and passenger vehicles used the air-road.

Genoa, on the foothills of the Apennine, stretched along a bay of the same name in a grand location. The road to the French border awaited a different masterpiece of a road-conduit at Ventimiglia: each lane was on a different level of the steep rocky coast, cutting its way through its own tunnels. At times, a third lane in between carried the trains on rails.

We crossed without any delay into France. The road continued now along the foothills of the Alps, the coast still partly steep and rocky. In Southern France we came past the Monaco Principality, a magnificent resort for mainly wealthy people from around the world with its exclusive privileges in banking, gambling palaces and harbours for yachts and luxury hotels.

Favoured by a weather that is more typical further south, Roman history still dominates the scenery here. The big white city of Marseille is an important commercial shipping centre of France. Its huge triumphal arch in the city centre was the first impressive sign of Roman Imperialism. The nearby city of Toulouse is a main naval base. Fertile land in the area introduced vineyards, citrus and olive groves and fruit plantations like in many parts of Greece, Southern Italy and Spain. "Midi France" as this part of France is called, enjoys extraordinarily warm weather due to climate conditions, which reach the area from as far as North Africa. In summer, the strong hot winds of the "Sirocco" blow up north into Rhone valley. In winter, the cold "Mistral" winds blow from the opposite direction bringing the rain into the area.

We cut across through Arles, Nimes to Montpellier, looking for a last chance to find a sandy beach for the remaining days of our holiday. The surrounding plains with their large vineyards gave us the opportunity to view the rich crops of dark-blue grapes. Vine-growers working in the fields had no objection to our overnight presence in their fields. People particularly in Southern France could still be identified by their own parole: "Laisser faire, laisser aller", which means:" Allow things to happen and move on (there is enough in the world to share). A superior view of life that cannot easily be found elsewhere.

Having been in Southern France a couple of times before, I'd like here to highlight on the city of Montpellier. In the past there were efforts made to create a second Paris in the South of France,where the climate was always more favourable. The opera in the centre of the city is a good copy of Paris, where magnificent buildings surround a large open area and street cafes add to a relaxed luxurious atmosphere.

It was, however, not the place we wanted to stay for the next couple of days. The Mediterranean was not far. This was the same area I had travelled 15 years earlier. It was here that I had pitched a tent higher up on the sandy beaches and occasionally met fishermen, who were working their boats, anchored along the beaches here and there. What we found now on these beaches surpassed any expectations: La Grande Motte had developed into a tourist centre packed with people along the beach as far as the eye could see. To the east, architects had given the area its special modern look with colourful buildings in the shape of a ship, a tent, towering waves—an attempt not to displace nature completely.

Amongst these crowds of holidaymakers it was difficult to find a place where we could stay. Thinking of an alternative would have taken too much time. So we put up with all the other people, trying to make the best of our remaining beach-time. But our dog seemed to dislike his restriction to the car. Did people gather here to watch each other? Our fellow citizens were naturally also amongst them. Heat, sun, air, sand and shallow seawater gave everybody the same starting point for a holiday. Most people must have enjoyed this beach life as they brought everything from home that they could carry: seats, tables, food, beer, radios, gas stoves and fridges. They made sure that life didn't differ too much from that at home.

As it is well known, people fortunately have different views. Regarding our view, we most definitely "did not take the home with us". We believe in a change during a holiday from the everyday demands, trying to catch up at least for a short time with a more basic life,where creativity in new life-situations becomes more of an issue. We restore our "batteries" only by shifting to different "polarities".

Inland, away from the crowded beaches we found freshwater lakes from the river Rhone estuary called "Etanges de Camargue". A rich variety of water birds lived here in peace, away from the hassles of our lives. Flamingos migrating from Africa can be observed here. Towards sunset, mosquitoes filled the air making life uneasy. As bird-watchers we received at least a good deal of freedom from nature.

Next morning it was decided to pack up and head back home. While packing our car, a couple said to us in German: "We watched all of you with interest and could first not believe, how you could store away all your belongings into the car and still have room left for yourselves. Now we have seen how it is done, you must be packing experts." We replied: "Experience from early boyscout times does help in such situations. The key is found in personal organization."

Only now, on our departure did the communication breakthrough happen. No-one spoke to us, when we camped there. Wasn't this like: "Missing the wood for the trees?"

Despite heavy traffic on the Rhone Autobahn, our progress back to the north gave wings to home. In Valence we bought a box of beautifully-ripened peaches before branching off towards Grenoble into the Alps. Large plantations of evenly-spaced walnut trees caught our eye before Grenoble which was already in the higher Fore Alps. Here the green meadow-hills changed to rocky Jura-stone slopes, which started the sky-rocketing Alpine peaks of the French Alps, where Mont-Blanc, Europe's highest mountain, exceeds 5000 metres. Heavy clouds locked into the mountains barred our views by releasing torrents of rain. The approaching night made us to stop at an "Auberge" (small restaurant) in the middle of a valley. During the week nobody was prepared for visitors, people carried on with their farm work after a day's work often in a factory. We had to negotiate our dinner that took time to be prepared. Our room remained cold, the emphasis was probably on savings. When the invoice came to our table, we understood, what Switzerland was saying: you want to see our beautiful country, we ask you to pay for it.

Serpentine roads and the heavy rain forced us to stop next to a lime tree for a rest. First daylight revealed a sign on the lime tree, which we could not read at night, saying: "Interdit pour le camping, le proprietaire". (Camping prohibited, the owner). We were back in countries with regulations, where every little bit was claimed by somebody and supported by rules.

Geneva showed its bright side to us, the rain was left behind. Beautiful green parks with their flower arrangements framed the city in front of the clear cold waters of Lake Leman with the highest part of the Alps in the background. A big clock arranged in flowers stood out on the shores of the lake. On the way to the city of Bern, bright green pastures rolled over gentle hillsides with dark green pockets of fir trees that created a perfect environment for milking cows to graze. We were in the Fore Alps again. Rainy seasons are quite common, but when the sun reigns, everything presents itself in astonishing beauty. Most houses are built in the typical Alpine style—the basement set in clean rock-walls with the upper part of the house built in a massive timber construction. A timber veranda with flowerpots along the railings supplied, under a gabled roof, the colours to a building.

A tobacco field in flower boasted many more plants than the drier fields of Epidauros in Greece. Everything was cultivated here to its maximum by its people in a totally clean environment. It is the basis from where the understanding of "Swiss-quality" comes from.

Zurich looked at that time like one big building site with a large number of Swiss factories calling it their home.

Where the river Rhine has left Lake Constance, the waterfalls of Schaff hausen create a spectacle of their own on the border of Switzerland and Germany.

The mighty river falls here in steps down to its continued level leaving a couple of rock columns in its thundery passage.

Having reached home soil soon after, the end of our tour to Greece came closer by the hour and with it the "exacting demands of a daily life".

A Spanish guest-worker told me on a previous occasion: "Germany is good to earn money, but not good to live." The economy is not an obliging measurement for a quality in life. It is usually difficult to have it both ways—a good income and quality of life; but quality can also be a holiday.

Back home our lives had to return to common rules. One rule, which had changed not long ago, was an equal family allowance, regardless of a social status. Earlier, only public servants received allowance for the first child—everybody else only after the third child; what a relic belonging to the Middle Ages. The reality of our small town was that the majority of children at school came from families with a foreign background. They hadn't lost the focus on their children in their materialistic endeavours. A correction in that sense will cost a society dearly. In contacts with other people, a lady came out with a note: "We must have forgotten about children; there are other priorities in today's world. Do priorities change, or do we change them"?

A new way of transforming a traditional life in Germany had started with an opening towards a United Europe, which was at that time still in its cradle. Foreign influence often created tension, when people tried to secure what was theirs with even more emphasis. This surfaced on an occasion, when my mother-in-law visited us early in 1980. Together we took a tour to the south into the Bavarian Alps.

*Mother in law-visit from Finland, Alps.*

Arriving in Fore Alp country with its green pastures across hilly countryside, it was decided to stop and have a walk on the wide pastures. Soon after, just when we started to enjoy a little bit of freedom walking across a meadow, a farmer turned up from somewhere shouting at us: "Get off my land, or I'll call the police." On my question: "Where are the signs you are not allowed to walk here?" The farmer went berserk: "You foreigners get out, we don't want you." We had nothing to say but leave, the unfortunate side of the encounter still remained. Perhaps the farmer must have had real-estate people inspecting his land uninvited before. Insecure people like our farmer try to secure their possessions with even more determination.

My mother-in-law did not understand the exact conversation, but she could not believe that in such a wide-open space our walk could have caused such a problem. Narrow conditions create easily narrow minds!

Leaving this unfortunate experience behind, we visited Neuschwanstein castle, a picturesque setting designed from the crazy dreams of King Ludwig II. High castle towers stood out between steep mountains. The castle was situated next to a lake with views to the north into open flat country and surrounding forest. Inside the castle no luxury was spared, for which the population had to suffer with their sacrifices through taxation. Today we conveniently forget about this part of history and look at the achievements as a miracle.

Sacrifices probably still remain today the underlying principle of all life forms. Life will continue with a number of unanswered questions.

At that time, back in Stuttgart, we rented a flat owned by the company I was employed with. Finding another rental accommodation in the Stuttgart area turned out to be impossible—not because of the dog, but because of the children. We went through all sorts of exercises in order to find another flat, with no success for over a year. Even offering bonuses didn't help. Buying a house for such inflated prices didn't cross my mind either.

Outside Europe we could easily afford a house, here in Stuttgart you had to be a millionaire to get you started with a decent house. The housing issue was, for various reasons, not on our agenda, because we didn't want to live in something of our own and put up with neighbours always putting their noses into other people's business. "When birds of a feather flock together" a neighbourhood can work. But if that is not the case, life could become unnecessarily difficult.

We were non-locals, therefore we counted less on the popularity scale. We were not running away from something, but reserved our rights to choose what suited us best.

In life, often we encounter situations, where we cannot change much for our personal needs. We are then bound either to live with it or act on it.

At work, the family, who owned the business was having disagreements that started to impact on the business. It appeared again that there is a rule in this world: one generation builds something up, another one brings it down again to maintain nature's cycles. Politics did not stop at the owner's door—it also came from outside. The company's business was lured into another place and even I was offered to follow.

Mentioning these developments in a proper way to the owner, I received only this answer: "It is not possible, you must be dreaming." This dream came true before I left the company. I was offered incentives to stay, but it was already too late. We had made up our minds to look for new horizons in Australia. Tragically, the owner committed suicide not much later—the pressure from family and business became too much to handle for him. The company could not go far any more.

## Spain and Portugal

Before reaching this point, we had another holiday in Southern Europe's summer domain, Spain, during summer 1980. Leaving again all the hassles of German progress behind, we tried to regain a more enjoyable life, even for a short time.

This time we didn't take anybody from outside our family with us. The constant presence of somebody from outside the family became on the tour to Greece a headache for everybody, despite best intentions from all sides.

Our tour to the sun in the south led this time to the west through Paris. The weather was so bad around Paris that we decided not to stay. Further south, the weather changed into summer heat.

Getting out of Paris we had to choose the right "national route" number. Number 1 came from the north into Paris, followed clockwise east, to south, the west and other outlets. A higher number was a direction towards the south. Number 6 was our route that led towards Orleans, the legendary city of Jeanne d'Arc, who helped free France from English occupation in 1429. At the mercy of England, she died a heroine without any help from her beloved France.

Signs along the river Loire indicated the locations of various palaces that were built to decentralize the Royal Palace of Versailles, extending the ruthless tax-squeeze of the country, that ultimately led to the French Revolution in 1789.

The country in the west of France was mainly flat with large areas of crop fields, but very little broadleaf woods. Limestone in the area had supplied material for many stone-set houses.

Large pine forests appeared around the city of Bordeaux, an important harbour-city of France and we enjoyed the vineyards of France, mainly to the south. The heavy traffic in Bordeaux encouraged us to continue our tour. Pine forests along the coast had been cleared on a massive scale, burnt to make way for maize plantations. The world needs food,but much is sacrificed in nature to satisfy this goal.

Biarritz, not far from the Spanish border, is a luxurious French holiday resort, where the Atlantic Ocean forms a fabulous coast-line against the green slopes of the Pyrenees mountains. We had planned to travel to Portugal because of its much less-expensive coastline.

The border at Hendaya showed how Spain was preparing to enter the European Union as there were no border control points. Bask-separate country lay in front of us in the mountainous Pyrenees. San Sebastian, near Biarritz, was another holiday resort. The road followed from there into a steep valley to Vitoria, an industrial centre of Spain. On the way, numerous heavy industries lined the road, many of them in a poor condition. Smashed windows could have been an indication of poor maintenance or of a place being abandoned. It became quite obvious that not much had been returned to this area despite its manufacturing importance. This was one of the triggers, that began the separatist movement of the Bask population. The linguistic and ethnic differences of the Bask added only to this imbalance of the economy,where everything went to help to feed the Spanish administrations far away in Madrid. Very little was invested in return to either the Bask industry or the external infrastructure. Moves to correct this imbalance were starting to gain ground promising better co-operation between Spain and its satellite Bask district. Unfortunately wake-up calls in politics mostly become effective only when conditions have become bad enough. For a ruling party it was always easier to live with a "status quo", because changes require renewed efforts across all societal party lines. Clear signs showing: "O Povo Unido" (United People's Power) gave an indication of where the problems came from: poor dialogue between the people and the powerbase in far-away Madrid.

Arriving on the high plateau of Central Spain, forests and green meadows of the lower coastal areas were left behind. Yellow-brown, sunburned country received us this summer. Widespread cornfields on both sides of the road were ready for harvesting.

On the side of one field, a row of old-grown olive trees gave us welcome cooling shade in the hot afternoon sun. Not long after having settled under one olive tree, an elderly man arrived wearing a hat and part of a uniform. As we found out, his task was to keep an eye on the field and make sure nobody set it alight by throwing a lighted cigarette from a passing car. "You can stay as long as you promise to keep the place tidy and create no fire hazard." A Peso tip helped the gentleman's decision to allow us to stay, which we appreciated.

Our campsite under the large olive tree was not far enough from the road and the constant traffic noise kept us awake during the night. Early in the morning the field guard was there and he farewelled us with "hasta la vista, felice tiempo" (see you again, have a good time).

Passing then through the town of Burgos, we passed a factory that made well-known machine tools. Many new houses accommodated the workforce, which has been recruited originally from the surrounding farmer communities. Past the city of Salamanca, the traffic was reduced considerably because the nearby capital Madrid absorbed most of it. During a stop in the small city, a lady showed us her collection of postcards. When we decided to buy them, she took the cards back and had a closer look, as if she had only just realized how beautiful her city was. Finally she found the heart to part with her postcards, adding the "serillas" (stamps) with a melancholy glimpse. In the afternoon the area became very hot and a "siesta" was the thing to do, like most Spanish people in the country. Cork oaks supplied the perfect opportunity for a shady rest. These vigorously-grown cork oaks in the large plantations were hundreds of years old, even their inner-branches reached solid dimensions. The thick-aged bark on the trees was deeply ridged. The light-weight cork is harvested for various applications including swimming support applications, sandals and wine bottle stoppers. The oak's trunk is cut half a metre above the ground with a curved knife. It is cut in sections around and straight up to allow the bark to regrow. These half-round sheets are stored on top of each other ready for transport.

*Cork-oak harvest, Western Spain.*

The leaf canopy of a cork oak is denser than that of an olive tree; the leaves of both are however quite similar. Staying under the canopy of a cork-oak grove during a hot day becomes a memorable experience especially because of the dominating silence. A smell of bark fills the air. Our "siesta" was extended into an overnight stay under the cooling leaf roof. At night a starry, moonlit sky sent interrupted light through the cork oaks' leaves. Patterns of bright light shined on the ground between the trees, bright enough for reading. The sounds of crickets chirping were all that filled the hot night air. Not far from our camping area, a small herd of young black bulls grazed. We did not notice the bulls until our dog, Mars, alerted us. They remained, however, out of our sight for most of the time.

Continuing on the next day after a great night in our "five-star cork-oak-grove hotel" we came across threshing places on the outskirts of small villages. The chaff sifted from the wheat was piled about 30 metres in diameter. Bundled straw bales outside indicated that the summer harvesting was over. A subcontracted machine probably threshed some of the wheat; some must have still been done by hand, as it was for thousands of years: threshing the corn out of the ears on to a mesh, which was put on an angle.

In Plasencia, we saw an early settlement of Roman history with an aqueduct high above the modern houses. When climbing up to the top of the aqueduct, we discovered that it no longer was full of water—just grass. Good soil and water from the "Sierra De Avila" encouraged colonization of the area at the end of armed conflicts some 2000 years ago.

For no known reason, here in remote countryside of Spain, a high-security police barricade stopped every car. Police officers were stationed in offset positions with machineguns on both sides of the road allowing no chance for any culprit to escape.

Similar approaches I had only previously seen in Brazil. In Germany, the police seemed to have been a bit naïve in control matters. Here in Spain they could have learnt how it was done. After our car interior was inspected, we were given the green light. The children and the dog in our car caused them to smile and bring forward a polite excuse. A good wish and a salute sent us back on our tour.

Vast cork-oak groves earmarked the area close to the border with Portugal. White building complexes appeared in between. These were called "haziendas" (larger properties) or "sitios", the smaller-sized properties. In some places the cork pieces were stacked in piles. Delivery trucks were loaded to an extreme height because of the cork 's light weight. These loaded trucks appeared menacing on the road with such a volume of a load. There was only occasional traffic here. The small villages along the road had drive-slow signs, because in the late afternoons many young people gathered on the road for a walk after a day's farm work. They had changed into their good clothing then—young men and women—enjoying each other's company at their "door to the world ", where they could catch each other's attention in their isolated countryside. Perhaps experiencing something together, something new that fed on their luck, imagination or even dreams.

Not far from the border of Portugal, we spent another comfortable night under the old-grown cork oaks. Flocks of bats introduced the start of the night and then disappeared into the dark sky again.

When the crickets stopped chirping, the night turned absolute silent—something we don't experience often in our civilized world anymore.

Here was the first time we could pick-up Radio-Lisbon, which gave us our first chance to brush up on our Portuguese language skills. The program was a conversation between a priest and a young woman—each side added humour to common life situations. This indicated well and truly that the Portuguese also like to look at life from the funny side.

The next morning we crossed another big Spanish river, Guadiana, that feeds from the mountains around the capital Madrid jointly with river Tajo. The latter we crossed the day before over a big concrete bridge, which spanned across deep riverbanks. Following the river Guadiana, another Roman ancient city appeared, where the river turned in a sharp bend to the south. An old massive stone bridge with many arches led across the river towards the fortress of Badajoz. At the end of the bridge there was an ancient triumphal arch. From here, small roads entered star-shaped into the historical part of the city. The new part of the city was built on an elevation behind the river's lowland. The border to Portugal was just behind the city. A surprising garden set-up with palms welcomed the traveller here.

The Spanish border-control didn't want to see our passports and we were given straight passage.

## Portugal

The Portuguese border control only needed some personal information on a form—but not much else.

As I addressed the guards in Portuguese, they asked if we were migrating to Portugal. I assured them, we were only visiting their beautiful country. Portugal had put a stop on migration from its colonies, even for its own citizens from there. The country was unable to cope with the influx of people from its colonies because of its small size. This could be seen as a double standard; previously it was good that its people colonized other countries, but today with the difficulties emerging out of the past, the country's leaders were taking short-term measures to fix those problems.

If we were from Mozambique, Angola or Timor, we certainly would have been denied entry into Portugal. This information was only gleaned by Portuguese-speaking people—not the tourist who could not speak the language. The palm island between the two border-controls could be interpreted as a sign of good relations between the two countries. As a matter of fact, their languages are not so much different—they can understand each other. Spain has today become the big brother, as Portugal has lost its colonial territories. The violet-blue and orange colours of the houses reminded us strongly of the distant country of Brazil, where especially the Portuguese used to apply colours to their houses. They highlighted door and window frames in a white or light green colour. Many windows had no glass, wooden shutters on each side instead. People here had yet no need to secure their houses.

This region of Portugal was a continuation of Spain with its regionally-associated cork-oak groves. In Spain, we always saw people around the houses, the elderly often in front of a house observing others going past them. This way they could connect to the outside world. Here in Portugal we hardly saw anybody in a village. They were either too busy with their "siesta" or at work somewhere else. To reach the coastal area didn't take long in the small country. Coming down from the "Alto Alentajo" (highlands), the cork oaks suddenly disappeared and pine trees took over the sandy soil. Dense old-grown pine trees gave excellent protection against the summer heat under their wide canopies. They left, however, a carpet of brown conifer needles on the ground, which gave rise to the many warning signs of extreme fire danger and for drivers to be cautious when driving across this needle carpet, because the tyres easily lost their grip on the ground and a car could eventually slide out of control.

Shortly before the capital Lisbon, an autobahn introduced everybody into a different world: houses had windows, were better built, the better built houses were surrounded by stone walls and cars outnumbered people in the street.

The entrance to Lisbon was across a grand suspension bridge over the mouth of river Tejo. At that time, the bridge was the largest bridge construction in Europe, surpassed only by the bridge in San Francisco. To the east, on its southern starting point, stands a monumental "Christus Rei" (King Christ) rock statue on a base spreading with its open arms blessing the entire city. A relationship to Rio de Janeiro in Brazil becomes obvious here, where a very similar statue resides over the city from the "Pao de Acucar" (Sugar Loaf).

During the summer months, Lisbon, with its hot sunny days, could be regarded as one of Europe's finest cities mainly through its sea and river-mouth position. Like most cities, Lisbon offers splendid places, museums and patrician buildings that hark back to a rich past in which the city was one of the most important in Europe.

Its history is also quite colourful, starting with its foundation B.C. and staying under Roman sovereignty, succeeded by West Goths, an Arabic reign and French occupation. Instead of driving around the city, I organized taxi rides. I quickly learnt, how to deal with the local taxi service. One had to be careful when the taxi driver asked: "How much do you want to pay?" I looked for a taxi that was prepared to put the counter on in his car. All taxis were black with a green roof. The polish of the car didn't reveal the make or the age, most were veterans. New cars were very expensive in Portugal,because it did not have its own car industry. Here was a thriving market of veteran cars maintained and polished in marvellous condition over decades.

One day in Lisbon was enough for us, so we headed further south to the Provinces "Baixo Alentejo" and "Algarve" along the coast. There was hardly any traffic on these country roads hugged by pine forests. A rest at a service station with a restaurant brought us into contact with a local farmer, who was sitting at an outside table under the shade of a huge pine tree.

In our conversation I asked the farmer: "Which Christ statue was first built, the one in Rio or the one in Lisbon?" He replied: "This wouldn't matter to me, it is still one and the same Christ."

Quite an interesting opinion, I thought to myself!

Continuing our tour, we left the flat country of the coast, which changed into hills and continued then into the "Sierra de Grandolla," where cork-oak trees again took over from pine trees. Houses were colourful again with no windows, the splendour of the capital Lisbon was lost in the distance.

Country people were living here with only the very basic necessities. How long they would stay silently happy, would only be a matter of time, when Portugal changes from a colonial power into an industrialized society at the unifying table of Europe. Lisbon will have to include into Portugal's efforts its country population. Social responsibilities across a wider society should be everybody's concern. How long shall we be able to meet poor, happy people? Will the happiness change also with the poverty?

Further south around Odemira eucalyptus trees were introduced into the vegetation, an indication of the existence of underground water. Portugal, not having introduced "daylight saving time", should be welcomed not only by country people, but also by parents with children. Fiddling with the hours of the day like in other parts of Europe, didn't take into consideration the needs of children. They are not clocks we can put forwards or backwards.

The road to the south was bordered either by pine or eucalypt trees, that gave excellent shade to the road. Crop fields with white farmhouses were in the distance to the east. Houses changed here, not painted any more in colours, they were either white or set in grey stone-blocks with glass windows.

The small city of Lagos on the coast of the Algarve, Portugal's most southern province, introduced us into a different world with foreign tourists everywhere. Having met no tourists on Portugal's country roads, they must have arrived here from another direction. Everything looked different again. The money tourists spent here, which is usually more than they would allow themselves at home, helped to create an environment answering more to tourist needs than local needs. This resulted in an artificial atmosphere. During our short stay, it came as no surprise that the alarm was raised about a robbery in town, in a place where we had been only a short while ago.

We encountered another difference here. As we moved out of the town, we found a petrol station set-up, where the petrol pump was on one side of the road and the cash office and small goods shop on the other side. Arriving at the petrol pump, you had to wait for somebody to come across the road to give you service. Helping yourself was definitely not an option. People took their time, which was demonstrated by two men painting a nearby fence. They must have concentrated thoroughly on every movement of their paintbrush. When we left a couple of hours later after having eaten at local restaurant, the two men were still painting the same spot of the fence. This was one way not to risk heart failure!

The local restaurant was also slow in service. According to local customs, we were too early at 4pm, but for the most expensive fish meal, the rules could be bent.

Tables and chairs in the restaurant were in carved brown-black timber, the floor in light flags, walls in brilliant white, interrupted by dark timber construction beams under the roof. Colourful earthenware jars decorated the interior, complete with the Portuguese rooster—their symbol of the clever countryman.

Our two children very quickly discovered the two Macao parrots in a corner of the restaurant. Only one of them responded to their visit, the other remained motionless. The waitress explained: "Both parrots came from Brazil many years ago. One parrot died and is now stuffed to keep company with the living parrot." Nobody could guess, what the parrot thought about this—it appeared rather absorbed and calm. It was a rare experience to come face to face with such a colourful creature out of the Amazon.

Later, other people came into the restaurant and a young lady joined our waitress. A lively conversation began. Did the young lady disapprove of our earlier start in the restaurant? After the conversation, a young boy handed us the bill on a plate. The other staff had completely disappeared. I would have liked to have had the bill explained to us. We waited, but eventually I put the money on the plate and left the restaurant rather than losing unnecessary time. The young boy collected the money from the table straight away. What started as a friendly atmosphere ended up as a purely business transaction. I knew, we were highly overcharged. This was not a good way to build on a restaurant's reputation by putting money before customer satisfaction.

The steep yellow-red rocky coastline made it difficult in parts to find access to the ocean beaches outside overcrowded spots with foreign tourists. At another petrol station, an African black man filled our tank. Talking to him, it was revealed that he was from Angola. He said: "My sister is across the road helping her German friend with a hotdog stand." She was indeed a good-looking black woman. The German friend hurried in explaining: "We love each other and need only a place to live together. At the moment we both just make ends meet with this sausage stand. I can only stay in Portugal for three months. Maria is here illegally. Portugal has stopped migration from its previous colonies. She won't be allowed to stay in Germany either."

While our conversation went on, we bought some sausages that were a far cry from a real Bavarian sausage. During our sausage meal we told them about our Brazilian experience: "In your case it would be no problem to find acceptance in Brazil, but how you would manage a living there without special qualifications, could remain a big question mark." Our friends were not exactly happy with this latest information, but they said: "We will check on our possibilities concerning Brazil." Tourism can bring all sorts of people together!

During our continued search for an easy access to a lonely beach, we came across several estates thoroughly closed off by rock-walls displaying signs in English "Private golf area", "Proibicao de Entrada", "David's star signs". Was this the start of a sell-out of their own country with people barred from entering the best locations in the area. We didn't give up looking for a suitable place to swim. The proximity of the Faro airport with its roaring aircraft-engines, bringing and taking out people in their thousands, caused us to look further around.

Further down the road, the gatekeeper of an insignificant railway crossing line gave us some entertainment. Like everybody else, we queued up before the closed railway gate. It must have been well over 10 minutes before a car passed through the gate, which was closed immediately after. Watching the area near the gate, I realised that the gatekeeper moved close to the first car before opening the gate and letting this car pass through. By the time it was our turn, we knew by then that we had to pay a toll. As long as no train came, this clever businessman spent his time collecting his pocket money. Some people used the horn of their car to voice their frustration. The guard answered this by returning to his cabin and only coming back when the car horns were silenced. Was this his message: If you are in a hurry, you have to pay?

Once past the crossing, we left behind the crowded places—rural country took over again, the original face of Portugal. Acreage properties showed up with rarely-seen fruit trees like the

"Para-nut-tree", the "Amourella", both originally at home in Brazil. The "Para-nut" is in the north-east of Brazil in the State of the same name "Para". It is the most successful fruit out of the tropics as its hard shell and inherent oils are highly-resistant to parasites.

"Amourella" is a blackberry-like fruit of a tree and as its name says, "sweet like only love could be."

Once we came closer to the coast again, we slowed down so as not to miss an access to a beach. The peninsula of Sagres showed with its fortress, complete with wheeled cannons in position, the historic importance of its position fighting intruders from the Mediterranean or the mainland. Today a lighthouse protects shipping traffic passing from the Atlantic Ocean into the Mediterranean.

Having returned to Sagres in our search for a place on a beach, we reached the most southern point of Portugal. This is a frontier surrounded to its west, south and east by the wild Atlantic Ocean, with its tumbling waves reaching far down the dwindling high rocky coastline. It was frightening getting close to the edge and looking down the vertical rock walls. Just when I told the children to stay away, a fisherman stood at the neck-breaking edge of the coastline and threw his fishing hook down about 150 metres into the foaming surf, not showing any sign of respect for this height. He certainly was free from giddiness, posing like this for a very special photo.

A stiff wind blew from the sea over the edge here, so we cut our stay short and went back to Burgau, where we found the only access to a beach, that was not crowded with tourists.

Colourful wooden boats anchored in the bay of this fishermen's town. Its colourful houses were lined distinctly along the bay, well away from the forces of the ocean. High-standing Algoa flowers were the only vegetation besides the grass, which tried hard to keep its terrain against the coastal winds.

At the inland end of the bay, where the coast went up steep again, we had chosen a place to put up our tent, enjoying superb views over the whole bay with the fishing village underneath.

The beach underneath us was not very wide; rock pillars in the sea along the coast limited the sandy shores. Our camp was like an eagle eyrie. We erected a quick fence made from nearby branches to protect our tent site. Everything seemed all right until we tried to get our cooking started. The strong wind from the sea success-fully hampered our attempts.

During that first night the wind increased so heavily that our tent was gradually ripped apart and we found ourselves in the morning without a useful tent. We received here a real setback in our attempt to gain personal freedom on an isolated beach. Our enthusiasm came to an end.

We were quick to pack up and try our luck on Spanish shores in the east. Even when leaving, the wind hadn't lost its ferocity. A nice spot was not always a good spot to stay. The cold water of the Atlantic and an approaching storm, told us to move to hopefully better fields. Leaving the rugged coast of Southern Portugal behind, we passed a rural area around Loule. This was the home of basket-making. Nearly every house displayed stalls out the front of basketwork in chairs, tables, pots and mirror frames. Only here the house-fronts showed colourfully-glazed tiles, a remnant of Islamic culture from the area's past.

Closer to the border town of "Vila Real" on the Portuguese side, the coast changed into a plain and the river "Rio Guadiana" ran in a wide mouth into the Atlantic, forming the border between Portugal and Spain.

## Spain

A ferry crossing between Portugal and Spain had a regular schedule and also took vehicles on board. The border controls were only minor, no delay was caused. On the Spanish side waited a picturesque small town with its white houses creeping up a hillside and giving an expression of a town in an Arabic country. No wonder, the place carried the name "Ayamonte". Andalusia, the largest provincial area of Spain, lay in front of us with the majority of its people working in the predominantly agricultural industry at that time. Olive groves started giving way to cornfields, which were less labour-intensive. Solitary large estates showed wealthy residences in the middle of a population, that was living on low incomes.

For centuries people had lived here with controversy. One cultural element from this can still be found in the ongoing tradition of the "Flamenco". Originally introduced through migration from today's Iran, Flamenco music has survived here in Andalusia. The elements of the guitar music and style hasn't changed much since, but the contents have: Flamenco music reflects also on the social problems, out of which the Flamenco is an escape into a tragic interpretation. This might be expressed through passion, determination or anger.

Years ago, I could still experience a real Flamenco gathering in Andalusia's countryside. Late in the afternoon of a hot summer's day, first the elderly of the village met in its centre, which was shaded by elm-trees with benches underneath. Later, the younger generation joined in. One guitar started, calling others to join. Depending on the atmosphere of the moment, a singer portrayed his role with his address through a song. Depending who was around at the time, other guitars joined in and a lady was encouraged to dance with the music. A young man accompanied her by knocking his heels to the ground, accentuating the rhythm by clapping the hard wooden castanets, one in each outstretched hand. The guitars played Flamenco variations, while the singer introduced new topics and awaited the audience's response. The words told about love, sorrow, hardship, loss and hope. The longer a flamenco session lasted, the more people joined in and the wine helped to keep the atmosphere buoyant. This was the real flamenco music and dance, born out of the moment. It could be difficult to find such an occasion today. Most flamenco we hear today is a copy and an imitation of the real flamenco music. It is a synthesis of Arabic and European music today, still transferred from guitar to guitar. The right hand of the guitar performance is close to impossible to document—it can be taught only by demonstration. Flamenco has its counterparts in

Negro Spirituals, Jazz and Gypsy music. They all come out of desire to sing away the hardship of life.

Andalusia is the country where Flamenco has survived over centuries dating back to the 11 Century. Flamenco still can be picked up only from another Flamenco player.

When we left Portugal it was cool, and yet nearby Andalusia welcomed us with extreme summer heat. The small villages we passed through were different from the ones in Portugal.

Roads had claimed most of the space here, so that only a small sidewalk remained in front of the houses,that were lined up in continuous rows. The houses were not colourful as in Portugal. Here wrought-iron work appeared in balconies and windows instead. Many locals were sitting in the small area outside of their houses watching the events in their neighbourhood and awaiting the cooler breeze of the night. Passersby had to keep a watchful eye on the many children, cats and dogs that ran around the sidewalks and roads.

The wide plains of the mouth of Rio Guadalquivir harboured along its shores the capital of Andalusia, Seville. Ships from the Mediterranean could reach Seville, making it an important port for shipments of goods from Andalusia.

Since Roman foundation B.C. under the Emperor Julius Caesar, the city has seen others to take foothold here: Arabic occupation in 712 left in its 500 years the floorplan of the city with its small dead-end streets, which caused at the time of our visit a major problem with the modern traffic. The gothic cathedral in the city's centre was built on the ground of a mosque. The minaret was changed only in its upper part to accommodate church bells.

This "Giralda" had become the city's landmark. Seville castle, the "Alcazar", is another remnant of Islamic culture. Its art in the construction is strongly similar to the "Alhambra" in Granada. Parts of the Roman city walls with its towers can still be seen.

The bullfight arena in the city was, in fact, the biggest in Spain. Its construction did not, however, go back far in history. Houses around the outside did not give first impressions of an arena. The inside of the arena had ranks of seats going around the centre. Only the top-most seats were under a roof, going all around with the support of column arches. With bullfights mostly banned, the arena is nowadays used for other purposes.

The summer heat in the city's narrow streets did not invite a long stay. We stopped in a children's playground, from where we undertook our excursions. The only quiet and cool place was besides the cathedral other churches. A priest conducted his mass in the presence of only a few worshippers. The only dim light inside the cathedral came through its colourful windows. This was like a refuge from the busy outside world.

Leaving Seville to the south, corn and sunflower fields bordered the road all the way in flat country. Only around the most southern point of Europe, Tarifa, did steep coastline catch up with us again. An interesting fact was that none of the locals could direct us to this most southern point of Europe. Nobody we met apparently knew about it. Some people tend to live in ignorance in their own backyard.

A similar scene happened to us in South America when we asked locals at the equator where to find a sign indicating that this was the equator. We found it on our own accord, people probably didn't even know that their country of Ecuador owed its name to the equator, which passes through there.

Back in southern Spain, Algeciras had developed into a much larger city since I had passed through 12 years earlier. New white houses climbed up the surrounding hills in big numbers with a direct view on to the huge rock of Gibraltar. Sea traffic across the Strait of Gibraltar had dramatically increased since the importance of the area has grown. The old point of controversy between Gibraltar (which was occupied by Great Britain) and Spain (which occupied neighbouring Ceuta on the African soil) had not changed. If anything, tensions had increased.

At "La Linea", the border to Gibraltar, all cars had to stop and only non-Spanish foreigners could pass through the controls. Everybody wondered, how long this situation could last with Spain having a foreign border within its own territory.

The area was undoubtedly prime land for all sorts of trade practices to and from Africa. This situation gave us a bizarre experience. I had our car parked not far from the shipping docks of Algeciras. While looking for some shopping facilities in the area, my wife waited with the children in the car, when a dark-skinned woman approached her with a tiny baby in her arms asking in broken Spanish: "Do you want to buy a baby, you can have it for only 200 US dollars." My wife instantly put the car window up, making sure she wasn't given this baby through the window. At the same time, she pointed into the back of our car and our four children. The message went across. The lady, heavily-pregnant again, moved on to somebody else. This was the first time that we had heard about a price-tag being put on a human—and at the incredibly-low price of $ 200 US. Poverty must have been a driving force here to adopt such desperate measures. One could have also asked the question: what else had been traded here between Europe and Africa? We left this answer with the Spanish police who controlled the area. We moved on in search of a beach location.

Algeciras was surprising in many of its places with dark-blue ornamental tile-work on floor areas, benches and fountains. The name, Algeciras, pointed to its Arabic history and explained the origins of the ornamental tile-work.

The last time I had visited Morocco was in 1967. More details can be found in Volume 1 of my book "Journey of a Lifetime".

Newly-established holiday colonies along the shelving coasts were of dubious construction. Watching bricklayers working on a building without a line or spirit-level explained how the bricks were lined in waves the higher up the wall went. Mortar over the bricks perfectly covered such imperfect work. The main focus here was on getting the job done quickly so as to keep pace with Real Estate requirements. Signs were everywhere: "Southern Spain's sun guarantees Ocean Views", "Quick profit returns for your investment", "The key to your success you receive from us". All these confessions of faith aimed at quick tourist dollars. Some earlier-built houses already showed the signs of poor workmanship, but this was not representative of Spain. The country demonstrated in many places its ability of proper building methods. The quick tourist-dollar had also introduced the shortcuts here.

In front of barren mountain-slopes, Malaga welcomed us in its wide Mediterranean bay. It was another pulsing southern Spanish city with a historical background going back to the Roman empire, followed by 700 years of Arabic sovereignty. The fortress of the "Alcazar" on a hillside above the city holds evidence of Arabic culture, which is again very similar to the "Alhambra" in Granada and the "Alcazar" in Seville—an arena also reigns above the city image. A magnificent avenue with a tropical park running through the city centre invites everybody for a rest in its cool shade. However, the tourist-presence also attracts unwelcomed elements of a society. Our car was almost broken into by a young moped-driver. He had started opening our door lock with some kind of tool.

If our dog inside the car had not frightened him away, he might have succeeded in breaking in. From that moment on, we didn't want to stay much longer in the place. Before leaving Malaga it is worth mentioning that in Spanish folklore Malaga had created its own musical characteristic with the lyric guitar of the "Malagena".

Past Malaga, we saw an aqueduct and a modern suspension bridge over a gully and thought we would investigate to find access to a beach. Not even a path could be seen leading down. Parking our car off the road, I decided to investigate first on foot and discovered a swimming place. I drove the car as far as I could into the upper valley. When the car was parked under the protection of green bush, we went down the gully with our belongings to a small sandy beach partly surrounded by high rock pillars in the sea. The steep sides of the valley ended here, we finally found an unspoiled place of our own.

A tarpaulin helped us to construct a home on a small stepped platform with a superb view, halfway up on the northern slope of the valley, down to the small beach-bay, the canyon to the right, the sea to the left. We found finally a bit of paradise. A basic kitchen with a fireplace became installed in a classic boy-scout manner, away from the living area, securing it with a fence out of branches against the steep embankment. Potable water surfaced from underground in one spot in the canyon. This was an important discovery for our stay on the beach. For safety reasons we still boiled the water before using it.

A serpentine footpath down to the beach gave everybody his share of fun. Once most of these preparations were done, a simple holiday-life in nature's paradise could start. The seawater was very warm and shallow. Clear seawater, sun, sand and hot summer air offered a holiday with a special quality. Nobody had to tell anybody what to do. We all found something worthwhile to do, either improving our campsite, playing with the sand on the beach, relaxing, swimming, reading, cooking or collecting firewood.

On the plateau, behind us, vast vineyards with dark blue grapes waited for our " judgment ", and there were capsicum fields to enhance our menu. Every day late in the afternoon we walked up the canyon to inspect our parked car and ensure everything was okay.

Then one day, just when we were getting used to our new holiday lifestyle, the children said: "Mum, there are naked people on our beach, what are they doing here?" Our "visitors "were actually out of our German neighbourhood. What else could we expect? One male and two female people had also found this place. They wanted to be as natural as possible, leaving their clothes somewhere else. This didn't mean we had to follow their example, when they came to say hello on the small sandy beach. The "Adam "introduced himself as a renowned soccer player in a German National soccer league. He was quite puzzled, when we admitted we had not heard of his name.

The two "Eves "had a much easier explanation—they were mainly concerned with the wellbeing of their soccer star.

The nudists were soon noticed by the Spanish locals. One local farmer asked one of the "Eves" whether she wanted to become his wife. He proudly outlined his possessions as two goats, one mule and one horse. The next day, the farmer turned up on the beach with a basket of food for his "Eve". She said she was a famous photo model and told me: "In my eyes the Spanish farmer is a funny bloke who cannot impress me." As neither of our nudist friends spoke Spanish, I became their interpreter. I urged them to take the farmer's intentions seriously and to be mindful not to create a disturbance in this Catholic community. I advised them to put their clothes back on—which they did!

Our 10 remaining days in this nature's paradise did not take long to pass. At the end of it our skin had turned dark brown and we had enjoyed a break from everyday life. Our "batteries" had been recharged in a wider sense. It was interesting to watch the children, how they spent their time mainly unsupervised without any quarrel. At home more supervision was needed to keep them from being at each other's throats. With very little material goods around them, they resorted more to their imaginations to have fun—sand, stones, water, shells, fish, self-made fishing lines, camp duties and swimming.

We kept in touch with everybody by sending a long, sharp whistle. Everybody knew to pay immediate attention, when they heard this whistle. My wife enjoyed swimming out into the sea more than the rest of us. On one occasion while Arja was swimming, I was at the lookout at our campsite and saw not far from her a shark-fin moving in a straight line out of the water. Off went the whistle as loud as I could, waving both arms, indicating for her to return. Fortunately the shark did not change its straight course, which gave my wife the chance to return unharmed. The shark could still be seen for a while in the water with the fin indicating its position. It must have been after fish and therefore preoccupied.

A lesson to our children followed, explaining to them the difference between a shark and that of a dolphin: a shark swims most of the time in a straight line close to the surface; the fin emerging out of the water is on its back in an interrupted line. The dolphin's fin is a close curved line.

Dolphins often swim with other dolphins and they move more in a diving-swim style. Sharks are dangerous predators,that don't only kill for food. Being territorial, they can deliver fierce attacks. Dolphins, on the other hand, are very friendly towards humans and, in some cases, they have even helped rescue people. There is also a basic rule: where dolphins are, there are no sharks. Sharks avoid dolphins because of their superior swimming capabilities and their possible hard-nose attacks. For these reasons it is vital to differentiate, without mistake, the shark from the dolphin—the foe from the friend. Sharks have a coarse sandpaper skin, the dolphin's skin is smooth—but we don't want to go that close to find out!

During our stay, an opportunity arose to watch dolphins in the sea and this helped my children understand my warning and explanation.

A meeting with a local diver brought us into contact with a catch of octopuses. The diver emerged out of the water near us wearing a complete black diving suit: facemask with snorkel, a harpoon in his hand, a knife fixed on the side of one leg. He sat down in the sand with his unloaded harpoon and pulled a bright yellow floating ring from the sea towards the sand. His catch of three octopuses included one with metre-long tentacles. We all listened to the Spanish diver: "There are all sizes of octopuses around here. Hunting them, you have to be always careful that they stay underneath you,when you harpoon them—preferably before the octopus body releases the black camouflage ink. If this happens, the octopus will attack with its tentacles in a downwards motion. Therefore it is important to stay above in case the ink interferes with your vision and the tentacles can't get you. A sharp knife is important to make a quick kill around the eyes and sometimes defend yourself."

The body of the octopus still moved slightly with the rows of rosette-formed suction buttons underneath each tentacle. The diver held only one button on my arm and asked me to try and pull it off. What a suction force this button still produced! One could easily imagine what would happen, if an octopus got hold of a diver with all its tentacles. The only way to free himself would be the use of the razor-sharp knife to cut off one tentacle after the other from the octopus's body. Such a struggle with a big octopus would be a life or death battle.

The glossy look of the tentacles made it hard to believe, once cut into slices and fried, they represented a special delicacy. The diver went back into the water to put his black rubber suit on, before getting ready for another catch.

Before he disappeared again, I asked him if he had seen the shark out there. He replied: "Keep well away from it, that's a big one!" After his words we looked at each other and realised we had been lucky again. We will always remember this lesson from an experienced diver.

One day towards the end of our stay we visited the nearby village of Nerja. I went with my eldest son, Risto, up through the canyon on to the road, which led into the village. On our way we said hallo to a farm worker in the area. He lived in a one-room hut surrounded by a small garden, where he cultivated his own vegetables. His garden looked rich in comparison with the surrounding fields, that he also worked for an owner.

This farm worker called Jose was actually the admirer of one of the Eve photo models on the beach. He had given up the idea of marrying her—the needs for his life kept him on his toes.

On the road to Nerja, there were not only cars rushing along and lifting the dust into the air, but also people on foot were sharing the dust and noise with us. Before the traffic slowed considerably down at the village entrance with its narrow "calles" (alleys), very little room was left in front of the houses. People in front of their houses, pedestrians and cars had to watch each other when moving in such limited areas. Entrances to houses were most of the time camouflaged by a row of sea and nut-shell strings allowing air circulation, but obscuring the views from the road into the house. The one-room house was usually extended to the back with another storey above. Its entrance was laid out with shiny tiles. Pot plants filling the entrance area helped to cut out the road noise and control the air temperature, especially when water was sprinkled on to the plants. Only a few houses displayed artistic fountains amongst their big-leafed plants. The immaculate cleanliness from inside did not extend to the road. The dust from the road and footpath forced the housewives to keep up a constant cleaning schedule.

A barber sitting behind a window and reading his newspaper with the assistance of daylight caught my attention. He seemed to be waiting for somebody like me wanting to demonstrate his hair-cutting skills with a proper shave. The old razor in his skilful hands worked marvellously—it was quick and safe and restored my civilized image. The "maestro" gave a special farewell-gesture. All this for a competitive price, which I honoured with an extra tip. We strolled with the barber's special recommendation to try another shop. Not much could be seen from outside, besides a few photo-graphical exhibits, funny souvenirs, perfumes and handbags. Only inside diving accessories were to be found. We were after a mask with a snorkel and a pair of flippers. The harpoon in the shop looked like the one the diver on the beach had used. Curious, I took the harpoon and investigated its function more closely. No spear was inserted, so I slightly pumped the cylinder. The harpoon suddenly released its pressure with a huge bang. Everybody else in the shop rushed out the door thinking that a shooting had taken place. The shop owner overcame his fright first and rushed out to call his customers back. Inside, a shop lady calmed the situation down and reassured me and Risto that nothing had happened nor was wrong.

Fright was followed by a surprise—how superbly the shop owners handled this incident! I didn't even receive a word of blame. Business continued as usual and we paid for our items—but not the harpoon. They waved goodbye in a friendly manner. We bought other groceries, but not milk, because it did not stay fresh in the sun even though it was labelled "long-lasting pasteurized milk". Milk very quickly went off our menu in Southern Spain.

Returning to our beach paradise, we visited Jose's hut and invited him to our campsite in the afternoon. We had organized Spanish wine for the occasion. When Jose arrived with his little son, Antonio, he carried a bag with something heavy in it. Recognizing our wine, he refused it and opened his bag, taking out his wine bottles with this explanation: "Wine is a Spanish affair, we bring it on!"

From the surrounding bamboo, he cut a piece and fitted it into the bottle with a cut on an angle at the outer end. The bottle made its round now in a Spanish fashion, releasing wine through the pipe in a controlled flow holding the pipe up in the air and not in our mouths. Kidney-shaped leather bags and clay jugs are used in the same way by moving them out with the stretched arms, while the water or wine from it flows in a bow to the mouth. This non-contact drinking method requires some training to direct the fluid only into the mouth. The trick is to start from a short distance and then move out with the arms.

As our wine party went on, the children had their own lemonades, Jose described his life as a farmer worker to us: "Life on a farm has never been easy for the workers. The owners often become rich. The income they pay is not enough for a living. Your own garden and a few animals like I have, my two goats, one mule and a horse are a necessity. In Andalusia nothing has changed in my life. I could not go to school 40 years ago, because there were no schools. Today our children have to spend eight years at school and where do they end up after school today? They are not better off with a school education than we were without school. Antonio still works on a farm belonging to somebody else for a small income. For us the world has not progressed. The rich have become richer and we were left behind."

A statement that is still current in many parts of the world. Changes happen most of the time as a last resort. Reluctance towards changes becomes rather deeply rooted. When I raised the idea of communism, Jose gave a blunt rebuke saying that, despite his poor financial situation, he still owned his hut, animals and garden, that he kept in high regard and was not prepared to give away. The landowners knew this, allowing therefore this private initiative. An ownership, no matter how small it might be, is still the key to a social freedom. Our discussions continued well into the early morning hours with the cooler breeze of the night. Touching the subject of a United Europe, Jose expressed his confidence that he would be able to get a better price for his garden products, because he currently sold to an oversupplied local market. What he didn't know, and what I kept to myself was that in today's Germany we could often buy Spanish agricultural products cheaper than here. What a bizarre economy rules our world!

When the subject turned to soccer, he let us know that Real-Madrid had just beaten Bavaria-Munich in a crushing 1:9 result, which helped to lift considerably the Spanish pride: "In soccer we are the best!"

During our stay in "paradise" we nearly lost account of the time.

Only with Jose's confirmation we were reminded that it was high time to return home. Our car had been over-run by ants during our stay and Jose came up with a brilliant idea of how to get rid of them. "We have to cut their support base. Let us dig holes around the wheels and fill them with water. This will make the ants disappear." Jose was right, the ants disappeared completely out of the car in a short time. Before the ants could regain the territory of our car, we had to carry everything back from the beach. Back on the road, we were absorbed by traffic. Our quiet days on the beach were definitely over.

We headed inland into the mountains of the Sierra Nevada, which was covered with eternal snow on its peaks. The farmers in the Guadelfeo valley grew pears, they sold at roadside stalls. It was a must for every bypasser to have a taste.

The yellow pears had a slight almond-taste giving them a top rank in their class. Stopping at one booth I looked at the honey jars. Picking one up to have a closer look, the lid came off and honey ended up in my hand and on my shoes. The sticky honey took a while to come off. My desire to buy honey disappeared. Even the lady behind the stand made no claim for the loss of her honey, but anxiously assisted in the clean-up process. She was quite happy that we bought her pears. Customer satisfaction was a priority here. The main road brought us to Granada and the traffic in its satellite townships. I might not have recognised the place any more, if the Alhambra fortress had not been above the city's houses and the mountains of the Sierra-Nevada surrounding it. Progress had brought a density and traffic chaos to this city. I did not want to spoil my memories from my earlier visit 15 years ago, when the Alhambra was not disrupted by busloads of tourists, who changed the silent atmosphere of this Arabic treasure-fortress. It was difficult to fully enjoy the art treasures because of the tourist crowds. Fifteen years ago, I could take selected photos inside the Alhambra with hardly any other visitors present. My earlier reception with a local guitar-builder at that time had also disappeared with the growth of the city and related pressure for progress. Our stay became only a short one.

The road out of Granada led to the north into higher areas— all burnt brown by the summer sun. A last glimpse back supplied a panoramic view of the whole city with the Alhambra fortress sticking out of its centre. The cathedral could not compete any more with its appearance.

Pine forest areas with their dark-green tree crowns took over at times from the burnt dry country. We arrived at Guadix, originally the ancient location of caves hidden in a mountain slope. Now souvenir shops filled the place right to the road. When stopping here, you could experience an overwhelming rush from merchants. Tourists also drove out here with money to buy souvenirs from the people living in the caves. I had good memories from 15 years earlier. We had no intention of stopping in front of a massive souvenir display. Spain could give also controversial impressions within relatively small distances.

Coming closer to the coast again near Lorca, desert-like country began. White-yellow soil was everywhere reminding us of stretches of the saltpeter desert in the Atacama on the south-west coast of South America; the white spots in the Atacama were concentrations of saltpeter. Soil conditions have an important role on the vegetation. For these reasons hardly any green could be found in the area, whereas on the plains further down the coast, around Murcia, exuberant gardens with citrus, grapes and peach farms appeared again in green vegetation.

In the late afternoon, it seemed the town's whole population regarded us as something of an attraction—four children and a dog in a car. As all the vehicles had to follow the pedestrians' convenient trot, our car quickly became an attraction for too many onlookers, bringing our progress nearly to a halt: the heat of an outgoing day, rows of palms bordering the main road on both sides and not, at least, the people asking us to slow down. Cheerful expressions from outside reached us inside the car while we took part in the slow domestic afternoon procession. People in Spain liked to dress up and gather together after a hot summer day in a public place, expressing their solidarity by watching, communicating and being watched.

Further north, the large city of Valencia became the unofficial border between Southern Spain with its high summer temperatures and the more moderate climate of its north. Grape cultures became more frequent again. The olive plantations from the south changed more into pine forests in the north.

An excursion into Tarragona to exchange money became a special show: A charming lady in a bank, who handled the transaction,was more concerned with her fashionable appearance than her job.

As an observer I could only watch how everybody else gradually became involved. The whole exercise took almost one hour to exchange a minor amount of foreign currency. Was this their first exercise in money exchange? I needed the Pesos to buy the petrol to get us through the rest of Spain.

In Barcelona we reached the "secret capital" of Spain, so named because of its location at the sea, mountain surroundings and a more favourable climate than Madrid, the designated capital, in Spain's highland centre.

Back on the French border with no control, we experienced the future United European spirit. Spain and France displayed their readiness for a good European membership. While in Spain there were olive groves, Southern France welcomed us with the world's largest area of vineyards.

Along the southern coast are inland lakes, called "etanges", close to the sea, some with a connection to the Mediterranean. Besides interesting wildlife, this area also featured a dominant historic fortress called Salses that protected the coastline along with other fortresses in Carcasonne to the west and in Aigues-Mortes to the east. It was said that from Salses on a clear day you could see as far as the large city of Marseille in the east.

In the Rhone valley of Southern France we caught up again with close Spanish climatic conditions. This was due to the "sirocco" winds that blew hot moist air from Africa into the Rhone valley during summer. Those strong winds can't be missed. They are a daily occurrence.

Roman history shows its marks still today in places like Nimes, Arles, Avignon, Valence, which I had visited in previous years. The Rhone highway, called "route du soleil" (sun route), brought us further north. A French rule caught us up after the city of Lyon: "All roads lead to Paris", which meant that we first had to follow in that direction, before we could find a turn-off to the west and home.

Cooler air, less-intensive sun, green meadows, cornfields and leafed-woods announced our proximity to Germany. The traffic density slowed everybody down until we reached the German Autobahn, where you could stay on the left side and "be part of the fast lane and not be overtaken." We were back in the "circus".

It was amazing, how quickly daily life caught up with us again, leaving the holiday a distant memory. The opportunity arose now to throw all "the goodies" gained from the holiday into a "balance pan" in order to hopefully manage life better. In our case, the "balance pan" started to point towards new horizons away from where we lived. The children asked openly: "Why do we have to live here? Before we came here our lives were so much better." Our judgement always refers to what we know! We put the question on the table: where can our family have more reasonable living conditions?

With the quest for a living standard, our country had lost at the time its priorities especially concerning the life of young families. Leaving this answer mainly to the foreigners didn't make life in the own ranks much better. We live "mainly today and tomorrow", which is also the time to make our decisions, if we wanted to achieve something in our lives.

Finding another accommodation for our family with the four children was an impossible quest. Our German shepherd did not present "a burden to that degree": the dog was more easily accepted than our children.

In German terms, with my income I was in the position to ask money institutions for the capital needed to buy a house and pay it off for the rest of my life. While others followed that path, it didn't mean we necessarily had to. Our past experiences told us that there were better options. I could not imagine living in something of our own in an environment where we lived at the present. We still had to face the special "humour" of the people around.

Before taking the decisive steps to leave the country again, we tested a number of options in other parts around Karlsruhe, Munich and even on the Swiss border. They all provided the same result: good job prospects for me, no affordable accommodation for the family. Our patience towards such conditions ran increasingly thin. My current workplace had developed its own problems with internal family politics as I have indicated previously. I was not prepared to wait for the end result.

"One mishap often happens with a connection to others to follow". Stopping such a process, a firm decision had to be made: Australia gave us the new direction in our lives.

An acceptance took its time, but in May 1981 I collected our registered migration acceptance at the local post office. The post officer behind his narrow glass-protected working area had to remark: "Again somebody leaving for Australia." I did actually remind the "gentleman "about his duty towards the sanctity of the mail.

Australia must have had an eye on families with children. Although I was turning 40 in 1981, the average-age of our family worked out to 19 years. My profession, personal health and English language were also important factors for our acceptance. We did celebrate this day. Even the children realised, we had started to move in a new direction, where our quality of life could only improve. The decision was made unanimously. We were going to leave Germany again. Australia had supplied all of us with visas. There was at least somebody, who wanted to have our whole family. The process to get there was, of course, not the easiest,but once all the conditions were met, we received the green light for Australia.

Busy weeks lay ahead for us. We wanted to take most of our belongings with us and therefore proper decisions had to be made to get everything organized in time. A move like this would be in everybody's understanding a big effort.

An inexplicable incident with the woman across our floor became the last drop in a series of hostilities: my wife answered the doorbell and received first complaints from this neighbour about our kids: "Your 'shit kids' have thrown rotten potatoes on to my balcony!" My wife's response was: "We have no potatoes in the house to throw around." With that, the "fat sow" attacked my wife nearly throwing her down the stairs. My wife called me at work. She was visibly shaken as I arrived. The "canaille" had already disappeared into her flat. Through her glass door, I passed this message: "You don't need to worry about our fifth child, we are moving anyway and will leave you alone." A medical check-up fortunately confirmed that my wife was not hurt, despite the nasty fall. How could somebody develop such a hate towards others? Our answer was to step aside and leave it to others to sort out such individuals. Renting an existing container for our household goods did not work out economically because of an uncertain waiting period until we could arrange a new address in Australia. We decided to use our own container. The steel frame, fitting into the garage next to the house, had to be properly manufactured in a local welding-place. Every day after work, I fitted a bit more of the sheet metal and plywood to the outside of the frame inside the garage. The car was left outside the garage, so I could work around the container with closed door undisturbed from curious neighbours: "We do not have to do these things ourselves, we can get somebody to do it for us properly", was the message from the neighbourhood even though they didn't know what we were doing. We didn't consider it necessary to inform everybody about our move to Australia. Everything went to plan. When August 1981 arrived, the container was fully packed, closed and additionally covered with a tarpaulin. It rested on round steel pipes so that it could be pushed out of the garage.

 My wife made a week-long farewell visit to Finland with Raija, the second eldest child. The other children assisted with the moving preparations. When the lifting crane with a truck arrived, one week was still left before our departure from Frankfurt.

 The crane attracted the attention of the whole neighbourhood. Opposite the crane, a neighbour was watching behind an open window and closed curtains. When the crane's diesel engine started, it directed its black exhaust straight into the neighbour's window. Faces black as coal, including the curtains, became the result. The engine noise drowned out the outbreak of swear words from behind the curtains, while the window was shut with a bang.

"Somebody had his nose too close in somebody else's business again ". This was a good lesson. After the mighty lifting crane and the truck with our container had left, silence returned to the place. The neighbour had time to "lick her wounds".

With our goods gone, we felt free. Only the suitcases and trunks were left to follow with us to the plane in Frankfurt. Before selling our car to friends, we still made the trip to Frankfurt with most of our luggage. We left this in an official storage area. Spending a number of hours at the airport taught our children more about airport departures. A big number of large planes waited along bays to take on passengers for destinations around the world. Every few moments a new aircraft arrived and another taxied on to the runway for take-off. No matter how often we see this spectacle, it is still amazing how these giant "birds" take off easily into the air, only after a not-too-distant run on the ground. "This is how we will head for Australia, as far as one could get on the planet, only stopping in New Zealand for an extra leg". From now on our children understood, why Australia was called "Down-Under".

Back at what we could not call home any more, our German shepherd, Mars, waited patiently, knowing already for a while that something big was going to happen.

Australia did not allow animals to be brought in from outside its territory. In other words, our dog could not come with us any more. Was giving him away an option? Under normal circumstances. No. Especially a German shepherd at the age of eight years, who had developed strong ties with its owner, which is essential for his instincts. This dog told us unmistakably, in a very direct way, about whether other people were trustworthy. Going to another person and having eye contact, was message of trust. Staying away from somebody and looking mainly at my wife, meant caution.

During our last weeks in the Stuttgart area we paid another visit to a family,who lived not far from us. We thought we should leave the dog outside their house, but they insisted: "Mars ought also to come in,because he belongs to the family." And, in fact, Mars knew better than anybody else, they were good people and on top of that had a special heart for a dog. Their dog had passed away only a few weeks earlier. They saw our dog and immediately fell in love with him. Was this to become a new home for our Mars? A test had to be undertaken to find out. The possible new dog-owners learnt only now about our departure to Australia and therefore offered us land, which they owned so that we could have stayed in the country. Even considering this offer, the current 1000 DM for one square metre of land in the area could only be met by a bank; and what about a house? Our decision had already been made. There was no going back. Wasn't this amazing, living for over three years in the neighbourhood of others and having had only occasional contacts that now as we faced a big change, there were also very good people around. Was this class-thinking, that kept people apart, until something broke down such barriers? In our case, did the dog, Mars, break down the barriers?

The way our dog accepted this friendly architect's family told everybody to give it a try and leave him in a new place.

The next morning, however, Mars waited patiently in front of our house. He returned before the friends had noticed. We allowed the dog to come inside to us telling him a long story, which he must have understood: "We are going far away and can't take you with us this time, it is best for you to stay with our friends across the road. It saddens us very much, but our friends will be very happy to have you. We go back to them now and promise to be a good boy." Said and done!

The dog remained in his new home, even when we paid another visit before leaving. The dog obviously understood us, how much did we understand this dog or generally speaking, other living forms?

Mars lived another five years in harmony with this wider family of three generations. He had his firm place in this family, but connected both families even through this distance. During the years we exchanged regularly personal notes with photos showing a happy Mars and his exact paw-print.

Only after the dog had passed away, did we have a chance visit the friends again. It would have been wrong to come and see our Mars again. He would have become confused and most likely very sad. Mars made such a lasting impression on his new family that they said later: "Mars was such a great dog, we cannot have another Mars, he was unique and our best friend ever."

A son of this family visited us in 2004 in Australia bringing real memories of Mars to us.

When the time drew closer to our departure, we felt like saying goodbye to "friend and foe". In my home town, my step-parents "woke up". They said: "We didn't know you had such problems."

We assured them: "We are doing our best to sort this out once for all."

There were also positive notes with our departure: a lifelong friend, a doctor called Hildegard, gave us her farewell present. It was a night's luxury accommodation in the Hilton Hotel at Frankfurt Airport on the night before our departure.

Having sold our car, we had no transport anymore. Our friends, who took our dog, Mars, helped out with our transport to Stuttgart. From there, we took the train to Frankfurt. All family members looked in a positive way towards our new future in far-away Australia. We were ready to board a Lufthansa plane, which was about to take us all the way to Melbourne in Australia, when a news team from the German magazine "Stern" approached us. The questions they asked and the photos they made, appeared over several pages in an edition of their magazine. Latest then everybody in Germany was informed of our move to Australia, which could not have happened in a better way. The same reporter —team paid us a visit in Australia 1984, wanting to find out, how a family like ours could settle in a new far away country. I can say here already in advance, we did not disappoint the reporters.

How we moved to Australia, lived with the problems, but finally succeeded, is described here only in a summary, because in a separate book called "Australia, a migrant-experience" I detail our migration process.

In front of us lay 24 hours of air travel after leaving Frankfurt. Our first stop-over was Karachi in Pakistan. One feature surfaced here, when local men and women entered the plane in their numbers, armed with banister-brushes and dustpans, cleaning seats and floor from the front to the back. It looked like an army of ants, doing their part.

Next stop-over in Kuala Lumpur, Malaysia, introduced us to tropical heat stored away in the airport buildings, as air-conditioning systems were not operational. Passengers suffered visibly from such a welcome.

# Australia

## Melbourne—Brisbane—Perth

Another few hours of flight time and Australia showed us from its clear skies its size, emptiness of human civilisation and the Outback colours. Melbourne in the south-east corner of the continent welcomed us. With the opposite seasons here in the southern hemisphere, August was winter and greeted us with cold and rain. The Melbourne weather informs you very quickly of its proverbial four-seasons-in-a-day. Nothing lasts for too long.

Our first free stay in a hostel supplied valuable assistance in our first steps as a migrant family. Despite having contact addresses organised from Germany, we reserved our options to look around. My family remained first in Melbourne, while I "cracked" opportunities further north in Brisbane with success.

It was also warmer further north and sunny, as it only could be in a State calling itself the "Sunshine State". The whole family moved north to Brisbane without delay. Renting a complete house was again something new for us. Also work and integration of our school-aged children could successfully be arranged. Life in Australia had started for us.

Now being far away from Europe, the irrevocable news reached us from Transylvania that my biological father Michael had passed away at far too early an age of 68. We still were banned from entering Romania because of the incident with the brother at the border of Romania with former Yugoslavia, and therefore we could only keep the good memories for the time that was given to us to remember.

It didn't take long to " hit our first snag". We had to move on to find more professional work. Perth was 5000 kilometres to the west and it became our next choice. We spent one year there but the better opportunities in manufacturing were in Queensland.

Returning to Brisbane, Queensland, through the north of the continent completed a tour around Australia for us. We gained a first good look into Australia, which gave us a better idea of what the country had to offer.

Judging by that, we could not be disappointed. The continent showed us its unique "make-up", which is a result of its age, isolation and mostly unchanged environment, not yet lost to human civilisation.

Its fauna and flora is equally amazing, transforming us back into an ancient history of our planet, displaying at the same time a huge "prehistoric museum", as the civilisation has only started in recent history to add a modern face to it. Our first impressions and later excursions in the continent with its seemingly vast and empty spaces was that nature's "showpiece" of a natural "unforgiving order" was still here in place.

Back in Brisbane we started all over again, but a bit richer in Australian experiences. As I have outlined in my book "Australia, a migrant-experience ", there is no valid recipe of how to succeed as a migrant in another country. Every individual has his own story to tell, making a migration a challenge in a migrant's life. It took us about six years to settle down into a promising situation where we knew we could succeed.

Life, particularly in Australia, was not meant to be easy because of its distance from everything else in the world. As long as Australia will maintain its pioneering spirit, it can provide with its wealthy background a prosperous standard of living. But only if own efforts and its wealth are not inverted by consuming the wealth first, before efforts are put in place. Politics also have a tendency here to go down that "easier road "for short political gains.

## Kabul-Tur (Caboolture)

*Whole family, start property in Caboolture, 1985.*

The purchase of land in countryside north of Brisbane was our starting point to settle in Australia after a partly difficult "run" through different stages. Land was still cheap compared with Germany. One hectare of prime undeveloped countryside was listed at AUS$8000. Our shire of Caboolture was a sleepy typical coastal country town, but not for long as developments already pointed towards rapid changes in the area.

Even with the improved employment situation, we maintained a cautious strategy towards our progress, moving ahead only as we could afford to. In our case it paid off in coming years and we did have the "headache" of paying off borrowed money. It was not the "modern" economical way, but it was a secure one. Instead of paying others, we could constantly invest in our property and as everything was done by ourselves, long-lasting results rewarded us.

Not many people in the area of the marvellous "Glasshouse Mountains" area ever queried the meaning of the shire name "Caboolture". This English-sounding name was originally "Kabultur" referring to its Aboriginal origin. "Kabul" in both Aboriginal and Afghan languages means "python"; "Tur" is the Aboriginal word for "home". The early settlers gave the area its name from their observations of its nature. Aborigines were the early Australian migrants. Nobody knows for sure, from where or when they exactly came. Of note is the sharing of the Afghan word "Kabul" which points towards a possible migration connection not necessarily from Afghanistan, but with Afghans.

Another feature of the area would be the fact that early European settlers had discovered here the Macadamia nut and its tree along the shores of the "Kabultur" river. The relatively small nut has a round brown and hard shell, a typical Australian, but when cracked, the light nut compensates for the effort with a milky, sweet taste. The nut is considered very nutritious, supplying valuable benefits in the control of cholesterol levels in our bodies.

The area north of the Glasshouse Mountains, with their striking volcanic formations, are part of a famous Aboriginal legend.

## Glass House Mountains—The Legend

"It seems that Tibrogargan, the father and Beerwah, the mother, had many children—Coonowrin the eldest, Beerburrum, the Tunbubudla twins, Coochin, Ngun Ngun, Tibberoowuccum, Miketeebumulgrai and Elimbah.

According to the story, there was also Round who was fat and small and Wild Horse (presumably Saddleback) who was always straying away to paddle in the sea. One day when Tibrogargan was gazing out to sea he noticed a great rising of the waters. Hurrying off to gather his younger children in order to flee to the safety of the mountains to the westward, he called out to Coonowrin to help his mother, who by the way, was again with child.

Looking back to see how Coonowrin was assisting Beerwah, Tibrogargan was greatly angered to see him running off alone. He pursued Coonowrin and, raising his club, struck the latter such a mighty blow that it dislocated Coonowrin's neck, and he has never been able to straighten it since.

When the floods had subsided and the family had returned to the plains, the other children teased Coonowrin about his crooked neck. Feeling ashamed, Coonowrin went over to Tibrogargan and asked his forgiveness; but filled with shame at his son's coward-ice, Tibrogargan could do nothing but weep copious tears, which, trickling along the ground, formed a stream, which flowed, into the sea. Then Coonowrin went to his brothers and sisters, but they also wept at the shame of their brother's cowardice. The lamentations of Coonowrin's parents and of his brothers and sisters at his disgrace explain the presence today of the numerous streams in the area.

Tibrogargan then called to Coonowrin and asked him why he had deserted Beerwah; at which Coonowrin replied that as Beerwah was the biggest of them all she should be able to take care of herself. He did not know that Beerwah was again pregnant, which was the reason for her great size. Then Tibrogargan turned his back on Coonowrin and vowed that he would never look at him again.

Even today Tibrogargan gazes far out to sea and never looks round at Coonowrin who hangs his head and cries his tears running off to the sea. His mother, Beerwah, is still heavy with child as it takes a long, long time to give birth to a mountain."

Credit: This legend is from "In the Wake of the Raftsmen" by E.G.Heap,B.A. as published in "Queensland Heritage", Volume 1 No.5, November 1966.

The name of the Glass House Mountains dates back to the early days when James Cook sailed for the first time along the east coast coming from the north. From the Pacific Ocean, Cook compared the view towards these volcanic rock formations with the glass houses—the glass manufacturing towers—of Glasgow, back in Scotland.

This ancient volcanic area has contributed with its lava to fertile soils, reaching to our land with its runners. First inspections of the soil on our land confirmed the existence of volcanic sediments. From a useful point of view we couldn't ask for anything better. As the land was also on a slight inclination, the heavy summer storms could easily run off.

## Work on Own Property, Home, Hobby Farm

*Home in Caboolture.*

Green Meadows as the area is called, lies 10 kilometres outside the town of Caboolture in a rural-residential area—and we were the first ones to move in.

Moving out of our rented place on to our land became a priority to get started. A family caravan with an annex under a quickly-built roof became the start of our home. The rural scheme under the Joh Bjelke Petersen government provided substantial assistance at that time for water, power and telephone connections on rural properties. Living in the caravan gave us time to start work on a house. While I could organize an owner-builder's license, which enabled me to do everything on the house by myself; the bureaucrats could not accept my own house plan. I was not a known draftsman, but once my plan had a signature of a known source, our home could get started.

Soil tests determined the structure of the foundation and gave us information as to how deep the fertile soil on our land went. We chose the position of the house right in the centre of the land that was higher than the highest flood-level mark of the 1974 floods. This level came to the swamp at the lower end of our property. A house, being a major investment in everybody's life asked for a good foundation. I could only manage this with the help of a concrete-workers team. Our start in summer 1985 required a fast approach to beat the stormy weather of Queensland. I realised, in time, that many things are driven like a race in Australia—the reason either the weather, time or money. We took our time, however, aiming to get the job right in the first place. This, of course, rang alarm bells in the bureaucratic circles, which had to interfere into our new established life with some unexplained warnings. Commonsense prevailed, when the local Councillor assisted us in our building efforts while we lived on the land. If somebody was to claim that we should not live on the land until the house was finished, he should also tell us where else to live as we had only recently arrived in the country. We didn't come here to be sent off from our own land.

With appropriate help, the message reached its destination—even with the help of some tricks. Building your own house on your own property can be like a dream come true in someone's life especially if you have been dependent on rental accommodation for a long time. A personal freedom developed from there in many ways.

Possessions are a major contributor to our viewpoint in life. While we look at them, they have a "return-impact" on us that is expressed in the definition of a "para-psyche". Without a doubt, the driving force in a migration move is also a search for a higher independency, once life's basic requirements have been satisfied by work, food, health and education.

Coming back to our own house construction, the finish in the rough could be achieved in as little as six months: a galvanized steel frame bolted together from the foundation to the top with insulation spaces inside and outside, bricked-up from outside. A cyclone-proof house was our aim to ensure our safety during possible cyclones in the area. The veranda around the house took a number of years to finish, actually longer than the house. The veranda became our answer to the all-year around warm climate, as it had been done in the older Queensland houses.

*House veranda, part.*

*Our indoor swimming pool.*

The banks won't like people building on their lives as one could afford and not ask for their "help". Doing everything our-selves helped us to save enough money over time so that we could add two sheds, three granny flats, one indoor swimming pool plus systematic landscaping to save us lots of maintenance time. Our own rainwater storage plus the existing town-water supply secured our irrigation needs, especially during the dry spells in a year. To consume rainwater in the house is also a much healthier choice. Finally the solar hot-water system on the roof helped to save energy.

But no matter how hard one tries to save in longer terms, a rule can come sometimes from outside to interfere. This happened to us with the mandatory installation of an electrically-controlled onsite recycling waste-water plant. Such a method demands constant energy and regular service from "qualified" outside personnel, making you to pay for every "shit" under the umbrella of doubtful efficiency. The environment, with its growing priorities, is increasingly addressed in terms of negotiated compromises, which lack simple solutions because of inherent expressions of interests. I will not go deeper into this issue because it effects many other community concerns.

Living in the countryside has its benefits, but also its down-sides like everything in life. Going to work every day of the week from the north of Brisbane to its south mounted to considerable travelling-time in my own car, by train and then pick-up by a company car. Not much time was left for anything else during the week. It became important to organize the remaining time in the most efficient way in order to be still able to enjoy other activities. Not only the house, but also the hobby farm and the family asked for their share of attention.

*Pair of King-Parrots.*

*Galah and Long-Billed Corella.*

Pets also joined our family: dogs, cats, sheep, donkeys and Australian parrots. In most cases they were the children's choice, which they were bound to look after responsibly. Our sheep suffered a cruel fate when in the early days of our settlement wild dogs " butchered " them. Even the buried remains were not safe from another attack. After this experience, sheep came off our pet list. How the two donkeys joined our family is a story of its own: on our way to town, another property had one of the donkeys. One day, the owner gave my wife a lift and the donkey issue was raised. She said: "You just won a donkey, which you only need to pick up." With the carrot trick, we managed to get the donkey into a float. The second donkey lived at a walking distance from us. Its owners wanted to get rid of it. When I returned from an overseas trip, this second donkey waited for me on our property. The family had, in my absence, convinced the second donkey to join us. I made the point, however: "We cannot become the refuge for other people's pets." But the joyful character of a donkey, its fidelity and easy maintenance compared with that of a horse and its alertness to any intruders on the property, also won my heart.

Australian parrots on our property had to be obtained through a permit system in which it is ensured that the birds are bred in captivity. Proper-sized aviaries were built around the house with Cockatoos, long-billed Corellas, Galahs, Crimson-, Eastern-, Pale Face- and Adelaide Rosellas, Rainbow Lorikeets, Red Wing Parrots, King Parrots and Superb parrots. The place looked like a zoo in no time.

Pets can also deliver surprises: Our first two sulphur-crested white cockatoos disappeared one Christmas Eve when they dismantled the aviary door and gained their freedom.

A lame magpie occupied the aviary for some time (after the door got fixed, this time with sheet-metal). The bird first lived alone and then was joined by two galahs, a white cockatoo and long-billed corella. According to bird experts, a magpie wouldn't be accepted by parrots and vice-versa. As the magpie was the first tenant, it was the boss, which the others surprisingly accepted. The magpie's boss-role came to a sudden end however: a carpet python somehow managed to get into the aviary and, how it happens in life, the most curious one, the magpie, ended up inside the snake. After that the snake was too fat to leave the aviary. The snake had to be removed from the aviary and this was not the easiest job one could have.

Even the dogs and cats have given us a surprise. When both had litters, the bitch was too lazy to feed and look after her puppies. Luckily the cat stepped in, after losing her kittens, and raised the 13 German shepherd puppies.

One of our donkeys also gave us a headache when it went too far into the swamp at the lower end of our property looking for the greener grass. It got stuck in the mud, sinking almost completely in. A neighbour's tractor had to be organised in a hurry. Somebody had to do the hard work to get the straps through the mud underneath the donkey's tummy to pull it out before disappearing deeper in the mud. The donkey was back on land. A mud donkey required a cleaning operation that lasted for hours. My wife became the heroine in this story along with the neighbour's daughter and the incident was reported with a photo in a local paper. I was at work in Brisbane and heard about it only after coming home. Hats off for the courage of my wife! Later she even stood up to the task of "cremating" the other donkey, which passed away. The remaining donkey started to look for greener pastures and a few times got out on the road—only pony pellets could get it back home.

## A Natural Life Shared with an Australian Nature

From the very beginning we planted trees, shrubs, palms and fruit trees on our property. The best planting results were achieved with young seedlings, planted during our winter, allowing the roots to get started before the summer heat and moisture took over. The small plants, however, attracted the kangaroos of the area. Until we could erect a good fence around our property, the plants regularly disappeared. The "roos" were quite clever, entering the property in a way that the dogs could not catch their scent with the wind.

The more our hobby-farm grew, the more birds came to visit the place or call it home. There were the magpies making their presence known during the months of August to October by defending their nests through sudden attacks out of the air. They are known for it and have to be respected to avoid any head injuries. Only just before an attack do they release their sharp, warning cry, making it often difficult to react in time and chase them off. Some "experts" claim to have the answer to this magpie aggression: wear a face mask on the back of your head so that the birds get confused with a face on both sides.

A young magpie from the trees around the nearby swamp must have fallen out of the nest too early and was picked up by our eldest son—but not without a fight staged by the magpie-father. At nighttimes, the young magpie occupied the top bar of a bed-frame in one of the children's rooms. Our "Maggie" exercised around the house and garden during the day, not missing the meal times indoors with our family. On one corner of the table, the magpie waited for its share and enjoyed everybody's attention. It was often with us in the house, always looking deadly serious until it decided to show-off with its incredible song variations. Eating very orderly from its own plate, Maggie used to cut up its food into smaller pieces by keeping one piece at a time in his beak vehemently shaking it from one side to the other. Maggie received the company of another magpie one year later. For over two years the birds lived with us, until they probably decided to look for mates and disappeared.

The magpies gave us much joy. A valuable lesson came out of it: a better understanding of another living form from around us.

The smaller butcher bird is of a similar nature, also a champion singer, whereas the larger plover bird could not be called a singer with its interrupted cry.

One of Australia's most typical birds is the kookaburra, known for its laughter, and indeed, they like to join each other laughing. The kookaburra is the largest of the kingfisher bird-family. Their eyesight must be outstanding: they regularly sit on the clothes hoist or on the veranda lattices, watching a distant soil-spot for worms, never missing to catch a curious one. When another bird joins in, they usually start with their distinct laughter, "an outlook on life, only Australia can deliver".

Then there is the "noisy miner", which in flocks can become so persistent in their noise-level that they have driven people out of their places because they couldn't handle their presence any more. The noisy miner is also an excellent catcher of food out of the air—and we often threw them breadcrumbs to prove this.

Another noisy bird is the "rainbow lorikeet", a small colourful parrot that likes to visit the dark-red flower stems of the umbrella tree for their honey. Many birds in Australia are noisy, especially in flocks when they irritate potential aggressors with their numbers.

Crows can be found everywhere in the world and also all over Australia.

I should not forget to mention that Australia still is a bird's paradise. In a place like ours in the countryside, birds are dominant. Even magpie-geese have, in recent years, established their home in our area because of the long drought. Pelicans and cormorants regularly visit our dam taking fish out of it.

The currawong announces bad weather is on its way with its call. This was immortalised in a country song by the famous late Australian singer, Slim Dusty: "... when the currawongs come down from the mountains to the warmer country down below a sign of rotten weather, rain or snow ...".

They and the ants on the ground know better about the weather than we do. Also the ants can tell us of the arrival of the wet season when they start to carry their eggs to higher ground.

I should not forget to mention the occasional appearance of the mighty wedge-tailed eagle, the presence of which sends off the alarm bells in the Australian birdworld—the first messenger being the butcher bird.

No alarm, however, is caused by the rare presence of the largest Australian parrot, the "yellow-tailed black cockatoo". On their migration they pass through the coastal pine forests looking for the seeds. Their cry can be heard from a distance as they communicate with each other in the air and strengthen their unity.

Fortunately civilisation in Australia has not yet pushed out the existence of its unique wildlife, however a critical point of sustainability in nature has been reached. We can see ourselves privileged to be able to experience on our property an unspoiled close contact with a part of Australia's nature.

Where else in the world can we see on a private property a Goanna lizard of one-and-a-half metres length rushing up a gum tree, or watch a long-neck turtle come out of the swamp on to higher ground to lay eggs in the ground, indicating that rising water levels will occur during incubation time?

Living close to nature can tell us useful information, but only when you can read nature's signs. The dry years in the beginning of the new millennium have created conditions neither right for the magpies to breed, nor for the long-neck turtle to lay its eggs. They are also able to judge conditions for their survival ahead of time. For a number of years both had retreated from their usual patterns. Only in June 2007, our winter, did we watch the long-neck turtle laying eggs again into the ground higher up on our property. Did it mean that the drought is on its way out and wet summers are coming back? Yes, because the rains came in the summer of 2007.

If we understood nature around us better, we could learn more than anticipated.

The recent Tsunami in Sumatra was recognised hours before by seagulls in Western Australia. They abandoned their territory in the Indian Ocean, flying inland, which was observed by attentive locals. Nobody wanted to listen to this warning until it happened, because it didn't come from "scientists". Then it was too late. In an increasingly specialised world, we "put our blinkers on more and more" and also look at broader issues from such limited angles instead of incorporating all the knowledge that we already have. "Everybody likes to ride his hobby horse".

Our hobby-farm received our attention over many years. Nature took its time in growing a garden out of an empty green meadow. Besides other nut trees, the local Macadamia found its way in numbers into our property. It is actually one of the few real Australian fruit trees and is highly nutritious. All good things need time to develop and so does the Macadamia-nut tree. The nut's oil has widely penetrated the cosmetic industry supplying a superior product to previously used ones. All the other fruit trees were introduced into Australia like: all citrus trees, avocado, mango, banana trees, guava, loquat, fig trees, olive trees, Satsuma plums, tropical peach, apple, pear, coffee, paw paw and mulberry. They all grow well in the sub-tropical climate of our area. Avocados were the most difficult ones to establish during past wet summer seasons. Bananas and Bowen mangoes benefited only from wet seasons. Our bananas are the little lady fingers—they have a slight apple taste. In Brazil they are called apple-bananas. Bowen mangoes are Queensland's own cultivated variety—their fruit flesh is string-free in contrast to many other brands.

The extensive landscaping of our large garden has reduced the work a garden often requires. In the case of a failed economical system around us, our hobby-farm of one hectare could help a family to survive reasonably. A dam for water storage during wet summer seasons secured our water needs during dry seasons, together with rainwater tanks of 40,000 litres installed around the large roof areas. Even an indoor swimming pool with a Finnish sauna came in time and this helped to keep our fitness and health levels up.

Not everything on the hobby-farm was for a purpose. Striking palms trees in varieties such as Bismarck, bottle, foxtail, royal, majestic, golden cane, triangular, wine, fan, alexandra, kentia, wedding, date, traveller, fishtail, sago and phoenix are attractive additions to our gardens. Bottle trees, poinciana, jacaranda, leopard trees, Bunya pine, Norfolk pine, white and red cedar, Wollemi pine, bird-nest, fern-tree, magnolia, oleander, bird of paradise, gardenias, azaleas, camellias, pony-tail, cardboard-plant and many hibiscus add to the beauty of our environment.

Solar-panels on the house roof help to keep the energy bills and the environment in better shape.

From the very beginning we began a tradition on our land: planting for a special visitor a tree of his/her choice. Some of these very early trees have since grown into big trees. Our next task would be to add identification plates to all the personalised tree specimens.

One of these trees, a rose-apple, which belongs to the Lilly Pilly family was planted personally by my step-mother in August 1988. Another tree out of this family, a Brazilian cherry tree, was planted by my mother-in-law on her first visit from Finland four years later. Ten years after this, the Brazilian cherry tree gave us a message when it started to suddenly, and uncharacteristically, lose its leaves. My wife realised this one morning and returned into the house telling me: "What is wrong with my mother's tree, it seems to be dying?" A couple of days later a telephone call from Finland announced that my wife's mother had passed away. It was not until my wife had laid her mother's ashes to their last resting-place that the tree recovered again, flourishing from then on.

*Brazilian Cherry Tree.*

What happened here over a distance of 20,000 kilometres? We have no answers. I am not referring to a miracle. The facts only point to a possible connection between living forms not yet known to us.

While creating a home for our family on our hobby-farm, our three girls and boys grew up without stopping to ask for their share of attention, too. My wife and myself had our share of activities. It never became "boring" and we never had to wonder what to do. A bit less of this challenge probably would not have hurt either! But we were kept on our toes—and fit and healthy as well.

## Possibilities for our Young Generation

What were the possibilities of a migrant family's children in a country like Australia? Should a new country provide also new possibilities? The new environment with its conditions plays an important role. While migrant-parents have to struggle more to adapt, their children born or not born in the country generally adapt easier, creating a possible divide between the generations. Parents have to be patient in such a process, hoping that their way of life is at least partly adopted by their offspring when they become older, more independent and return out of their own decision to values held in a family. A migrant life is not spared from changes. Children go to school in Australia like in many other countries to learn to perform early enough to their capabilities. Parents should give their support, not their ambitions. School uniforms can actually help towards the integration of a migrant child into the mainstream by taking out external differences. Unfortunately also in Australia, school is not a warrant for success in a life. In many cases participation at a school is often good enough, avoiding the strict censure to wrongly protect young students from later demands in their lives. Life will catch up with everybody sooner or later. It will then be decided how an individual is ready to stand up on his own.

As parents we supported strongly own decisions of our children, probably because I could not enjoy such a freedom in my life. Everybody needs to become creative in his life and do something he can identify himself with. One child became an aircraft engineer in the Australian army, another found her hobby in a specialised bookshop, one had chosen a shortcut into their own family life, one more became a salesperson in a Japanese organisation, another child found her way in performing on a classical concert guitar through music studies and the youngest one learnt a trade first, continuing in computer design.

After school also comes the decision of which direction to continue in. Early interests can be helpful towards such a decision. The focus on a higher education is changing since the costs have risen beyond "normal people's" budgets. Two of our children achieved university education on their own accord, the others entered professional education.

Success is rarely imminent. Our children have to go their own ways to get there eventually. It is not sensible to make comparisons about what they would have achieved if they had their education back in Europe. People often refer to future possibilities that cannot always be right because living standards change increasingly from society to society in a modern world. Fortunately there are also other vital directions in life that are worth focusing on and therefore achieve relative satisfaction and some happiness.

Everybody should aim for something different from the mainstream in his life. This happens, with no doubt, in a migration decision.

To find out more about this migration issue, you can read my book: "Australia—a migrant experience".

## Australia- "A Big Real Estate"

In 2001 we met in the Outback of Australia a German family who lived in Hong Kong. During this meeting the question was raised: "What makes people visit Australia in large numbers today?" They answered this question in a surprising way: "It is so rewarding to see so "little" in such big distances and not have a concrete-jungle vision like Hong Kong."

Nature in Australia is still dominant, our civilisation is still confined to the few city centres from where people in the past have moved out only in small numbers into the vast continent. Life in a city provides for most people a more secure environment than the wide, open continent with its climatic contrasts. The density of the population around cities sparked a demand for new land to be developed far beyond real needs. Speculation from beyond Australia's borders introduced an artificial demand, raising land prices as a result. Foreign investors found, through increased commodity prices in capital growth, a welcome economical environment in Australia. But this was not so much the case for the resident Australian population. A typical example of a real estate "bungle" was in 1985 just after we had bought our land. On the road in front of our property, a car stopped and a young couple asked us in broken English: "We just have bought a land not far from here. We need a contact to somebody who could look after it when we are back in Germany. We plan to move on it later."

The first question we asked them in their more familiar German language was: "Do you have permanent Australian residence?" Was it our response in German, our question or both together that caused the couple to become visibly confused? Nobody had told them that they needed Australian residency. At that time tourists were tempted to buy land in Australia, mainly outside city centres. The landowner's pride of the young German couple did not last long when they found out about the strict Australian residence requirements. This cheap land situation changed more quickly here than in many other parts of the world. When we bought our land in the "rural residential area" in 1984, its undeveloped value was AUS$8000, which had risen to AUS$275,000 in 2006. Only in 2006 city dwellings in Brisbane went up by 100%, putting the Australian dream of owning your own home almost out of reach. It is already becoming a political issue to stop the spiraling costs of home-ownership and find ways to ease this burden for the Australian population. It remains to be seen which of the powers are greater, internal ones or efforts brought in from outside. Our present neglect towards own manufacturing efforts will be a potential missing factor in our balance for economical efforts. Soon we will be asked to tighten our belts, but the tide will turn around again with time.

## Australia, a Magnet for Visitors

Tourism can help the economy only for a limited time with employment and balancing the books. It probably comes as no surprise that many things in Australia work differently from other parts of the world, because of its distance to other countries. Everywhere else in the world tourism is a starting point for other developments to follow, in most cases industrialisation.

In Australia, however, tourism has grown especially in the last two decades with a decline in manufacturing activities. Where such a reverse-trend leads to is an open question. We could run into an unwanted dependency towards foreigners who want to come to us only for a holiday. When it comes to selling our sunny days during a year, we have a good bargaining power for foreign holidaymakers. If we invested the gains of our natural wealth in a better way, we could easily become "the Switzerland of the Asia-Pacific region". A considerable number of visitors from overseas have relatives or friends in Australia. Besides family, many other people have visited us in the past years, even people who never visited us in Germany; what a difference distance can make! "The closer we are, the more distant we can live from each other?"

Our family and friends usually received their own choice of a tree planted on our hobby-farm before leaving Australia. We therefore owe a number of trees to our overseas visitors. It could be suggested that most of these trees will still be around long after we are gone, carrying the memories eventually further. Little steps like this in a migrant's life help towards establishing our own traditions, which are vital for our identity search. Through our identity we find our wider acceptance in a new country.

There have been special visitors worthy of a mention who all took great memories back home after meeting a unique natural environment, found in the South-East of Queensland, around Brisbane.

It is a big mistake to try and see Australia in only a few weeks. There is already so much to see in our area, which calls for a person's restriction in order to see more. A young couple from Germany, whom we had never met, turned up with a rented campervan at our gate on Boxing Day in 1988, after having received our address from my youngest brother. Their journey to Australia fulfilled the woman's Australian dream for their honeymoon. During their stay with us a lasting friendship was established so that they also decided to try to gain permanent Australian residency when back in Germany. That part of their Australian dream could unfortunately not become true. Sometimes it does appear that getting Australian residency might be more difficult than winning Lotto?

A friend, also called Martin, came from the Philippines to see us. Being an artist, he spent time expressing his impressions with paintings of the country. His few contacts with local artists gave him the impression of a high standard of artwork in this country, created by artists who were not internationally recognised. There is quite a creative force within the people of Australia. They need only more support and exposure to gain international recognition that in return could benefit the country. This is the case especially in Australia: "No man is a prophet in his own country."

My former boy-scout leader, Bernhard (the brother of artist Martin), himself a musician in Germany, came to see us on his mission to Australia. He confirmed the comments I made before when he met local musicians, most of them struggling in Australia despite some of their quickly-recognised high standards.

I should not forget our very first visitor in Australia, Dirk, who witnessed the very beginnings of our lives in Australia. Dirk found a clever way to see Australia and us by consulting a group of prospective investors from overseas in the sugar-cane industry of Queensland.

In the family ranks, my step-mother had the courage to visit us at the age of 80. My step-father had passed away one year earlier and so it became only natural for her to seek out something that was missing in her life. As long as we live, it should never be too late for a change. Spending a few weeks together under our own roof, at least gave us the start to bridge so many years of unnecessary misunderstandings. On her farewell, she received her tree on our property, a rose-apple, which has grown since into a vigorous Australian tree, keeping her memory still alive.

Not only first impressions have an impact on our memory, but also the ones near the end of someone's life that are carried by wisdoms, usually weighing more in their significance. I remember my stepmother saying at her late 80s: "I am perfectly fine. If it tweaks a little bit here and there, it tells me I am still well and alive, our worries are getting us nowhere."

My mother-in-law came twice from Finland in the company of my wife. The long distance to Australia was difficult for her to comprehend since she belonged to a generation that has lived most of their lives in their own country.

She expressed her joy while living with us for a while, calling out: "Your place looks more beautiful than the photos you have sent over the years."

One weekend we visited an animal park, where one Emu had a special welcome ready for us. It followed us persistently with its funny trumpeting noise coming out of its beak; was it looking for a mate or warning us off? The incident attracted a lot of Japanese tourists and their cameras at the time. My mother-in-law's tree, a Brazilian cherry tree, developed a special significance when it signaled to us her passing-away after having returned to Finland the second time in 2002—a phenomenon I mentioned already before. Traveling the second time the long distance to Australia showed her determination at the age of 85 to connect again to the family of her daughter, because it was to become her last visit. Just three months later after returning to Finland, "her final journey" began.

One more remarkable visit I would like to mention here was a lady doctor who knew me since my early childhood and brought the music into my life. Hildegard continued with a family tradition that started already during World War I when her father received shelter in Transylvania and a friendship between our families started. Her outstanding personality based on knowledge, human qualities and gifted talents carried her through a whole lifespan. She remained a steadfast friend and did not change even in the face of "heavy blows" like the sudden tragic loss of her husband, who fell victim to an electrical failure of a hand-drill, only days after they married. Wolfgang was a World War II captain of a submarine. His brilliant stories encouraged a cousin Fred from an early childhood to become a captain as well. Nothing can be better for young people in search of a role in their lives than the model of a strong personality. Hildegard has travelled the world a lot, probably to maintain the widest possible dialogue with others and to keep her life on centre stage. Two nut-bearing Macadamia trees on our property carry her memory further than we could expect to live. Besides many excursions together with our family around our area, she asked me also to retrace a tour through the Top-End of Australia's Northern Territory which was a lasting impression. Charles Darwin described it as a journey to the origin of where evolution started (despite having never set foot there himself). In the chapter "Road to Nitmiluk", my description of this part of the Australian Outback can be found.

Philip, an exchange student from my home town in Germany, lived with us for six months in 1999 and regularly visited the local high school. Young people like him also welcomed the different life in Australia from that in Germany. Before going back home, his mother and siblings visited us as well experiencing a special holiday in Queensland, always to be remembered.

## South-East Queensland, a Natural Treasure

What makes people visit Australia each year in their millions? To answer this would be an immense task. By describing the area of South-East Queensland, I restrict myself only to this area but can highlight better the richness, natural beauty and diversity that can be found here. It is not only the natural treasures of the area that attracts visitors and encourages people to live here. Contributing factors to the image of the "Sunshine State" are pristine conditions of its nature with a clear atmosphere for the sun to shine as much as hardly anywhere else on earth.

Along a green coastal belt stretches a new developing area from the Gold Coast in the south right through to the north of the Sunshine-Coast. Between these two coasts is the city of Brisbane—a city with a rapidly changing image, all in the name of progress.

The constant flow of new settlers mainly from the southern States puts pressure on the satellite-developments further south, as well as north of the city.

The hope remains that the whole area doesn't grow without leaving sufficient natural undeveloped spaces. The development of Los Angeles should not be repeated here, one huge area without nature's corridors. Today in 2008 we still have these undeveloped corridors, but for how long? Development pressures take their toll on the environment—something has to give in such a process. The first mountain range of the Great Divide that runs along the east coast of Australia from Tasmania up to New Guinea is still covered with its dense forests. Ancient rainforests can be found in the Gold Coast hinterland, around Mount Glorious overlooking Brisbane and also in the Sunshine Coast hinterland.

Leaving behind the pulsing life in the coastal centres for an excursion into a rainforest is like an escape into a "forgotten world", where we can listen to birdlife in a total silence. This is only experienced in these areas. Tree giants with lianas look from a high forest canopy far down to us on the ground, making us appear smaller than we consider ourselves. Nature's cycle shows us here a constant growth and decay in balance—still maintaining an image that can be described as amazing beauty.

The mountains and the forests are also the lungs of South-East Queensland. The Glass House Mountains dominate near the Sunshine Coast. Sharp pointed, steep rising cores of ancient volcanoes rise into the sky. The fertile volcanic soil in the area has supported the farming of pineapples, avocados, macadamias and passionfruit. Small farms cultivate these fruits in a picturesque environment, only found here. Experienced climbers can reach the top of most of these Glass House Mountains. From up there in a cloud-level, the whole South-East coastline lies underneath. The green mountain ranges rise on the west, culminating in the south near the New South Wales border in a cross-mountain-range of the Granite Belt, around Stanthorpe. Many pointed volcanic mountain-formations tell of an ancient history. Some areas can still deliver unlimited views all around only of mountains and forests—a green natural carpet not to be expected in Australia, the driest continent on earth.

The two main long-islands (Bribie and Moreton) in front of Brisbane in the Pacific Ocean are the result of a constant southern ocean current which has built these islands out of sand in millions of years. Fraser Island, the largest sand island in the world, is further north. Halfway to Fraser Island is Bribie Island, located in our shire, which can be reached from the mainland over a bridge. They are all built of rich mineral sands supporting a growth of dense forests across each of the islands. A visit to Moreton Island delivers a view through a coconut-palm beach towards the metropolis, across a blue-green bay in the background of its green mountains. Where else in the world have we got such views?

The Gold Coast presents itself with the highest residential skyscraper in the world, as of 2007. Several amusement parks including Dream World, Sea World and Movie World offer diversions for everybody.

The Brisbane city-centre offers a rainforest on its river shores opposite its skyscrapers, an Arts Centre, Botanical Gardens, a Carl-Zeiss planetarium. And, in today's world, a casino has to be also on the map of a prosperous city.

The Sunshine Coast has developed in the past with a slightly stronger emphasis towards privacy. Buildings are not as high as the Gold Coast. The Sunshine Coast's Underwater World is worth a mention, likewise the Australian Zoo (formerly Reptile Park), founded by the father of the late Steve Irwin, the "Crocodile Hunter" who fell victim to a stingray attack in the coastal waters of North Queensland in 2006. His fate reminds us of the dangers waiting in the non-protected beaches of Queensland.

All this and much more are the reasons why so many people visit Australia and its specific areas like South-East Queensland to still experience a world we have thought to be lost.

## Re-Connecting to the Rest of the World

The distance from the other parts of the world makes Australia a "Mecca" where today people make a "pilgrimage" to it and also an "exodus" from it to other parts of the world. The difference between a "pilgrimage" and an "exodus" is that a pilgrimage is marked by an aspiration, whereas an exodus by "needs". From Australia we need to connect to other parts in the world to demonstrate our readiness for global membership. We like to live in our relative isolation, but also go away from it, only to return as pilgrims; a natural cycle in Australia.

Once my professional credentials had found a field in Brisbane, it didn't take long that I also went overseas to connect with business people. Although English is widely spoken around the world, it also proves beneficial for Australians to speak another language. It took a while to recognize this, mainly because of the multi-cultural society in Australia. People thought: we got it all in the own country, why bother? Everybody will eventually find out the benefits of talking to other people in their language, or at least making efforts in that direction.

The business where I started after a "necessary Australian learning curve" was still small, but very progressive. Having passed my probation time, the owner asked me one day: "Have you got your passport ready, we fly out on the weekend to Hong Kong and Taiwan".

Asia is our neighbour. We are part of it. England is today further than ever, because of its commitments to Europe. Clever business people don't go past Australia's neighbours—we are bound to make our future with them. Our first contacts were made overseas with the help of an already-established business partner in Australia and Taiwan. In Asian countries it also matters, who you know. This can be achieved only through regular bilateral contacts. On the first visit to Hong Kong in early 1988 British rule was still in place. A special experience for everybody arriving or leaving Hong Kong was delivered by the airport of that time, opposite the city-centre across the bay. Before touching down on the runway, an aircraft came breathtakingly close to high-rise buildings, where washing-lines hung partly out of windows. The brakes of an aircraft had to work well to stop in time on the airfield. Every other international airline arrived here, adding to the dense air-traffic. Aircrafts, people and car-movements gave the impressions of chaos, but obviously a working one. Everybody seemed "to give a little bit "to allow this "chaos "to move.

The city-centre across the bay with its mountainous background reminded me of Rio de Janeiro. On a later visit to Hong Kong after the change from the British to the Chinese rule the new airport far outside on an artificially-created island took with its modern new layout all these previous expressions away. An English gentleman joined me at that later date in a taxi across the huge suspension bridge to the main land. The bridge's cable and suspension dimensions were enormous. I've never seen a bridge of that size.

Knowing Hong Kong very well, the English gentleman assisted me greatly to find my hotel in the city-centre. We arrived in the middle of the night and the activities of the day on the streets had not died down at all, people and cars were still everywhere.

My hotel room was in the top-level of one of the highest buildings. I can't remember the number of the storey, but looking through the glass-wall of my room to the outside made me giddy, because the top of the building on that height was visibly moving. With closed curtains, the impression disappeared.

One major difference I experienced during that later visit was contrary to previous years that locals must have forgotten English under the new Chinese-rule making communication somehow difficult.

Returning to the first Hong Kong visit, a connection flight took my boss and myself to Taipei, the capital of the Taiwan island (formerly Formosa).

The plane leaving the runway just gained height, when the water of the ocean appeared underneath. There was no margin for any take-off-error.

Taiwan and its people were in many ways a Chinese copy with the difference of a democratically-elected government. The people seemed to be the same as those in Hong Kong, everybody spoke Cantonese. Our host, a Taiwanese contact person, (a very important pre-condition for a successful stay in an Asian country) made our visit a pleasant occasion. Most business people have their business cards also printed in English, using very often a common western first name. In our case, it was Simon.

The level of activities in the country was astonishing, not stopping even during night hours. We visited many manufacturing places. It was quite common during these meetings to be asked technical questions, which were generally-speaking wise to answer carefully.

People were very proud of their achievements, their efforts could be seen everywhere. In return for our appreciation, they invited us to their first MacDonald restaurant, demonstrating that progress has happened also in Taiwan. The food was the same like in every other MacDonalds in America or Europe.

Chinese dinners had become on the other side a regular event with only sticks available. The more difficulty one had in picking up the Chinese food with the two sticks in one hand, the more hungry he ended up. My boss spent years of his life in Borneo and handled the stick-business like a champion. I had to learn it quickly or stay hungry. The only food I could identify clearly in the beginning was the hotpot with vegetables and noodles on a carousel in the centre of the table, which was kept hot with a burner underneath. Many other little bits and pieces of food, besides rice, I had to ask about their origin, which was explained very kindly to me. I picked up Chinese words fairly well, but to remember them was much more difficult. I must admit never feeling full after these lengthy dinners, communication was the main point. It became apparent that all restaurants were at night busy with families especially on a weekend, when each family member invited in their turn the others for dinner, also for meeting purposes. A potential customer was treated here like a king, they knew how to support us in decision-making and were expecting, in return, to meet with a business agreement. This did not happen on every occasion, but an agreement helped to spread the news around.

People were very obliging when they could see a way to secure a business for them; giving business to us however, appeared possible only through our Chinese/Taiwanese contact-host Simon. Business on a mutual basis was otherwise difficult to achieve.

On one occasion, a Taiwan businessman who had previously sold us one special machine, a copy of a German one, invited us into a special coffee restaurant after hearing that I had lived for a number of years in Brazil. He wanted to show me that they had all the coffees from around the world so that you could taste them in one place. I knew and kept it to myself: Brazilian coffee was not necessarily all the time the best of the coffees. Regardless of that, the invitation went ahead and we enjoyed a lengthy tasting of well-known highland coffees from around the world, served in stylish Chinese cups. The gentleman showed no disappointment at all when he heard that we were not buying anymore machines, but had started to manufacture them ourselves with our technical expertise in-house. It appeared to be accepted as long as one side could "outsmart" another one without interfering in their business.

Despite an obvious widespread business-sense in the city, other scenes indicated that people had their interests also somewhere else. There was, for instance, a factory owner giving his German shepherd a thorough wash in a baby-bath on the footpath in front of his factory. He had taken a break and sat down comfortably on a chair enjoying the sparsely penetrating sunlight washing his pet with a sponge and shampoo, while his machines were running in the background. As we came closer, the dog remained in his bath, as the factory owner indicated with a smile that he would show us around in his factory. Ballpens were manufactured here on a large scale, of which we each received a special sample. The owner rejoined his patiently-waiting pet as we left.

When business allowed a couple of hours extra-time, a visit to the Chinese Art Museum became a worthwhile break. In a multi-storey-building Chinese arts and crafts were exhibited, focusing on details of porcelain, paintings, silk dresses, furniture, stone-mason work, woodwork and vases. All exhibits were on sale for a reasonable price making a choice difficult in front of such a huge selection.

Taipei is surrounded towards the sea by a wall, protecting the city from the effects of typhoons mainly during the summer.

On a later visit of mine to the country, the city's progress could not be denied. The main traffic arterial had gone up into the air, providing also a lot more space for parks and new buildings. The airport had developed in a short time into a mega-transfer-centre of incoming and outgoing air-travellers. Things don't take long to change here.

Before my boss and I left Taiwan, our host gave us tour through the country. Taiwan has been developed with a clear concept: all industrial activities with most of its population take place along the west coast of the island. In the north, lies the capital Taipei, from where an autobahn goes to the south to the other industrial centre of watchmakers, Tainan.

High mountains covered with dense forests rise to the east of the island. Halfway to the south a road went through a rocky valley into high mountains to a resort, called "Moonrise". On the way, big boulders on the road gave an indication of the forces the water masses from a typhoon had unleashed. The road could be cleared only from time to time by blasting-off the rock-monsters which were left on the road. We could only hope that it didn't happen, while we were in the area. This could have delayed our stay for a long time. At present, the road was redirected in many places.

At Moonrise an unspoiled nature welcomed visitors in a luxury hotel-accommodation. The traffic, the noise, the people masses were left behind. The only noticeable human presence was a Buddhist monastery some distance through the forest.

Listening in the early morning hours to the deep sounds of monk-voices reaching the hotel, I went outside to listen to these impressive messages and found, at the same time, our host also on the road to the monastery. Simon gave me a very good briefing on Buddhist culture, which has a very tolerant view towards life. I want to mention only one piece of information that Simon told me during our walk: the number of the pagoda roofs on a temple count for the happiness that was dedicated to it. More pagoda roofs on top of each other display more happiness in the Buddhist belief.

Our stay in Moonrise over a weekend became a memorable event through its isolation high up in Taiwan's mountains, away from the progressive rush in its cities.

Back in another southern city, Tainan, showed us in its watch-making places, how to make watches. The Taiwanese produced at that time in 1988 many of their products in methods that were in connection to the skills and diligence of their workforce. Taiwan has since also moved to automation, taking the human-factor more and more out of manufacturing. We are all taking part in this "race". Do we really know, why we compete with each other?

From the hotel room in Tainan, I could look into a schoolyard where mixed students in uniform congregated in rows for the start of their school day. Everybody had arrived in time for outdoor gymnastics. The discipline was visible and also for that reason Taiwan has earned a reputation of high education standards world-wide; discipline should be the start for every education.

Our time in Taiwan came to its end. Before our departure from Taipei, we used a couple of hours visiting the aircraft museum next to the airport. There were also military aircrafts on display, pointing towards the defence-determination of Taiwan mainly against its mighty "brother", China. Simon said to us during our first visit: "Every clever Taiwanese business has one leg already in China. What the politicians can't work out, business has already done."

Having returned from Taiwan to Australia, other trips of a business and private nature to the country became a reality in my 19 years with the Brisbane company. I do not want to go into detail with each overseas trip, I'd like rather highlight a trip I took with my boss, this time to the familiar territory of where I came. Visiting two different polarities in the world becomes here the main focus.

Beside business interests, my boss wanted to experience, with my help, how people live and work in this part of the world. He had been to Europe before, but not with the personal guidance of a former local.

We were part of a business group from Australia invited by a major machine-tool manufacturer in Germany. I am not going into all the details of this event, rather pick out occurrences which stood out and made a difference to the journey. Who travels, can gain new experiences.

A chartered bus brought us to the Alpine southern part of Germany, where we have been accommodated in a luxurious mountain-pasture hotel after busy factory visits around Munich. Coming from Australia, we had initially the usual acclimatizing problem to the much colder conditions, especially in the Alps.

Snow still lay mainly in the higher regions, sending the temperature below zero during the nights.

The hotel was built in the Alpine tradition out of solid timber from fir trees. Even inside were huge wooden exposed beams in a workmanlike fashion, giving to the building a solid image. Everything inside was in rustic timber, tables and chairs, chandeliers with their basketry or leather screens, heavy stylish curtains and heated rooms delivered a cosy atmosphere, which many hotels, restaurants and pubs in Germany are known to offer their guests.

Roast deer, dumplings, sauerkraut and the famous Bavarian "liquid bread", called beer, took special care of a stomach's wellbeing.

Beer is often served in a glass boot to a group of guests. The boot makes its way around the table, one person to the next one, by touching off the boot carefully with the back of the hand. Who keeps the foot of the boot up, while drinking, will receive an instant beer-shower out of it, passing on the boot either too hard to the next person, makes the boot tumble or who takes the last gulp out, has to pay in all these cases a new boot filled with beer.

Germany has found its regulations even for the fun.

As we could find out during our day-tours in the highly modern and clean factories, beer in Bavaria is "liquid bread" which is allowed for a controlled consumption even at work. It is said that people are disciplined enough not to consume too much. Is beer also one secret for Bavarian quality like their BMW?

Anyway, next morning the bus took the Australian contingent around other places in Germany. Leaving the mountain area, a hangglider tumbled high up in the sky between steep snowy slopes, a crazy hazardous undertaking in such an environment. All kinds of sports attract daredevils here.

While driving through the hilly green pastures of Bavaria with islands of forests everywhere, crop fields in between, our bus driver had put on Bavarian "pub music" which went unfortunately too far for one person who could understand the Bavarian dialect.

People from Australia usually originate from different parts of the world and we all speak English. Therefore it was likely that other people could have understood also the wording of the music. Its content was unfortunately highly-racially motivated: it could not be understood as a joke at the beer-table with these words in the song "…we are the greatest, the rest in the world are a- holes." I asked the driver to stop his music immediately.

He certainly was a good Bavarian. He never left his village for the "uncertainty" of other places. Fortunately the tour could continue without any unpleasant interruptions. The Aussies, who could eventually understand the "rough joke" could more likely afford to ignore it. Wasn't this a typical sample of different people coming together, when one side "hasn't lived their lives on a journey", but "put the blinkers on" instead.

Rain in Germany is more of a normal event. It was my boss who caught a glimpse of a road-workers unit from the bus: "Look at that, they keep working here in pouring rain, we don't see that at home." Germany is probably one of the countries that "invented organized work " which gives the capacity to perform. If this mentality was transferred to Australia it would most certainly become "the Switzerland of Asia-Pacific ". But what would be left of the Australian way of life? Australian people are happy as they are capable of living their daily lives also with all sort of problems, which they rather try to ignore, if nothing could be done.

Germany "functions" only with everything running close to perfect. Australia keeps running regardless of perfection. People around the world like us, the way we are, coming therefore in their numbers to visit us.

One factory in Aschaffenburg inspired my boss by watching CNC-machine operators, how they continuously handled the manufacturing processes on each of their three machines. He had to say: "Mate, if we worked like this at home, we would run out of work soon."

Our stay in Germany also brought us over into the recently reunited eastern part of the country and its northern part. Modern and clean factories continued to be cast like out of one mould. The canteens in factories invited also visitors at lunchtime to have with the workforce different meals on a menu. The food became more than enough for the rest of the day. In the eastern part of Germany huge investments were directed to bring it in line with the west.

We also know, everything has also its price—progress sounds good, but is not all. A balance in other needs of a society is the keyword.

On such visits it is always interesting to see how others work on their balances. With open eyes we can learn only from others.

During a visit to North Germany, we received an invitation to a five-star restaurant in a big haybarn of a farm, which was transformed into luxury leaving the barn-character intact. It was indeed a great presentation. What this part of Germany could offer to its visitors were their specialities of smoked meats.

The remaining time of this business trip took our Aussie group also to North Italy to Bergamo, an ancient town, where we learnt that progress could be taken one notch even higher than we had seen until then. The invitation to a factory and its presentation showed us perfectly how only the Italians could possibly manage. The welcome lunch left nothing missing that could be called style and excellence. A successful business had spread its wings also here into other horizons, putting it ahead of others by that margin. Knowing how to run a business economically is one thing, but to "sell" it can be an art.

With the focus on both, manufacturing and "art", the Brisbane company back home in Australia grew, within a few years, from a small cell to a car air-conditioning manufacturer of an international reputation.

What we can learn and incorporate into a business, which respects also the special requirements of its nature and market location, makes a business in Australia successful. Australia has always been a testing ground for business through its offside position and a relatively small domestic market.

Australian businesses have not the privileges of established markets like in Europe or North America and many emerging parts of Asia, including India.

It will still count for years to come: who ever had made it in Australia, could have made it also anywhere else in the world.

Back to our stay in North Italy; my boss as a Ferrari-fan also got in touch with other Ferrari-collectors in its homeland. The collectors were very anxious, whom they showed around in their state-of-the-art Ferrari-collections. Not being an owner even of one Ferrari, I could live with the fact that I could not gain access to one of these "showrooms". My boss at least learnt that he had to build on his car collection to match what he saw.

A person's hobby can often say more about him than his other activities do; but then again, don't make your hobby your profession, you can otherwise lose a crucial balance in your life. Balance is the key to everything in our lives, which means, we have to look at "things "also from different angles.

Visiting other places and their people has the effect that we can connect to others to find out in our search, sometimes a partner or at least an access to new ideas, which can help to solve problems. When we returned to Australia, a "circle" had closed again; noticeably what goes around, comes around; it is up to us, what we gain in such "circles".

I have described intentionally two business journeys into two different areas of the world, one in Asia, and the other in Europe, where I came from. Beside other business trips, I'd also like to highlight on some private visits mainly to Europe. It does appear, going out of Australia, is to go also to Singapore. Having connections also there, I experienced together with my wife a private tour through this model-city-state. It started already at the airport that everybody had to pay his respects to this achievement, which could be only classified as: big, well planned, incorporated tropical nature, clean, easy to find one's way and all perfectly maintained. Singapore is also known for its strict regulations; traffic in the city is moving on speed limit, smoking in the public is banned, possession of chewing-gum is an offence, any trafficking of drugs is followed by a death sentence, graffiti is prosecuted, littering is an offence.

Out of the many ethnic groups living in Singapore, the Chinese emerged as a leading force, giving the directions for the future. Progress and prosperity speak for the city-state. As a foreigner, one can feel safe in this city, crime is hardly known. The multi-cultural society creates also here a tolerance, which a visitor can only benefit from; across the city people are friendly and helpful.

The highly-efficient automated harbour, and an automated train system at the airport and in the city are developments pointing already into a future.

In cooperation with other countries education and industry are established in a most modern way. Singapore is a future model-society. This can be only achieved with rational restrictions attached to the life of a society.

I realised that Singapore visitors to Australia enjoyed, to a certain degree, the much less restricted life in Australia. Singapore is not larger than the Brisbane area in Australia, but has many more citizens, asking therefore for more regulations in order to stay on a progressive path. What could we learn in Australia in "our way of life" from Singapore for our future?

Leaving Singapore usually on a hot and humid day makes the world change again, because of its proximity to the equator, no matter, where one flies out.

When arriving in Germany, it is much cooler and modern images don't become so dominant, because the "old" and the "new" have lived there for longer, making the place and its people again different.

As my wife once arrived in Germany, the railway system was on strike, making further travelling rather difficult. After a taxi driver became available, a conversation took place: "Where do you come from?"—"From Australia"—"How did you come here?"—"Definitely not on foot!"—"How come that you speak German and tell me, you are from Australia?"—"Originally I am from Finland." Now the driver became completely confused asking more questions: "What do you speak in Australia?"—"My mother-tongue is Finnish, we speak at home German and outside home English. Over 70 languages are spoken in Australia mainly in private, everybody speaks otherwise English." The taxi driver stopped asking questions.

Our connections back to Europe didn't spare us some painful reminders, when loved-ones passed away far from us. My step-father passed away at an respectable age of 84 only a few days later after my visit in 1987. I was unable to go back after only a few days.

My strong-minded step-mother lived 90 years and I accompanied her on her last journey in 1998. When we go on our last journey, everything else should be forgotten, only respect should prevail. If we don't respect each other during our lives, we have failed in our destination.

My mother-in-law had put all her strength together in 2002, when she came from Finland accompanied by my wife for her last Australian visit. After returning to Finland and having seen not only her eldest daughter's family, but also her own thriving tree on our property, which indicated to us her demise.

How much do we really know in the face of such events? How our journey after life continues is not a matter of knowledge any more, we have entered a cycle, which we still cannot comprehend.

In a wider sense, we are only world-citizens, borders with other countries and the languages is what we have created. Therefore we should be able to call home every place on earth, a home can be established also in Australia. In our lives we have to develop the strength to look at the positive sides, that can carry us further.

## Outback—Australia—Tour

It was decided in 2001 that my wife and myself would go on a "pilgrimage" through the Outback of Australia to Darwin in the Northern Territory, where our youngest daughter, Gucki, studied music at the N.T. University. Her chosen main-instrument is the classical concert-guitar. Darwin calls every three years the best concert guitar performers from around the world for a concert-week in its university-premises and also wild backyard.

We travelled to Darwin in July 2001 to attend Gucki's first concert. The distance between Brisbane and Darwin is on the road 4000 kilometres.

Going on this road, I'd like to start with a trial "poem" that I have put together to introduce the Outback of Australia, which makes up for most of the tour from Brisbane to Darwin:

## Outback—Poem—Trial

Time must have stopped, life has fallen silent, a far cry away from every days' life in a city. The sun reigns all year, the views are wide and open, the eye can search, we are in the Australian Outback.

A day starts here like every other one, sunlight opens the sky in a colourful display, from dark-orange direct above the bowed horizon, to orange, red, yellow, the higher this fire-ball climbs. Shades born by individual bush out of the dark, shorten, until daylight makes them disappear.

Birds, single, small, large, in flocks—white, black, pink, rich in striking colours- Cockatoos, Magpies, Ravens, Galahs, Finches, Lorikeets, the occasional Wedge-tail Eagle, they all fly into the sky of a new-born day, not with-out announcing it very sharp and loud. To whom the birds make their announcement? Nobody is here to listen! Have they got the window to our creator?

The sun rises in a crystal blue sky, sending heat-waves towards Mother Earth, on the increase, large red-kangaroos, small wallabies, emus, wombats, brumbies, cattle, wild pigs only occasionally, they all move into hiding in the vast bush, looking for the protection from the heat of the day.

In a contrast, the large family of snakes and lizards search for the early sun of the day, feeding off the heat waves.

Few people only move after a business in the early hours of a day. Not long will it take that Mother Earth sends back the heat, it cannot take more in the middle of the day, shifting then the air and creating distorted pictures of the Outback, everything turns totally silent.

From its highest point in the sky the sun has penetrated everything. Travelling in a car on a road, with or without dust, makes you then best moving. A breeze through a car can keep minds alive. Stopping with a car in summer, the sun will hit you hard. The law of the Outback is support and help. It is nowhere written down, it is a must for a living, travelling, surviving here.

With long hours on the road another car appears, hand signs speak for everything being o.k.-Stopping generally indicates a problem ; in a changing world, caution is also here not out of place. Changes from outside take a foothold only slowly in the Outback. Heat, drought, floods, winds, a resisting nature, successfully have put on the brakes on our development needs, so far.

2000 kilometres distance from the tropical coast of East-Australia, the border of Queensland and the Northern Territory is not far. Vast rolling fields of wheat around Longreach are just behind us, the green bush has claimed back its territory for a while, only grassland, high standing after a wet season, yellow when mature.

On the road are also the road-trains, moving goods, life-stock, harvests in long truck-chains. They are the kings of the Outback roads, demanding the right of a lane, up to 5 long trailers can make up a road-train.

They move very fast, have long distances to go and won't stop. Sidewise moving trailers ask oncoming traffic better to stop, on the side of the road. The driver of a road-train cannot see, what happens in a dust-cloud behind. Massive bull-bars on the front of road-trains keep everything off the road: kangaroos, cattle, better not another car.

At night it can be only recommended to stay off the road. The animals hiding during the heat of the day are moving and feeding then. Surprisingly much life is waking up during an Outback night. Human presence is disturbing it, animals flee from us, putting them and us in danger on a road.

Towards the end of a day the sun starts losing power, heat remains however well into the night. Shades become longer until darkness of the night takes over.

Only in the early morning hours does cooler air move across the Outback.

A caravan-park near a hamlet is a welcome stop for a night. At the shed of the entrance is visibly attached: "Owner is out, leave your fees of $8 in the mailbox, thanks." City-folk, foreigners, Interstate-travellers are found here of a sudden, but hardly any locals.

Everybody experiences the Outback his way. Therefore people and their stories in caravan-parks differ like the people themselves. Locals have less stories to tell, because they know. The nearby road delivers during the night only the occasional thunder-like passage of a road-train. The dark night is otherwise immersed into silence under the roof of a glittering sky.

People in the caravan-park sit together around a small fireplace, exchanging their stories and waiting long into the night, before the heat of the day gives way to a cooler night. Crickets rub their wings out of their hiding, sending messages in waves through the air of this night.

A sudden fast moving shade between the few Eucalypt and Acacia-trees make up this caravan park in the endless grass and bushland surrounding it.

There are also the curious bats; sometimes even kangaroos come out of the bush very close to the people, making their inspections on what is happening in their territory.

Another morning does not fail to announce a new day. The far horizon sends again the first cautious light into the black uprising sky-dome.

This is the moment, our new day starts. Everything is packed away into the car in its own place. We allow the engine to run warm only for a moment, not to disturb other people in their sleep.

Shortly after we are back on the road, alone, lights of the car show us the way. A pair of close red points in the light beams announce a kangaroo on the side of the road, where the only green grass is at the bitumen—border.

Speed immediately is reduced to watch the kangaroo anxiously waiting in the dark. Will it keep feeding or jump? "Roo" is a master in sudden movements. Strong back legs give them the power to jump a few metres out of the bush on to the road right in front of a car. The red colour of our car made the "roo" to stay, reminding it eventually of blood, when hit by a car.

The morning spectacle is repeated once again, daylight consumes the dark in a colourful display. Two and a half hours have pioneered us into a new day, before the first car passed us. A sign of a homestead attracts our attention on the side of the road. We stop, move off the road, despite hardly any traffic.

## Home-Stead Visit

There is a small piece of bitumen leading off the road into a stony dusty track. Two timber logs carrying a long cross-bar, high enough to let a loaded truck get past. The name of the homestead is also shown in white letters: "Robertson".

On the side of this obvious entrance, a smaller post holds a milk-jug on a chain in a horizontal position; this is the Outback letterbox.

Yellow, green, brown grassland rises to man's height out of the dark red soil, as far as the eye can see. The land rolls in continuous waves towards the horizon interrupted only by mountainous elevations. Islands of green bush emerge to the searching eye, small bands of trees stoop in lower areas, yet there is no house visible.

Just behind the track-entrance shows a sign on another post the distance to the homestead: 120 miles. Underneath these numbers is a note: no petrol for 186 kilometres. A firm decision is required to make the way to this homestead.

Our day is still in the early hours, petrol is sufficient in spare tanks on the roof-rack besides two spare tyres; toolbox, steel-wire, hammer, rope, axe, spade, clean and safe water stored are the essentials from now on.

It is decided to start this 120 miles journey.

The track winds gently towards the north from where the sun will reign in a few hours. The car tyres follow the red-dusty tracks to the right and the left, leaving in the centre grass standing, rubbing noisily under the car. Our movement is rather slow. We need time to make the distance to the homestead. Wheat farmland comes up as far as the eye can see, the crop stands low out of the ground, there has not been enough rain so far.

From the distance, the wheat looks like a carpet, from close this carpet is thinly scattered. A flock of white cockatoos fly low in the air right in front of us, as if we didn't exist. The cockatoos take their share out of these vast fields as they like. A power line next to us shows in the distance, where the track runs. A dust cloud rises not far from us, coming closer, it has moved already to the west. A stockman appears on a horse, directing a herd of cattle from behind in half-circles. Under the wide brim of his leather hat a dark face can be noticed. An Aborigine is usually very good in overlooking, guiding and dominating such a powerful herd. We must be now closer to the farm.

Massive black-brown cattle make the ground tremble, one can hear out of the dust these rolling hoofs.

During one circle-movement the stockman comes with his horse closer to us. Both sides waving hands simultaneously, he disappears into the dust cloud. We continue on the track to the homestead.

The sun is setting closer to the horizon, while the heat demands to keep moving, we must have been over five hours on this track. In the lower part of this territory, next to the dry bed of a creek, appears the main wide roof of the homestead. The grass is here low to the ground. Small numbers of high eucalypt trees with their thinly scattered leaves form small green islands around the house. This large shade-area invites a visitor to leave behind the scoring heat of the sunburnt land. We roll-in closer with the car, roofs of other buildings appear out of tree-crowns. Only the road gives free passage, the rest around is barred by log fences to keep the cattle out of the homestead.

The wind-wheel on a steel-tower on higher ground next to the main building is spinning slowly. Water is pumped here from deep underground into a huge round steel-tank. Water means here more than anywhere else; no water means no life.

Tall round corrugated iron towers in a group look over the trees from behind the homestead. They store the harvest and will take in more, as soon as time will be ready again for harvesting of the wheat.

Nobody can be seen on this wide farm. Cautiously I set my foot into the property. Other buildings and sheds catch the attention, surrounding in a near-circle the main building. Nobody could have expected in the oasis of these trees such a well-organised farm set-up.

I turn towards the building to the left, where the front leaves a wide door open. Before getting there, a quiet big black dog comes out of the building towards me. I stop. The dog keeps trotting further towards me. Talking a couple words to him, the dog stops, looks up, but stays quiet. A German shepherd must have been in his family as he turned in a circle around me in a distance out of reach. Finally we come opposite each other, where I face the wide open door. Dog and myself stay in one spot motionless.

The afternoon sun sends hot waves of its radiation to the ground, still saturated from the whole day's heat. Not much later a woman appears in the dim daylight of the veranda, which surrounds the homestead: "Greg is over in the machine-shed." She points with her raised right hand into the direction of the shed with its wide open door. The dog is still in my way as the woman leaves the veranda, calling the dog by his name, which I could not understand.

The dog moves slowly to the side of the woman, but keeps an eye on my movements. Before reaching the large corrugated iron shed, a man in his fifties comes out through a smaller side-door in the shed's front. The man puts straight outside a leather hat on his head. I cannot see his face first, but his words still come out: "What are you doing here?"—"I want to have a look, how life is on a homestead 120 miles off the road."- "Do you bring rain for us?"—"It is waiting on the horizon for you."—"Is this a promise?"

During our first exchanges this tall man with wide strong built shoulders comes towards me so I can see in the shaded daylight his face.

"I am Martin, how are you?"—"I am Greg, where do you come from?" Greg's hand reaches out towards me, I receive a short handshake, as if my hand is put between the jaws of a vice. "Is somebody with you in that car?"—"My wife tries to stay out of the heat there."—"You make sure, she is all right and get her down here, will you." I go back to the car under the Coolabah tree. By sheer habit I lock the car, becoming aware of it only halfway down to the homestead. There is most certainly nobody around here having an interest in our car. After a short walk I arrive with my wife in front of the veranda carrying an "esky" with us.

The sun is setting again closer to the horizon, its shallow light penetrates through the lower branches of the surrounding eucalypt trees into the veranda.

"You are lucky, we have done most of today's work, let's go inside out of the sun."—"I have out of my car-fridge a cold beer, I am sure, you like also one."—"You keep your beer in your fridge, come in and try mine."

I introduce my wife not without explaining that Arja is a Finnish name and Finland is the country where she comes from. "We need people to come and see also us in the Outback, we are on our own, but don't mind to have a good company, which today is not always coming out of the cities."

"How is the crop going this season?"—"It all depends, whether we have that bit more rain, neither too heavy nor too much. The last couple of years were too dry for a good harvest, but we manage. The young people don't want to stay on the farm any more, they all move into the cities. I am running with my wife the farm in the third generation, I can't be sure if one of my two sons will carry on. As long as they don't forget us here in the Outback, everything should be all right. Tell me about your kids and what you are doing."

Lights are switched on inside the house early, a nice orderly furnished living room with a kitchen next to it give a homely atmosphere, the dog stays outside on the veranda. "We have to do everything by ourselves here, there is nobody around to give a hand, except my stockman, when he is in the area. The cattle business is also not too flashy. We have dinner, if you want to join, you are welcome. It is nothing fancy, we don't live with this sort of fancy staff."

Our conversation carries on into the night, but at nine o'clock Greg stops and reminds us:" Tomorrow is another day, we have to get up early, our work doesn't go away, we have no holiday on the farm. Are you right to sleep in your car tonight? If I don't see you tomorrow, have a good trip. Your stay has been a welcome break for us, we will remember you."—"Thank you for your hospitality, we also move tomorrow back to the road at first daylight.

Stay in good health and have the rain soon needed for your crop."

The homestead we have visited was partly in the Northern Territory and partly in Queensland. Farms and their cattle don't know borders. As soon as we arrived back on the bitumen road to the west, our tour continued with the first destination Darwin. I am describing here only briefly the course of events, because our Outback tour in Australia is described in more detail in my book "Road to Nitmiluk ".

Further west we entered the Stuart Highway, which we followed to the north. Traffic was still low, but moving on a high speed without limit in the Northern Territory.

Further north the bush started to spread on both sides of the road. If fire hasn't burnt the land, the bush is always green despite long dry and hot summer seasons. The tropical oasis of Mataranka becomes a recreation for a traveller. Hot natural springs in a pool give the opportunity for a swim in a surrounding cabbage-palm forest.

In Katherine, the Top-End of the Northern Territory starts. The town is a centre for the whole region. Its river created the Katherine Gorges (Nitmiluk), which can be regarded as the Grand Canyon of Australia with the difference that its gorges are filled with the water from the Katherine river, making a boat tour a special experience, but asking respect for the crocodiles, which call every water area in the

Top-End their home. Eucalypt forest soon took over from the bush, cycads spreading in between. Where fire had burnt the land black, cycads are the first to stand out with their fresh light-green leaf-shoots against the black-burnt surroundings. A water pipeline runs gradually with the road down to the coast, reaching Darwin, the capital of the Northern Territory.

The city of Darwin owes its name to the scientist Charles Darwin, who actually never visited it, but documented his "theory of evolution" from reports out of the Top-End. In recognition of his pioneering scientific work, the city honoured the scientist, adopting his name.

The Top-End is all year around warm and in summer very hot and humid. Winter is the only travelling time for it, when the monsoonal summer-rains have stopped. Darwin has been completely rebuilt after the 1974 Cyclone Tracey destruction. Today it is fairly easy to find your way in Darwin, because the city is built around the airfield.

Our mission in Darwin was to see our youngest daughter, Gucki, performing her first classical guitar concert. We were not disappointed, Gucki received applause for her interpretations of Sor, Bach, Albeniz, Vivaldi, Giuliani and Villa-Lobos.

My wife and myself visited also the university and were allowed to attend several lectures in the faculty of music, experiencing a little bit of today's university atmosphere, which refreshed memories from our time at a university.

The Northern Territory University was probably one of the few universities in the world that could take more students. Many lecturers were appointed from overseas, connecting the university with the rest of the world to high standards in its teaching. Darwin is still today a pioneering field; who can live in Darwin, must have survival qualities, when the heat and humidity starts to build up in October. Everybody experiencing it, will understand, what is special about it.

A couple of days gave us also the opportunity to look around in the Top-End. Not far from Darwin can be found in the south-west,

Berry-Springs, Litchfield National Park with the Florence and Wangi-Falls, surrounded by eucalypt forests and bush. Spectacular views, rest places, swimming in controlled areas make a visit worthwhile. Where there is water, there are also the crocodile warning-signs. The biggest termite-mounds in the world can be found as well there, indicating that there is a lot of heat in the area, which makes the termites build their "air-conditioning systems" to such a height.

The Kakadu National Park is located in the east of Darwin, a visit not to be missed. Even in winter the temperature can reach 40 degrees Celsius, heat is here constant. Even the road has its own croc-warning-signs. The "crocs" seek the heat on the bitumen and it would not be a good idea to drive with the car over a crocodile on the road. The Alligator rivers show from the road crocs as well in the water as on the riverbanks. They are good hunters and ask for respect, it is not advisable to ignore them.

Pandalus-Spiralis palm forests give the area a special look out of an ancient earth-history. High grassland surrounds the gigantic rock-outcrop of Nourlangie Rock with pre-historic Aboriginal rock-paintings dating back 60000 years. The sunny weather of the Outback reaches the Top-End in winter with a guaranteed sunshine, making a visit to Kakadu a memorable event.

Special four-wheel-drive skills are required to reach on land the Jim-Jim and Twin-Falls, where water falls stepwise into a massive deeply washed out canyon surrounded by forests and steep rock-walls.

Ubirr is a rock-plateau in the north, not far from Jabiru, the only major settlement in Kakadu. Rock-caves in Ubirr show also Aboriginal rock-paintings. Throughout ancient history, the area has been for Aborigines' nature's temple.

Visiting the area today with respect, can give some understanding of its cultural expressions.

Jabiru at the east-end of Kakadu is a well-planned settlement with some tourist facilities, being at the same time the starting point of the controversial uranium-mining in the east of Kakadu.

There are more Aborigines than in other parts of Australia, their population is only in small numbers mixed. They represent still today their originality both in appearance and culture.

The alert observer can also catch a glimpse between the flocks of native birds in Kakadu, the Top-End-stork, called a Jabiru, which has posed for the symbol of the Northern Territory. It can be found in swamps of the territory, mostly single and very shy.

With our Darwin mission coming to an end for this time, we returned to the south of the Northern Territory, remaining on the Stuart-Highway. The dry land with its rocks, bush, often red ground received us again. Our daughter, Gucki, joined us in Tennant Creek, coming from Darwin with the bus. Together we wanted to visit Ayers Rock, also called Uluru. On the way we passed also the landmark "Devil's Marbles", an outcrop of rocks, not far from the road, flat country surrounding it. Sun, wind and rain have shaped the rocks, some single ones standing huge off the ground in a nearly perfect ball-shape.

"A Town like Alice" (Nevil Shute) recalls a special place in the Australian Outback which can be understood only by those who have seen the place and discovered it : "There is no other town like Alice Springs."

On the foothills of the MacDonnell Ranges shelters a city, with an image imposed through a nature, which has survived so far all of nature's furies: heat, bitter cold, winds, droughts, fires, floods. The city-mall is like a dream brought into this harsh environment, allowing visitors some escape and to briefly forget about the conditions.

The Todd river cuts the only passage to the south. Boat races during Spring-time take place usually in a dry riverbed, when the competitors stick their feet through their special boats and run the distance with the boat.

It has happened only once lately that the "boat race" could not be held, because the Todd river carried unseasonable water.

Leaving Alice behind, not much later the road was indicating the direction to Ayers Rock in the west. The world's largest monolith appeared soon on the horizon, first small out of the distance in a vast flat land surrounded with low bush, which struggles to keep its role in nature. The closer the road brings a visitor to the monolith, the bigger it grows out of the ground.

*Top of Ayers Rock, Olgas in background.*

After an admission point already close to it, one can only try to comprehend this world-wonder. The Aborigines of the area do not like to see people going up the steep path on the rock-face. Despite this understanding, it was officially in certain times allowed to go up on the rock. The views from the top are fascinating: in the west lie the Olgas, another worthwhile visit, in the north can be seen on a clear day Alice Springs with the Mac-Donnell Ranges, to the east and the south are in a far distance other smaller monoliths. The eye can see as far as the Ranges on the Western Australian border. A road is running like a thin line through a carpet of green bush, no cars no humans can be seen from the top of Uluru; this is a "sacred view" into the world, the horizon shows the bend of the earth all around. A view on to earth like out of space.

Close to Ayers Rock lies to the west the Olgas. In front of the naked huge rock-mountains stand scattered desert-oaks in the middle of high yellow grass. The colours stand out here, the sky is blue, the rocks are red under a special daylight, the desert-oaks are dark green, the grass is yellow, scattered bush is black and light green, the ground is red.

The desert oaks in front of the Olgas are unique, they are the only specimens of its kind in the world and have survived through ancient history, possibly millions of years. No passage is allowed into this area.

On the return journey to Alice, it cannot be missed a sign to King Canyon, a colourful rocky canyon. Time is needed to experience the centre of the Australian continent. During summer extreme temperatures occur, whereas in winter the temperature goes at night below zero, making nights very cold, but the days through the sun are still fairly warm. Winter is a good time for a visit.

Travelling north again, there were a couple of places of interest past Alice. A pioneer had established a garden Eden's along the road in the middle of desert bushland. A vineyard and a fruit plantation looked healthy out of a fenced farm property. Somebody had achieved here, what is considered the impossible.

The artesian underground reservoir of the continent has undoubtedly done its contribution also further on a camel-farm, which is divided into lots with camels around a building complex with traveller accommodations. The whole place stood out with its green meadows, but also with an intensive smell from the camels. The owner had brought from former Rhodesia their pet ostrich, which fitted nicely into the environment here in Australia.

The historical rock-buildings of a Telegraph Station from the early pioneering years is worthy of mention.

The roads to the east to Queensland were in an uncertain condition, most were only dusty stone tracks, requiring four-wheel experience.

The faster better way back to Queensland was at Three-Ways to go east to Mount Isa and Townsville on the Queensland coast; this was the longer travelling distance, but the quicker way.

The coastal ranges of the Australian Great Divides started after Richmond and Hughenden, where everything becomes lush green and forests cover mountains. After travelling thousands of kilometres in the Outback, the coastal ranges of Queensland are like an entrance into a different world.

We didn't see even one drop of rain in the Outback, but it didn't take long to catch up with the rain again along the East Coast.

As our eldest son, Risto, lived with his family in Townsville, we paid him a visit. He showed us around north of Townsville for a few days: along the coast is Innisfail with its sugarcane fields and banana plantations in front of mountains covered with rainforests, Atherton Tablelands with coffee and tea-farming, Kuranda's tropical rainforest-oasis located high above Cairns, both are visited by large numbers of international tourists.

The tropical coastline of North Queensland is magnificent, classified as one of the most natural beautiful places on earth.

Everything must come to an end and so did this first tour into the Australian Outback. Returning home to Caboolture with a camper-trailer behind after 14,000 kilometres of travelling, it became an exciting moment to find out how our property had "survived" our absence. The "zoo" at home required to be looked after with an individual attention to each of our highly-regarded "family members". It was a pleasure to come home because our youngest boy, Micki, who was still at school, had done well his job as "property administrator" only with one hiccup with the station-wagon left in the garage. Weighing the "goodies" against the hiccup, spoke still in favour of our son Micki.

A more detailed description of this tour can be found in "Road to Nitmiluk", which could be a good preparation for somebody planning a similar tour. Australia can offer something that is entirely different from the rest of the world. Who knows to appreciate this, can collect immense experiences and impressions.

## In Eighty Days Around the World in 2003

Following the leitmotiv of this book "Lifetime Journeys", I took the opportunity in 2003 to travel with my wife around the world in 80 days.

The company I was employed, gave me three months time off after 15 years of continued successful service. A tour around the world would be a once-in-a-lifetime experience in everybody's terms.

Instead of going back to Europe the common way from Australia through Singapore and continuing north-west, our tour started into the opposite direction, to the north-east. We had chosen the northern hemisphere summertime. Vancouver on the south-west coast of Canada became a destination on the North American continent. Air Canada received our bookings to take us there.

As Air Canada operated only out of Sydney, we had to make our first leg of the journey from Brisbane to Sydney with Qantas.

Arriving in Sydney one day before our departure, gave us the opportunity to catch up with the family. Our son, Peter, lived with his Sri-Lankan wife, Gowry, and their little son, Abhay, in the Sydney suburb of Lane Cove. The next day we were all at the International Airport on our departure.

After the long flight over the Pacific Ocean, we received a welcome break in Honolulu. During our flight we crossed also the datum-line, which means, going east, the global time turned one day the clock back. In other words, we started in Sydney on the first of June and arrived in Honolulu on the 31st of May!

The plane was full to the last seat, but we were probably the only passengers on a tour around the world.

Back home we had planned to make this tour a comfortable one, with hotel accommodations, where we had neither friends nor family and to hire also, from time to time, a car to stay more independent.

## Hawaii

A mild summer night temperature welcomed us on our arrival in Honolulu. The plane left again without us two on board, because we had planned a first holiday in Hawaii. A taxi could be still found to give us a lift to the hotel on Waikiki Beach. The driver reassured us, there was no crime in Hawaii contrary to the mainland of the United States, as there was nowhere to escape.

Our hotel room was in a high-rise building, from where we had a bird's-eye view on to the surrounding ocean of lights in this part of Honolulu. Not many tourists had come to Hawaii, because of a global fear of a SARS-epidemic.

When most people stay at home, had become the best time to travel around the world, as we found out.

The island of Oahu, where Honolulu is located, woke up next morning under brilliant sunshine, as we are most of the time used to at home in Australia. A brief visit to Waikiki Beach, just next to the hotel confirmed that the calm water was warm enough for a swim.

Instead of trying to see all the islands of Hawaii, we decided to concentrate on its two furthest-apart ones: Kauai in the north-west and the Main Island in the south-east. Travelling between the chain of Hawaiian islands is mainly done by air. The wide Pacific Ocean displays in many parts along the islands its monstrous waves, making sea travelling hazardous.

A plane took us from Honolulu to Kauai, where we had booked a stay for one week in a beach resort. Once the plane had gained height over Oahu, its mountains and coastlines appeared clear underneath, everything was covered with a green carpet, the blue Pacific broke in a white foam-line along the island. One hour later the plane touched down in Lihue on Kauai island.

A friendly taxi driver from the original Hawaiian Polynesian population gave us a lift to the resort near Kapaa, not before handing each of us a shell necklace as it was the tradition to welcome a visitor to Hawaii, adding also: "You are on your honeymoon? "Why not", were our thoughts and we left our driver in his belief. The driver took also the opportunity to inform us where to stay, eat or buy in his opinion. He recommended naturally his Hawaiian colleagues, indicating a competition between American civilization and Hawaiian way of life. Our taxi driver's suggestions were generally cheaper, than the better-known names like Woolworths. Hawaii was quite expensive, most products had to be brought in from the American Mainland. Local Hawaiians could not afford these costs. They created their own markets, which they could afford better.

The reception at Aston Island Resort was also very friendly, and we were mainly served by indigenous Hawaiians. They were full of joy. And when we picked out of our dictionary sentences to address them, their joy was real.

The resort buildings spread in a circle near the beachfront, giving out of every room a view into the tropical colourful flowering garden, its palms supplying the shade. The view continued to the edge of a sandy beach dropping slightly down to the sea water. Sand on the beach was widely mixed with stones, fine sandy beaches are not common on Hawaiian islands.

Ocean currents have also to be watched, but not so much other dangerous marine creatures, which haven't made it that far in the Pacific. Sharks however can be found in all parts of Hawaii, asking for caution.

Being islands in the vast Pacific Ocean, the climate in Hawaii is not too hot, it is during the day just under 30 degrees Celsius, which makes it with a sea-breeze very comfortable.

Our room in the resort had also an air-conditioning system installed. Switching it on required a good bashing on its box to make it stay on, was the instruction given to us. Nobody would come here expecting to meet perfect technology.

The first few days were committed to a rest on the beach and smaller excursions into Kapaa town and the closer surroundings. Coconut trees grew here to a respectable height, asking for the attention to stay away, when they had in their crowns nuts. A coconut coming down from that height would cause a considerable problem for the one who meets it.

In the centre of Kauai rises the volcano Waialeale. Its surroundings are daily visited by short heavy showers and are classified as the world's wettest area.

*Waimea-Canyon, Kauai.*

*Hawaiian Fashion, Martin and Arja.*

On a tour in a rented car to the north of the island we stopped near Hanalei, when it rained like cats and dogs for only half an hour. As soon as the rain stopped, the views to the mountains cleared again and water cascades became visible on all the steep mountain slopes. Lush green fields of Taro, a stable food of the indigenous Hawaiian, spread in the plains, disrupted only by a winding road and river. Further on came Hanalei, where the road led close to the beach again with exuberant tropical vegetation ending in Wainiha. The coast became from here so rugged that no road could go further. The tropical environment serves very often here in the film industry. Many tropical images in movies come from this area.

On another day, the south of the island became a destination we wanted to explore. In coastal plains around Koloa are Hawaii's first successful sugar-cane-plantations, already since 1835. The continuing road to Waimea Canyon runs again along the coast, stopping in the west before the rugged Napali Coast. From a high located lookout on the border of Waimea Canyon, an overall view can be gained into its deep ridged canyons. The impressions don't stand back much from those at Grand Canyon in Arizona. Green vegetation in its valleys is however a major difference between the Grand Canyon. High rainfall in the area forms still the canyon. Between the few onlookers the presence of two German tourists could not escape our attention, in their opinion: Waimea is as good as Grand Canyon.

We spent the day before our departure from Kauai in the area around our resort, visiting the small Waioli-Huiia Church, which was built out of timber and painted green, another building surrounded by a veranda, called an Assembly House, was next to it. The veranda-benches invited us to sit down and admire the pink flowers of the surrounding trees. No bird could be seen, only a few native birds have accidentally found their way from the American Continent across the Pacific. Animals are not existent on the islands of Hawaii, unless they are brought in. The main food-source came in the past out of the sea. While resting in the shade of the Assembly House, a Hawaiian man came out of it and joined us. He was keen to hear from us where we came from. After asking him questions, he started a very interesting conversation: "As you probably have found out already, we have here only two speeds: first speed is slow, second one is slower. Hawaii is the nucleus of all human civilisation, human life started here. Our language is the easiest, we have only 12 letters. A similarity to our language is found also in Japanese on Hokkaido, which points towards an ancient migration. You are doing the right thing, we like people to use our native language, even if only a few common words like: aloha (for hello), aloha kakahiaka (good morning), pehea oe (how are you), mahalo (thanks), aloha ahiahi (good evening).

# MARTIN KARI

Today we belong to the United States of America, but we do not want to lose our identity. Have a look at this poem by Mark Twain, which I'd like to give as a friend's gift, take it with you and don't lose its memories:

> *"The loveliest fleet of islands that lies anchored in any ocean*
> *No land in all the world has any deep,*
> *Strong charm for me that one ; no other land*
> *Could so longingly and beseechingly haunt me*
> *Sleeping and waking, through half a lifetime, as*
> *That one has done. Other things leave me it*
> *Abides; other things change but it remains the same.*
> *For me its balmy airs are always blowing,*
> *Its summer seas flashing in the sun; the pulsing*
> *Of its surf-beat is in my ear; I can't see its*
> *Gar-landed crags; its leaping cascades; its plumy*
> *Palms drowsing by the shore; its remote summits*
> *Floating like islands above the cloud rack; I can*
> *Feel the spirit of its woodland solitudes; I can*
> *Hear the plash of its brooks ; in my nostrils still*
> *Lives the breath of flowers that perished twenty*
> *Years ago."*

—Mark Twain

"During early explorations the Dutch missed us in the vastness of the Pacific Ocean. It was James Cook in 1778, who discovered Hawaii for the outside world. From then on, our indigenous Hawaiian population has suffered a dramatic decline. China and Japan brought also their people in, today we are a minority on our own Hawaii. Take my story home and tell the rest of the world about it." We responded: "Mahalo nui" (thanks a lot).

An old established farm in the area had maintained its traditional Hawaiian style buildings with high ceilings and a large roof area, shading the house walls with trees and tropical gardens. A huge mango tree had grown near the house well over one hundred years to a size, I had never seen before. Standing under the tree, one had the impression of a nature's house with a gigantic roof over it.

Besides many waterfalls on the island we visited only the nearby Walua and Opaekaa-Falls. Native Hawaiians showed us in one place, how they skillfully cut a coconut with their machetes and shaped out of its hard shell a spoon, used to cut the flesh out of the nut after drinking the milk.

A good size coconut supplies liquid and food for at least one person's half-day needs. The island of Kauai pleased us in particular with its vigorous fresh green growth, a real tropical paradise.

Lihue airport waited for us again for a departure to Kailua-Kona Airport on Hawaii the Big Island with a stopover in Honolulu. The waiting time at Lihue airport was filled with a presentation of Hawaiian guitar music, an original way of saying "Aloha" (good bye). The metallic sound of the guitar strings reproduced in a melodious way the waves of the wind and the sea.

We had to change the plane in Honolulu. Flying over the island-chain, all their mountains, coastlines and their wide green carpet appeared clearly visible from the aircraft. As we landed at Kona Airport on the Big Island, our plane appeared very small next to the Boeing 747 from Japan Airlines,which had just landed before us, bringing into the island tourists in their numbers.

During World War II, some 160,000 Japanese had lived in Hawaii, fuelling that time the suspicion of a secret involvement in the outcome of Pearl Harbour, where Japan attacked, inflicting in one morning of December 7, 1941 the worst damage to American armed strength in the history of the nation. Japanese must still like Hawaii today for a living or a visit. A rented car from the airport made us immediately independent. In the direct surroundings of the airport, green lawns and palms were maintained, straight after barren land rose inland, yellow, brown and black were the main colours. It looked first like we had landed on the moon. Towards inland hung in higher levels of the mountains a dense cloud layer, of which the origin was from volcanic activities further inland.

*Royal Palace, Big Island, Hawaii.*

*Mauno Lea Volcano, Big Island, Hawaii.*

As we learned during our stay directly from Hawaiian people, they never worry about the volcanic activities. They regard it as a part of their daily lives.

Royal Kona Resort lies south of the airport, a huge hotel-complex on the coast, very different from the smaller resort on Kauai. Masses of tourists can be accommodated here in Kona Resort, but because of the SARS epidemic-fear worldwide, tourists had stood away also from Hawaii, which became only a bonus for us. Swimming was provided here in a pool; the black rocky coast with its big waves from the ocean didn't allow swimming.

Besides short walks in the town, where we visited also the very modest Royal Palace, we had a plan to the whole island. The Royal Palace did not stand out much from other buildings. Hawaii had abandoned in 1894 its monarchy, when Queen Liliuokalani surrendered her power in an unbloody open revolution and gave way to a Republican Constitution. An occurrence worthy of mention is that in 1882 the Hawaiian King Kalakaua made an expensive round-the-world tour, becoming the first King to be a circumnavigator. But he sent the country bankrupt with his life on a "properly royal scale".

In 2003 our round-the-world tour didn't send anybody bankrupt, because conditions have changed since, but not excluding a proper planning.

As a result of the Spanish-American war the annexation of Hawaii by the United States became a fact. Since then the American stars and stripes banner reigned over Hawaii, declaring it US-territory. Relating to the international law of today, this annexation was questionable, but history has always been difficult to change.

An American V8 rented "tank " took us in comfort on the tour around Hawaii, the Big Island, starting with the northern area. The area remained more of a dead rocky landscape with very little spots of vegetation. In the north, we cut across to the other side of the island on a road, which went up on the side of a mountain range. The higher we came, the more green pastures began changing towards the other side into a lush tropical coastline.

The mountain slopes on the island are most of the time barren volcanic rock stripped off any vegetation. In the lower plains of the coast however, on the eastern part, fantastic tropical vegetation thrived due to the ocean currents. The hamlets along the coast were orderly and clean. Houses had often pagoda-like roofing to ventilate the interior better.

A botanical garden before Hilo, the largest city on the east coast, gave us a good overall view into the rich flora of the area. The flowers were particularly outstanding with specimens of native plants only found here.

*Kilauea Crater, biggest active volcano on earth.*

*Black Lava Beach at Kamoamoa, Big Island.*

A view from the coast into inland didn't let you miss the high mountain formation of Mauna Kea. Its peak with an eternal snow-cap sticks out of clouds, where also an important observatory can be seen. We turned inland to Hawaii's Volcano-National-Park after leaving the town of Hilo, which is located within a beautiful tropical flora. As we came closer to Kilauea crater, the air started to smell strongly sulphuric. Kilauea is the largest and most active volcano on earth. A path high above the crater gives a view of its dimensions. The outer ring between the hot and the cooled-down lava was from above clearly visible. A lava-tube could also be visited at the southern end of the crater. Vegetation struggled around the crater, but the very first plants taking foothold again on cold lava, were ferns springing up in a light fresh green, making a deep contrast to the black lava.

The volcano decided to stay calm during our visit, so we could continue our tour around the island. Hawaiian philosophy of their volcanoes can help in many life-situations: "In nature is our God, who takes care of us".

Forests in the Volcano Park were stripped off their leaf-crowns through the effects of the air. Black lava-beaches could also be found on the west coast, a very unusual appearance. Coconut trees on the upper edge of the beach looked very bright, green and healthy. Walking on the beach didn't leave any marks like coal does. A turtle demonstrated to us that life was also on the beach.

As we came closer again to our resort, the population density started to increase, macadamia plantations flourished on the coastal slopes of the volcanoes, all having their origin in South-East Queensland. Coffee, a variety special to the area, was also widely cultivated here. We met a coffee farmer, who took us with his truck up into the mountains to his coffee farm. The truck rattled up the steep stony track surprisingly well, despite its slow climb, without coming to a stop. The coffee was here so far different from other coffee bushes that the berries grew directly around the stem and not in branched off twigs. The coffee-rows, on hill-terraces supported by stone walls, were visibly thriving well in this volcanic soil, but not without a lot of hard work put in first. We were even shown, how the coffee was processed.

Back on the coast, the gentleman invited us to his coffee shop, where we could easily give him top-marks for his product. He also told that coffee was again taking over macadamia-plantations, because the money was better.

Our time for Hawaii came also to an end. We had to return to Honolulu to catch our Canada Airlines flight to Vancouver.

Our flight was delayed for many hours so that the plane arrived first in the early morning hours. On journeys, hiccups happen as a firm part and not much can be done about. It shouldn't really matter, as long as safety is still in place. Some funny things can also take place: a number of passengers were asked to stay longer in Hawaii at the expense of the airline because of a bungle in seat allocations. We however didn't cast our vote to stay, fortunately other people agreed to the proposal, so we were on the flight to leave Hawaii for Vancouver. The farewell from Honolulu was tailored more for dispatching masses of passengers, not like the personalised farewell in Kauai. Five and a half hours flight—time separated Canada from Hawaii.

## Canada

Snow-covered mountains on both sides of the aircraft were the first impressions over the Straight of Georgia, towards the Pacific Ocean lay Vancouver Island, inland the Rocky Mountains. Snow on the mountains in the summer month of June indicated that they must be fairly high. On landing in Vancouver the snow had disappeared. Sunny and warm weather welcomed us, not often experienced in this Canadian city.

Despite the SARS "epidemic", Vancouver Airport had at the time of our arrival several others from the Far East, which gave an impression of having landed in an Asian country. Leaving the airport for the city, this impression of an "Asian invasion" disappeared, people were also here a mixture of different nationalities. Were the arrivals at the airport visitors, migrants or both?

Opposite to Hilton skyscraper, our hotel building appeared small.

Vancouver was said to be the fastest-growing city in the world at the time, which was underpinned by its skyscrapers and new high- rise building sites. All streets of the city centre ran down to a bay of the Straight of Georgia.

The unusually warm weather in the city made our hotel room uncomfortable, because everything was here well insulated against the cold Canadian winter and not above average temperatures, which ask rather for an air-circulation.

The mountains and forests surrounding Vancouver made the place look nice, especially in sunny weather. Our intention was not to spend time in the city, instead, we wanted to see the Rocky Mountains. A car was rented, some shopping done and we were ready to move on.

The Number one Trans Canadian Highway started outside Vancouver, going first along the Ocean Straight, before turning inland. Dense fir-forests along the coast turned more scattered in mountain regions. A well-maintained road led through a deep valley, the powerful Thompson river rushing through it.

Erosion has stripped partly steep mountain slopes of their vegetation, on the other side of the valley appeared the Trans-Canada Railway with its double deck-outlooks, one of the great train journeys in the world.

During a stop in Kamloops, I had a routine look at our rented car and found out that the motor was running without nearly any oil. The local agency fortunately changed the car for us, because I could not afford to get stuck here in the Rocky Mountains. While signing the new paperwork, my wife had started a conversation outside in the parking area with a Finnish gentleman, who was on a contract with a Finnish company. Finnish people can also be found everywhere in the world, but not in big numbers. Once our car-exchange was sealed, nothing stopped us to continue to the north, Jaspers National Park.

The road followed a valley, in its centre a torrential river. The density of the fir-forests varied, snow came closer to the road. Resting places along the road had usually the bear-proof rubbish containers. The bears in the region had previously quickly found out how to get to the rubbish left behind from travellers. As it happened occasionally that bears confronted people in a competition for the rubbish bin, the Canadians came up with a solution: the lids of rubbish bins are locked under a protective cover, which the bear can't reach. This measure helped to eliminate confrontations with bears.

We were lucky to meet "Mister Bruin" crossing the road easily just in front of us and disappearing into the uphill forest. The road led in a long straight pass down to the wall of gigantic Mount Robson and its massive glacier, demanding to divert in front of it into a 90-degree change of direction.

*Rocky Mountains, British Columbia, Canada.*

Clouds were trapped in the mountain walls, the outside temperature had dropped close to the freezing point, making us switch on the car-heating.

In Jaspers it was decided to stay a day or so in a Bear-Hill Lodge, a single furnished log-cabin for visitors. The locals must have thought it was warm, when wearing only shorts and t-shirts at a temperature of just eight degrees Celsius. We had one small problem at night to get warm, because locals didn't heat any more, as "summer" had arrived.

The houses were partly built in an Alpine-style like in Switzer-land and Austria. Looking around the place on foot, the seasons of the year couldn't make up their minds into which direction to go: 10 minutes sunshine, followed by a shower and sometimes even snow. When the sun managed to stay around for a moment, we watched a couple of young men put a sofa through a house window on to another house roof underneath, sitting down on the sofa to catch the sun at least for a few moments, before they were disrupted by a sudden shower. Back went the sofa, until the sun appeared again. We could only think, these people must be tough.

A local Greek restaurant helped us with a great dinner to regain the energy to withstand the cold. The owner, who came from Greece, had found the right idea of how to show his guests without feeling the cold the beautiful mountainous green area with its snow-caps: the restaurant was completely behind glass, well heated and tropical plants inside made a pleasant stay, showing also up, of course, on the bill. At least we got something for our money. The excellent meal in the warm premises helped us to get through the second night better in our Bear-Hill Lodge.

Before leaving Jaspers, we took our chance to call back home in Australia. From the public phone we couldn't get a connection with an operator on the line, it was not easy to understand what he was suggesting in his fast response. At the lodge-reception they connected us with Australia: "The Australian lines might not have connected easily to the cold Canadian lines?"

The continued tour to the south through the Rocky Mountains explained easily why the area was given the name "Ice Field Park ". Rugged mountains covered with green fir-forests only in their lower parts, snow and icy lakes welcome a visitor with over-whelming expressions: high-pointed mountain peaks, snow fields hanging on the steep rocky walls, glaciers blocking the forest, icy water in lakes lies silent reflecting in black silhouettes the nearest mountains, where the ice-layer had not closed the surface and mountains left space in the sky for the sun to break occasionally through cloud-fields.

*Lake Louise with glacier, Rocky Mountains.*

Lake Louise, narrowly locked between steep mountain-walls, turned up on the road. To one side in the north, from where we came, rises a huge hotel building in front of the lake, giving accommodation with its special luxury to a large number of guests. The Swiss owners followed a tradition of Swiss enterprising spirit, dating back to 1899 when the first Swiss mountaineers "conquered" the Rocky Mountains out of sheer enthusiasm.

The Canadian Pacific Railway has devoted a memorial plaque stating:

> "In 1899, CPR brought the first Swiss Mountain guides
> to the Canadian Rockies,
> Inspiring worldwide appreciation
> Of Canada's rich mountain heritage
> And sparking a mountaineering tradition
> That continues to this day.
> Dedicated to the memory of the Swiss mountain guides,
> October 1999."

A brief visit into the hotel reception area gave a warm heated atmosphere with a luxury asking for well-paying guests. The lake with a green lawn between the hotel and its shore lay totally silent, reflecting in a turquoise colour.

The cold climate made wildlife here rather tame: on our arrival a heavily air-puffed bird sat on the roof of our car and had no intention of moving. Earth squirrels emerged on the lake's shore from rock-crevices, standing up high on the back of their short legs, as if wanting to say: "Look, how affectionate I am!"

The cold air imposed silence everywhere: a visitor's presence could hardly be noticed.

Across Lake Louise posed a massive glacier on a mountain-wall, closing off the southern side of the Ice-Field Park.

*Banff National Park Hotel, Rocky Mountains.*

Banff National Park with a torrential mountain river followed, raging down into a valley opposite to another hotel building, which looked like a huge castle in the middle of a forest on mountain-foothills. Following the valley down, mountains gradually gave room to larger meadows, leading us from the Canadian State of British-Columbia and its Rockies into the State of Alberta, Canada's prairie, called "Chinook Country". Huge farming land in the east left the mountains behind. Calgary appeared in the countryside on an elevation like a huge castle with its skyscraper city-centre. At the entrance of the city, the Olympic Park was a reminder of the 1988 Winter Olympic Games with the ski-jump.

On a building site, before the city, we became a bit confused in the traffic. A policeman realised it and went on to the road, stopping all the traffic, giving us a free passage; what a great gentle-manly gesture!

## USA

We had planned to continue from here to the south into the United States, wanting to find in the State of Washington an old friend, Chris, whom I met 37 years earlier in some controversial circumstances, but had still positive memories, which are the essentials also in a friendship.

The Canadian prairie changed towards the United States into dense mountainous forests, giving its State of Idaho similar impressions of Black-Forest scenes in Germany.

On the way south to Spokane, Priest River Lake offered for holidaymakers in a large area boating, fishing and swimming. The city of Spokane showed on a huge poster this recommendation: "Life is short, eat ice-cream." How right is that!

People we spoke to, recommended us strongly to stay in Idaho: "There are no lakes and forests any more in the State of Washington, you will only meet monotony."

*Connell, USA—Outback.*

If Chris was living in this monotony, we still wanted to see her even there. Her farm home address was in Connell, in the middle of the Washington State, which is a large wheat-farming area. The people in Idaho were right: desert-like countryside welcomed us in Connell. A sign on the side of the road marked the existence of the town, which hides in a depression of the hilly farming land. Green tree-crowns in the town became from the road first visible, surrounding fields looked brown without any crop. I had never been in Connell before, therefore we had to make enquiries about the address of Chris' home. Starting at the local bottle-shop, we received first information on the whereabouts of the family farm: "The son sold the farm after the mother passed away at a high age, then the family moved to the coast, but I don't know where." It looked like we had lost the contact.

The fairly warm weather let us quickly forget the cold of the Rocky Mountains. Our first unsuccessful enquiry didn't mean that we couldn't find the present address of Chris. While thinking to contact a clergyman about the address, we found out that this small village had six churches. We must have arrived in American heartland of sects, where people in isolation worship religion. Looking at the churches, Spanish sounds reached our ears. A Mexican workforce obviously also lived in town working the fields.

We visited the cemetery, because it holds usually information of a town's population, it lay on a hill outside the town. We couldn't locate however the family name, which indicated, nobody of the family was laid here to rest.

Instead a disturbing discovery was made that many gravestones carried names of young children. One of them showed a whole family with their seven young children. Was this the effect of the underground nuclear tests of Pasco in the west, not far from Connell? Nobody wanted to answer this question.

Everywhere we asked, Chris and her family was still known. Passing on foot over the railway-line to the western side of the town, a young man watering with a hose the garden in front of a house, also received our enquiry, responding: "Across the road lives Richard, who played with Chris when they were young. He should know where the family is now. I go and get him for you." Richard just had finished a job in front of his house and came to join us: "Ah, you are from Australia coming all the way here to us in order to find Chris and her family? We never had somebody from Australia in our place. How is life over there? Anyway, I am Richard, and what is your name? Chris and the family live on the coast, they moved after the mother passed away a few years ago. I can find out the address and phone number for you. My wife Kathy is unfortunately very sick at the moment, I can't invite you into my house, but when you come around again tomorrow morning, I will try to get hold of both the phone number and the address. Where do you stay tonight? The M & M Motel is a good place to stay. See you tomorrow at eight. Is it too early for you?"

The motel owners were also very forthcoming and friendly. Connell reflected the atmosphere of a big country-family, where everybody knew each other and was friendly, the best way to beat the isolation.

A second-hand shop in the neighbourhood attracted our attention before closing. It was loaded with household goods from family estates. Lots of antique items in a good condition were on display, which could have had a sad story behind, because mementoes of one generation were not passed on to the next one. The shop was so full, you could hardly move on the premises.

Probably the prices were for that reason very low. Of course, we couldn't take anything with us on our round-the-world tour. This overflowing shop was most likely in the wrong place; in a city these antiquities would certainly have attracted more attention and better prices. Was this a blank-point in a market opportunity?

Next morning we turned up at Richard 's place at eight o'clock sharp. He was already waiting outside with the good news for us: "I got in contact with Warren, the father of Chris, whom I occasionally speak to. He is living with Chris and her husband in La-Conner on the coast. Here is their telephone number and address, give them a call, before going there." How lucky we were!

An Australian picture-book and a Queensland coffee was our thank-you to Richard with wishes that the coffee should help his sick wife, Kathy. From now on we were ready to continue our tour, west to the coast.

A huge bridge over the Columbia River took us on to a very good highway in a rapidly-changing environment. The water of the river irrigated model-farms of apples, pears, cherries and peaches. On the horizon showed up Mount Rainier with its snow-peak-cap, pointing 4600 metres high into the sky, the highest mountain of mainland USA. Before travelling further to the coast, we turned south towards Mount Rainier.

Dense old-grown Douglas-Firs surrounded the foothills of the mountain. In higher regions they became scattered until they disappeared in eternal snow.

The coastal area is dominated by four major volcanoes: Mount Rainier, Helen, Olympus and Mount Baker, of which Mount Helen became known in 1980 for a huge volcanic eruption. Interesting studies took place that time in finding out how primitive living forms started again from volcanic destroyed life; primitive bacterial forms started again on lava through environmental and biochemical conditions.

*Hotel Paradise, Mount Rainier.*

*Beaver on hill site of Mount Rainier.*

Our gradual approach to the higher region of Mount Rainier delivered great views: lower mountain ridges, valleys, dark green Douglas Firs, spots of green meadows changing higher up into snowfields, until a wall of snow stopped the road in front of Paradise

Hotel. In some regard the large hotel building was special, it gave the whole place a warm homely look, having entirely been built out of solid Douglas-Fir-logs. A smoking-ban in a building made perfect sense in front of so much timber.

The evening atmosphere in the hotel lounge set everybody's mind to rest when a grand-piano performer played to individual wishes quite confidentially.

A brief conversation with the pianist brought out that he also spoke some French and German, which only added to his musical talent.

The night in this height of Mount Rainier with masses of snow around was dead silent, which gave the hotel guests a good resting time. Next morning a perfect clear sky continued, which was very rare in the area according to local information. Clouds from the Pacific Ocean stop most of the year in the four volcano ranges from moving further west. The result is here the green belt of the coast.

As soon as the sun rose in the sky, the night-chilliness disappeared and warmth reflected intensively from the glittering snow-surface. We spent some time relaxing in a safe distance from the hotel further up on Mount Rainier, leaning with the back against single dwarf-pines and soaking in the sun's warming rays. The echoes of gunshots broke occasionally the silence in the surrounding mountain gorge, reminding of the existence of mountain lions. As we kept quiet, a badger came out of its snow-den only a few metres from us. It watched us first and moved then confidentially across the snow field.

The summit of Mount Rainier seemed touchably close, but it would have been a great underestimation to try to conquer it through the deep snow. One needed to know more about this snow-covered volcano.

After two days in this Mountain Paradise we returned to the coast through the silent dark-green Douglas Fir forests on the mountain's foothills. The time of the day told us not to head any more for the large city of Seattle, but to the coastal town of Aberdeen, where we found overnight accommodation in a Korean-owned motel. Telephone calls from a public phone were of pure luck for a foreigner. The Korean gentleman helped us out with his mobile phone to make the first contact with the address given to us in Connell; in America you needed a new sim card for each State. All we could do was to leave a message, because nobody answered the phone.

Next morning we went again on the road to tackle the traffic through Seattle during the morning rush-hour. Once past the skyscraper centre of the city, we moved freely with the traffic further north, getting closer to La-Conner.

Before arriving there, we also passed Everett, the home of Boeing.

Fenced-off hangars with new aircrafts waiting outside on large concrete fields could be seen from the highway. Boeing was undoubtedly one of America's most successful enterprises, which I was very close to joining in 1966.

I should also mention that even before starting our round-the-world tour, we searched at home in Australia for the whereabouts of Chris. Only in her former hometown of Connell we succeeded, because she had re-married.

Why connecting to a friend? In life we should not leave behind our past and disconnect ourselves from it. If we can maintain a friendship during a lifetime, every effort is worthwhile, because by not doing it, we will not have in a later stage of our lives many friends left. Friends are people we can see at any time about anything, alone and also with everybody. A hidden agenda would not support a friendship. It was actually my wife's logic, which helped to find the address of a friend after 37 years. Women can have surprisingly their own logic!

As we approached La-Conner, my wife saw first a sign with the name we were after in front of a specially-built house, still in the surrounding crop-fields of the town. A man with a beard, probably in his sixties, answered our call in front of the specially-featured timber house: "Wait here, I call Warren." An old man soon came to us explaining: "I called the motel in Aberdeen, but you had already left.

Chris is on a mountain retreat, she will be back on the weekend in three days, please come into the house."

At the time Warren was 90-years-old, still very determined and strong-minded. A stick, Warren's third leg, helped him to move around as he wanted. A wide stairway led up into a large living-room, of which one side was a complete glass wall, allowing views into the surrounding fields.

My wife made a coffee for us three from the sample we brought from Queensland. For visits during our tour we had with us various small presents. Besides this, we also carried pocket albums with photos from our family and our lives to support a conversation. Lunchtime of the day had passed and I suggested to Warren: "Why don't we have lunch together, do you know a place around here?"—"You drive and I'll show you."

*At lunch with Warren in La Conner.*

Said and done! We spent some time of the afternoon in Warren's favourite restaurant, had lunch together and told each other's life stories. Warren must have been confused by the occasion, when he recalled good memories of my visit in Connell many years ago. This actually never happened, but we left Chris' kind father in this belief.

The order of the day requested that Warren have his rest in the afternoon. We left him at his home, while we moved to return on the weekend, when Chris was also present. After driving around for a while, we visited the town and found out that the place was a home of artists, exhibiting their work in a few shops. No exhibits could be found relating to any work of Chris'.

The days until the weekend became a bit of a waiting-time. As we had continued plans after that weekend, a rest-time was decided only with minor excursions on foot around Mount Vernon, close to La-Conner.

An American town was different from an Australian one, especially in Queensland. A modern look was here mixed with a lot of ad-signs, which disrupted an impression in a way that the signs seemed to dominate; business was present everywhere. Outside town-centres, however, homes could be found with a more personal style, like Chris' barn where we returned on Saturday morning after confirming our visit on the phone. Contrary to our visit a few days earlier it became all of a sudden cold, which indicated that the temperature could change here very quickly even in summer, possibly because of the surrounding high snow-fields of the region's volcanoes.

*La Conner, Arja-Chris-Martin.*

This time Chris was present and it became an interesting moment, standing face to face. She hadn't changed much in so many years, I could have recognised her anywhere. Other people said the same about me and my wife, Arja, whom I introduced to Chris. We shook hands, as if we had seen each other not long ago. This was the external impression, I am sure, internally much more was moved, when memories started to set in.

Coffee came on the large table and on a plate were prepared apple-pieces. Chris received a kangaroo-souvenir and a picture-booklet from Queensland, in which I left a personal note after a request from Warren. Our time for this meeting was limited to two hours, because we had to drive still the same day to Vancouver in order to catch our flight to Alaska. Our photo-albums and stories told about our lives. Chris showed us around in her studio in the top of the house, where she had a well-organized artwork setup.

Before saying goodbye to keep these memories, photos with different combinations were taken from all of us. Warren suggested that

Chris should accompany us to Vancouver so that we could have more time together. As Chris didn't respond, the issue was left unanswered. She gave a heartfelt hug to both of us on our farewell. For some unknown reason, her husband was not present. The moments with him on our first arrival didn't leave much of an impression, which was not for us to interpret. As Chris wrote later, she mutually could connect to us like good friends. Warren bestowed upon us to keep in touch and write to each other again. A long period of a silent friendship was reborn through our visit, including now also my wife, Arja, which made it only more precious. Why shouldn't we reconnect to a past and incorporate everything on its way?

The Canadian border was only two to three hours drive away. At the time it was recommended to have spare-time for the border-crossing because of strict controls between Canada and USA. The "Damocles-sword "hung already over international terrorism.

Before reaching the airport of Vancouver after a straight border-passage, we stopped for the night at a Highway Motel, so the last leg to the airport could be continued in the morning without any delay. People with a different outlook were accommodated in the motel: the room next to us was occupied by a group partying well into the night. To join them was not an option for us because we needed a good sleep before the next leg of our round-the-world tour, Alaska. I was determined in my response to the motel-management and told them: "I am not prepared to pay for such a disrupted night, but rather sleep in our car." My insistence paid off, the noise went somewhere else.

In USA and Canada there is a slight difference when looking for a public toilet: in Canada they are called "Washrooms" and in the USA "Restrooms". Do they focus in one place more on "washing", in the other one on "resting"? The new day in Vancouver started overcast and miserably cold. What a difference between now and on our first arrival 13 days earlier!

## Alaska

It was my birthday—Sunday, June 22—when we flew to Anchor-age, Alaska. It was, without doubt, a special birthday present. The plane of Canada-Airline followed the Pacific coast to the north with views over the entire Rocky Mountains. We had never seen such a huge area of snowy, icy mountains, glaciers and deep valleys. To pass over all this was a "piece of cake" for the aircraft. It still remains a "miracle" how we can rest in comfort and see all that. The tour like this on the ground would ask considerably more in personal efforts, involving more risks as well.

It should never be forgotten by using progress, what efforts went into it and we should try at least to comprehend a little of the ingenuity behind the progress and never take things for granted with an superficial understanding.

There is always more behind something than we know!

*Welcome to Anchorage.*

Anchorage had a surprisingly big airport with heavy air-traffic. The North-Pole Route from Asia to Europe goes through here. Mostly large Boeing 747s landed and took off constantly towards an icy mountain-wall, not failing to turn in front of them to the side on a flight-path out of Anchorage.

A rented car made us also here independent. Streets in this fairly big city had instead of names, numbers and alphabetic letters, making it difficult to find your way. Here on the border of one of the last wilderness-frontiers one could find shopping facilities of equal standards to any other modern city.

The accommodation-place near the city-centre caused us however some headache: our bookings from Australia were ignored, we were asked to pay again. On which account this hiccup went, we could find out only back in Australia. The management didn't move from its position, making sure to get the most out of the short summer period. This was the Alaskan-way of doing business, as we experienced also later on.

Despite the cold weather on our arrival, flowering lilac had managed in some places of the city to show its splendour, indicating that summer was on its way. At 11pm it was still daylight, as this is the case in the very northern part of the globe, in the middle of the summer. At 3am, in the first morning hours, daylight had started again after only a semi-darkness. Life didn't seem to come to a rest, constant noise in the city made us to start our day short after 3am. Good roads directed traffic fairly fast out of the city. A three-lane highway on each side with virtually no traffic led into the wilderness of the north.

Birch-trees made up the forest near the coast, their white trunks, spotted black and light fresh green leaves gave the region an own image against sharp rising barren rocky mountains, which appeared even in the daylight dark with white snow-fields higher up. Ferns and grass grew in some places to a man's height.

It is amazing the strength behind this vigorous growth: the longer nature hibernates, the stronger new life regenerates.

Rivers with lots of icy cold water from the Rocky Mountains continue also here. Salmons could be seen from the road jumping in the clear water. Wasilla became a welcome first stop with a well equipped and clean rest place on the side of the road. Its shiny marvellous timber floor caught also our attention.

Conifers took over soon after from birch-trees, growing smaller and increasingly thinner scattered further north to dwarf-pines as we entered the tundra-region. Very little green on the ground and low bush struggle here for their existence. Arriving at Denali Visitor's Centre after hardly any road-traffic, one could only wonder where all these people came from. Busses in parking-areas delivered partly the answer. Tourists were concentrated mainly in a few places, commonly recommended by guide-information which doesn't necessarily provide individual experiences.

A number of buildings with accommodation units lay in a terrace of a mountain-slope, providing views into lower areas and the horizon out of balconies. Mountain peaks in the south-west announce Mount McKinley, 6500 metres, the highest one of North America. Most of this giant is covered with eternal snow and ice. It is also the highest mountain in the world, which can be seen in one view from the sea-level to that height.

*Mount Mc.Kinley, 6500 metres, Alaska.*

Despite being located further north, Denali was at the time much warmer than Anchorage. Long into the night the sun prevailed here on Latitude 63, which compares with Middle-Finland. Due to the influence of the Golf-Stream, dense fir-forests still grow at this latitude in Scandinavia, whereas in Alaska the tundra struggles with no trees and only little bush in low laying areas.

The long days of end-June gave extra holiday time; sleeping was not much in anybody's mind. The sun dipped only for two to three hours on the horizon and this was all the night. Meeting locals revealed that many of them came to Alaska for the simple life to escape civilisation. In the souvenir shop of the Bluff Hotel Resort served a former female university professor, who had given up teaching in Heidelberg/Germany and was seeking the life in Alaska. Hearing from us about our time in Heidelberg, she said: "I wouldn't go back into this racing-world, nobody competes here with anybody, everybody can be more individual. The only challenge to us is nature; when it is rough, we have to give in; when kind, we have a good time; nobody would stand up against nature here. In this respect, all people in Alaska have a common ground: live, help and stay together. Alaska is one of the last frontiers, not yet changed by civilization."

My wife was quick to point out that she came from the same latitude in Finland, but wouldn't change it with Queensland in Australia any more. Here in Alaska a lady was escaping into the icy world of Alaska and my wife Arja to sub-tropical South-East Queensland. Everybody was also here on a journey in his life.

It came to our attention in a grocery shop that milk carried a Russian name "Matushka", which must have been a remnant of Alaskan history with Russia.

Alaska belonged, in fact, until 1867 to Russia, when the Americans bought it for 7.2 million dollars from Russian furriers, who regarded Alaska worthless.

What a historical mistake and underestimation on Russia's account! Imagine, Russia having a common border with Canada today and the political fallout of it! The USA had already demonstrated in the past that their own interests were always the first priority.

An excursion during the day on foot brought us closer to the views of Mount McKinley. To experience only this view is already worth to come to Alaska, nowhere else in the world rises ice and snow to such a height straight from the sea-level; we can feel in front of it quite small, insignificant and lost.

My wife and I were light-minded alone on foot, considering the presence of Alaskan bears. The honey in our backpack might have worked distracting them in the case of an encounter. Alaskan brown bear and grizzly are the biggest of its kind in the world.

At Anchorage Airport are stuffed samples of each Alaskan bear on display, including the polar bear, which gives a good idea of their colossal size and power. We didn't see a bear and I assume, it didn't see us. A caribou however could be seen grazing undisturbed in the bush of a valley.

Back in Bluffs Hotel Resort, a number of people reported to have seen a bear from the bus, which appeared unlikely for us as we were alone on foot in their territory. Our stay in Denali had plenty of warm sunny hours, which didn't change even during the short night. On the way back to Anchorage we made a couple of stops to meet locals. Many houses not far from the main arterial road were built in solid timber-logs, showing from outside the round shape of a log, whereas inside and on top and bottom the log had received a flat cut surface to close the inside-wall smoothly. On the corner the ends of the logs overlapped from outside each other giving a solid and effective insulation.

A family sold in their beautiful block-house drinks and souvenirs expecting their customers to stay for a while and exchange news with them from other parts of the world for Alaskan news. All prices everywhere in Alaska were rather high and not negotiable, because the short time for tourism in summer was in many cases the only time to earn an income.

Most work had to be done also in summer, keeping the Alaskan people very busy, before winter forces everybody to slow down and hibernate.

Contrary to Alaskan countryside, people in Anchorage could be seen to soak-in the sun. The warm days were a present from heaven. There was no visible rush, Alaska was quietly worshipping summer.

## Canada

On the afternoon of June 25, an Air-Canada flight took us back to Vancouver along the same scenery over the Rocky Mountains. My wife had only to say: "I have seen enough mountains, ice and snow to last my lifetime." In Vancouver civilisation started to catch up with us again in a test of patience, while some transport workers had gone on strike. The few rushed-in workers in the luggage— dispatch area made sure everybody paid his attention to their importance, which didn't help to cut the waiting-time. Once in the aircraft, everybody became disappointed in his expectations that from now on everything should go smoothly. Canada was at the time not in a hurry to move its passengers. The ones who had time were also the winners here.

When the plane took off from Vancouver for Toronto across the whole country to the east, the flight path took us over the volcano Mount Baker, which was covered with snow not far underneath, so that the crater on its top became clearly visible. Snow filled also the crater.

Despite the proximity of the Boeing factory, it became obvious, Canada must have had given its preference to Airbus, because all the aircrafts were Airbuses. How much had the French element in Canada played its role here? It can't have been only economical considerations determining this picture.

Four hours flight-time were enough to cover the distance. On landing in Toronto the weather was considerably warmer than in Vancouver. The arrangements with a taxi-transport worked here as it was arranged to get us to Niagara in the south. Big highways with busy traffic led out of the city and it was good to have a local transport, which knew the traffic conditions. Air-crossings with other highways presented easy confusion for non-locals.

While our transport left the city behind on its way, Toronto Tower stuck out in the city's skyline, at that time the highest building construction in the world. The city was obviously planned to a chessboard. Further out of its centre mainly modern factory buildings lined the sides of the multi-lane highways.

Reaching the countryside of Niagara Peninsula, the road followed first along the large glittering surface of Lake Ontario to the east. Fertile soil supports here the wide cultivation of wine, apples, pears and vegies. In summer it can become very hot, but also extremely cold during winter.

According to our driver, the "Russian Mafia" had used Toronto lately for an organised car-theft racket for the purpose of sending the parts out of the country.

Unfortunately big cities around the world have not only their "sweet" side, but often challenges can be found close by.

Our bookings at Niagara, Comfort-Inn, Clifton-Hill, were orderly waiting for us and our stay started to look promising. Leaving the usual show-business aside, Niagara offered, with its well-established parks along the Niagara River, an attraction worth visiting. Niagara River feeds from Lake Erie in the south falling sharply 50 metres down into its lower riverbed mainly on two places into Lake Ontario in the north. The Canadian part of the falls has a horse-shoe shape limiting the deep riverbed to the road with a solid rock-wall. Where the river edge falls, its course is level with the road being separated only by this rock-wall approximately of one metre height. The water can be watched from close, rushing smoothly towards the edge, and how it falls down all along the horse-shoe with a big thunder, spraying foam into the air during its down-trip and landing in the bottom of the falls. Boats with spectators wearing yellow raincoats approached the falls from the lower river, while sunlight created a rainbow with all its colours in the rising foam.

The constant sound of this thunder kept everybody's attention to follow the rushing wall of water. Only a little further up the river-course, a metal-plaque could be found neatly fitted into the rock-wall with a poem of a Cuban writer, Jose Maria Heredia (1803—1839). "He sang to Niagara and, as Jose Maria said, awakened—An Ever-Burning Passion For Freedom—in the hearts of all Cubans."

(Not to be mixed up with the French poet of the same name living from 1842 to 1905).

## NIAGARA (Fragments)

THOU FLOWEST, ON IN QUIET, TILL THY WAVES
GROW BROKEN MIDST THE ROCKS, THY CURRENT THEN
SHOOTS ONWARD LIKE THE IRRESISTIBLE COURSE
OF DESTINY. AH, TERRIBLY THE RAGE, -
THE HOARSE AND RAPID WHIRLPOOLS THERE!
MY BRAIN GROWS WILD, MY SENSES WANDER, AS I GAZE
UPON THE HURRIYING WATERS, AND MY SIGHT,
VAINLY WOULD FOLLOW, AS TOWARDS THE VERGE
SWEEPS THE WIDE TORRENT, WAVES INNUMERABLE
MEET THERE AND MADDEN, — WAVES INNUMERABLE
URGE ON AND OVERTAKE THE WAVES BEFORE,
AND DISAPPEAR IN THUNDER AND IN FOAM.
THEY REACH, THEY LEAP THE BARRIER, THE ABYSS
SWALLOWS INSATIABLE THE SINKING WAVES.
A THOUSAND RAINBOWS ARCH THEM, AND WOODS
ARE DEAFENED WITH THE ROAR.
WHAT SEEKS MY RESTLESS EYE? WHY ARE NOT HERE,
ABOVE THE JAWS OF THIS ABYSS, THE PALMS, -
AH, THE DELICIOUS PALMS, …THAT ON THE PLAINS
OF MY OWN NATIVE CUBA SPRING AND SPREAD
THEIR THICKLY FOLIAGED SUMMITS TO THE SUN.
AND, IN THE BREATHINGS OF THE OCEAN AIR
WAVE SOFT BENEATH THE HEAVEN'S UNSPOTTED BLUE?
HEAR, DREAD NIAGARA, MY LATEST VOICE!
YET A FEW YEARS, AND THE COLD EARTH SHALL CLOSE
OVER THE BONES OF HIM WHO SINGS THEE NOW
THUS FEELINGS. WOULD THAT THIS, MY HUMBLE VERSE,
MIGHT BE, LIKE THEE, IMMORTAL! — MEANWHILE,
CHEERFULLY PASSING TO THE APPOINTED REST
MIGHT RAISE MY RADIANT FOREHEAD IN THE CLOUDS
TO LISTEN TO THE ECHOES OF MY FAME.

*(TO THE NIAGARA, FROM THE CUBAN PEOPLE. OCTOBER 1989)*

By watching the crowd along the river course, nobody seemed to take notice of the Niagara poem. The powerful expressions in the poem describe this spectacle not only for a moment, but also for as long as the Niagara River falls down marking the border between Canada and the USA.

A bridge further down the river crossed into the USA. The Niagara Falls on the American side are less dramatic, because less water reaches that side, which falls down on a straight rock-wall, continuing in a not far distance to the Canadian horse-shoe falls. America had built a tower on one end of its falls, allowing visitors a bird's-eye view over its part of the falls.

Visitors from the Canadian side were subjected however to such a rigorous control that we decided to stay on the Canadian side, visas were required for foreigners. Besides safety, there was most certainly an issue of a stiff competition behind the American control.

The weather was sunny and hot here, close to 40 degrees Celsius. Dinner in a restaurant opposite the falls finalized our stay in style. It was the rule in America and Canada that waiters/ waitresses requested with the bill their share, officially 10%, never failing to let you know, more was expected. Locals blamed also the SARS-fear for the lower visitor numbers. But we rather welcomed that, because there were enough people around anyway.

The next leg of our round-the-world tour became Europe. A rather expensive return-transport to Toronto Airport put us in queues of waiting passengers. The departure-scenario of Vancouver repeated itself, too many people wanted to be served with a preference.

It wouldn't be good to get excited in such a "waiting game", it could take away too much of a benefit expected from a holiday. People can be watched returning straight to their "daily-fighting routine" in these situations, which is usually expressed red-headed and colourful, achieving at the end nothing.

## Germany

Our delayed flight over the Atlantic followed all the way above a dense cloud-level appearing with its innumerable small grey-white cloud spots like a flock of sheep underneath us. On arrival in Frankfurt, Germany, the hot weather continued, but coming from Australia, we were heat-primed and had no problem. We could find out again: what others consider hot, can often be just fine for Aussies.

A rental-car brought us also this time out of the airport on to the Autobahn to the north, Kassel, where a good old friend lived with his family. Beech-tree forests on surrounding hills, green meadows and ripe cornfields in the plains gave the city of Kassel a natural image, not all cities could claim.

The friend's house with a garden around in a small quiet street was in Germany a special achievement, not many could claim. Two more friends came from other parts of the country to join us on that weekend in a memorable reunion: one ran his own Engineering Consultantancy business, one a professional musician, another a catholic priest, myself a technical manager and if the reunion were complete, a school-teacher would have also been with us.

*Kassel, Germany, Dirk's guests: Bernhard, Otti, Dirk, Frank, Martin.*

*Heidelberg, Germany, Harro's guests.*

Banjo and guitar were pulled out to recall the old days. Even with the best of intentions that level could not be reached any more, because we all had changed during our lives, connecting instead to old memories and more recent stories. Reunions are not only to remember the past, but also to give a new outlook into a continuous friendship. They will not work in every case, it depends on how much every individual has changed.

The weekend offered plenty of good food so that an excursion on foot into the nearby forest hills became a good exercise. A waterfall spectacle at the Hercules monument didn't want to take place, leaving most of the visitors disappointed, showing that not even in "perfect "Germany everything went as planned.

Germany and its beer were also in this part of the country a stable element, as we found out in a nearby village at another place. A summer cottage in the garden underneath the house delivered views into the green countryside, while beer drawn from the wood was flowing more than enough.

The only exception to a party presented a view right into the village's cemetery, which our host knew to play down: "This is only a useful reminder, anyway as a tax consultant I bought the land at a very attractive price. If you don't want to see the crosses, don't look at them." This could be called, "a view down to earth ", couldn't it?

Time reminded us again to continue with our round-the-world tour.

If things are at their best, this is also the time to move on, isn't it? Friends from Brazil were at the time also in Germany on a visit in Regensburg. Their son lived with his Brazilian wife and daughter on the outskirts of the city. Our meeting was rather short.

A "reconnection" didn't want to work in this case. The problems in Brazil had moved the former friends so far apart from our lives that our meeting remained only a formality, telling us however, it was a good decision for us to leave Brazil 26 years earlier.

Well-off people of previous years in Brazil experienced changes, since a social government gained power and started to change for many the situation. At least the grandchild could visit a ballet school in Germany under less restrictions.

Conditions in the world seem to change like a round-the-world tour does, with the exemption of an uncertain timetable.

The area of Stuttgart, from where we started our journey to Australia 22 years earlier, became our next destination. Our old German shepherd, Mars, was not with the architect family he had lived the rest of his life. A heartfelt reception gave us the opportunity to visit other acquaintances in the area. The elderly architect-couple was still active in their daily lives. Gerold showed me his latest architectural projects and his art-creations as an serious artist. Dinner in their special home was an event marked with broad discussions in their highly personalised cultural environment of architectural and art-expressions.

*Wernau, Germany, Martin, Arja, Rose, Gerold.*

Rose and Gerold belong to those non-changing people, remaining always ready to help and be kind. On the recommendation of Rose, a decision was made to visit during our stay the heated mineral indoor-pool of nearby Leutze, which helped to regenerate some of the lost energy and get ready for the next visit at the Daimler-Benz Museum on the factory premises of Mercedes. This exhibition was not only a Mercedes' one, it also showed the history of the car in which it played a vital role. Daimler and Benz started the car-evolution and ever since Mercedes has aimed to be a front-runner through its design and quality. It was also no surprise to meet visitors from all over the world in this modern museum with a majority of Japanese tourists.

Not far from our place of stay lived also a family friend, retired lady doctor Hildegard, who was waiting for our visit. Her universal intellect in music, arts, botany, history, languages besides her medical profession connected us again intimately with local cultural places of interest packed with history, which is quite common in many German places. Tradition as a history-creator has so far continued to claim its firm position in the German society.

Hildegard promised to visit us again in Australia, her age had not stopped her from an active life.

Another visit was paid to a neighbouring town, one of my 2/3 brothers, Alfred and his family. They had moved some years back from our former native country Transylvania to Germany instead of joining us in Australia. They had received Australian permanent residence with our help, but decided to stay finally in Germany on the request of the rest of the family, a decision they regretted later. A permanent residence in Australia not followed up, is void forever. Other members of my biological family had also arrived to this meeting. As it turned out, they had unfortunately some tragic news: their eldest daughter had died in a fatal car crash, reminding all of us how fragile our existence has become particularly in a modern progressing world.

As humans we have not moved far from our past, but the efforts for progress have distanced us from our creativity, leaving benefits and dangers increasingly closer in our lives: "The powers I unleashed, I can't control any more." (Goethe).

Many people asked us for possibilities in Australia, which we bluntly answered: "Life has become a battle everywhere, it all depends, what an individual can achieve with given conditions. Problems never go away, they only change their nature somewhere else." This was our advice to keen migrant-hopefuls to Australia. I never wanted to become accountable for other people's efforts in a migration process.

I could not miss a visit to my hometown Ettlingen. The family of our previous exchange student gave us accommodation. The ancient town-centre with its narrow alleys hadn't changed at all since it was rebuilt to its early image. Frame-houses looking back a thousand years were no rarity. The last resting place of my step-parents received our visit, giving it the respect we all owe each other.

The weather had become unusually hot again in the area and as we learnt during our stay in mainly Germany, Finland and France, this had been the hottest summer on record. Temperatures were hopping around the 40-degree mark, fortunately with dry air and not humidity, which makes life uncomfortable.

A brass-band entertainment in a marquee in a neighbouring village brought us and the host family into close touch with local traditions: music in full swing, extremely loud in the closed tent, packed with visitors of all age-groups, consuming German beer and fried sausages, sitting on long benches in front of long tables. After listening a couple of hours to this collective-traditional entertainment, my head became "so blown up" that I couldn't take much more. It was time to leave. Another family, that had joined us at a table, had shown us before their new house during daylight hours. Both worked full-time, the husband in China for a German company and the wife locally in order to pay-off their new home; the three children played their role in between. The couple claimed: "There was no other way to get your house in Germany." Well, we had found a way around it in Australia.

Before heading to Frankfurt Airport to catch our flight to Finland, we went to Heidelberg and visited my teacher-friend Harro and his wife. They lived in the "old city" in their own house of three storeys, built in 1770. The room-size and stairs made the width of the house allowing in the back still another room. Very thick stone walls ensured the house would be around for a long time. The steps in the narrow cobbled alley in front of the house sounded like drums specially in the night-time. Neighbours across the road were nearly in reach of a handshake. To keep your privacy good curtains became a necessity. The back of the house offered on the second floor a balcony with flower arrangements, a good refuge from an indoor living. Sunny weather made an idyllic atmosphere in my friend's place, which the art-painter Spitzweg (1808-1885 Munich) illustrated best in his petty-bourgeois-art.

To connect back to our years in Heidelberg and other periods of our lives became special with a guitar and singing: school, boy-scouts and canoeing to Southern France. It was not possible to continue into the night with respect to the neighbours around. Rules set in here and we had also to get out early next morning to catch our flight from Frankfurt to Helsinki.

## Finland—Norway—Sweden

Bad weather was left behind in Germany, not only sunshine but also friends welcomed us on our arrival at Helsinki Vantaa Airport, being so far the first welcome on an arrival during our round-the-world tour. The Finnish couple were friends from our time in Heidelberg and we have been in touch since. Pirkko and Kalevi invited us into their home outside Helsinki in Finnish country-side. Everything was in summer here fresh and green: meadows, birch and fir forests, bright yellow flowering canola fields, homely Scandinavian timber houses, mainly outside of a city. Homemade fresh strawberry cake waited for us on the table. The cultivated strawberries in Finland have very limited time to ripen during the short summer, tasting very aromatic like the berries found in Finnish forests: blueberries and cranberries.

Finnish people are generally willing to help out with another language, if somebody like me lacks praxis of the Finnish language, making it at the same time difficult to learn more Finnish. Our friends spoke both fluent German and English so that our communication could take place in more than one language. Kalevi, who is a professor of astronomy at Helsinki University, knows a lot of answers to the many questions the universe poses for us.

A significant difference between Germany and Finland is that most of the time Finnish people do not use their titles (Dr. Prof.) in dealing with other people; they are more modest, reflecting also on human relations: it takes time to gain a friendship in Finland, but once established, it is normally for a lifetime.

During our stay the three grown-up children of our hosts also joined us. Two of them lived their lives outside the parent's home following successful higher professional appointments, whereas one son lived with the parents. Two dogs, a Dalmatian and a fox-terrier, were permanent family members asking for attention which was very much in line with the different characters of the two dogs; a ball-game with the fox-terrier could have lasted all day, if up to the dog. Pets can bring that break into daily life, easing some of life's burdens.

The sunny weather in Southern Finland invited us for a swim in one of the many lakes the country can offer. As summer was still "young", the water in the lake felt still fresh for us, inviting however a tough Finnish swimmer, who takes even on the elements during an icy winter. Finnish-Sauna attracted at the time our interest, relaxing us more. From the unit of our hosts we had straight views across fields to a forest, where an old church became visible. The days were long like in Alaska, sending the sun to the horizon shortly before midnight. Intensive daylight in summer gives nature the strength to grow everything fast. You can experience during springtime in Finland dead looking trees turning green overnight. In autumn the reverse happens, especially in the north, Finnish Lapland, when the leaf-canopy changes from green to its autumn-colours overnight, called "ruska". It shows us that in the nature even "death" has its beauty.

Before leaving our friends Pirkko and Kalevi for Turku, a rowing boat took us out on a choppy lake-surface to check out the fish. We also visited two museums in the area, one of the Finnish composer Sibelius and the other a women's war veteran museum (Lotta Svard Museum), which remembers the brave contribution of many Finnish women, including my mother—in-law.

Back in our friends' place, fresh fish and new potatoes came on the table, a speciality not to be missed.

As we were leaving Helsinki with the bus, it was agreed to visit them again before our departure from Finland. The next step in our Finland tour came to visit my sister-in-law and her family in Kaarina, close to Turku. The bus drove along the southern coast of Finland passing only through smaller places in a lovely hilly countryside with forests, lakes, green pastures and ripe crop fields. On our arrival in Kaarina, the only sister of my wife and her husband welcomed us at the bus stop. They have a big three-storey house, sitting typically on a granite out-crop in a light mixed forest. There was plenty room for us. In this place I had to polish with no excuse my Finnish knowledge to communicate personally with my in-laws, who had not much knowledge of other languages.

Connecting to friends of the past, my wife and myself visited first a nice 95-year-old lady, who was a nextdoor neighbour and a good family friend, who helped my mother-in-law raise her two daughters. It is always useful for a younger generation to connect to the older one, no lesson can be learnt better than from them. During our visit an observation was made, how well organised also the home of this old lady appeared. When asking her for the secret of her healthy and long life, she answered: "A simple, active life and never worry too much about something we can't change anyway."

We rented a French Renault Laguna at a good price through the connection of my sister-in-law's husband and used it for our next three weeks in Finland. The rented car gave us the independence to move around easier, first around the city of Turku. As I had introduced my wife to my American friend, Chris, in return Arja presented one of her former friends, Kullervo, who welcomed us in a very friendly manner with his wife and one daughter. They invited us sailing with their 24-foot boat. For the time being, the boat-trip had to be postponed and we had instead good talks in front of Finnish coffee and home-made pastries. Travelling people have always something to tell, and so had we.

Most Finns live in their own houses, but there has been a tendency to move into flats or units, especially in the city. House affordability was quite good, young people could still look forward to owning a house in a reasonable number of years, which certainly adds to the high living-standard the country's small population of just over 5 million enjoys.

The tour got on its way with sunshine on the 12th of July. Middle Finland continued with mixed forests on both sides of the road in between pockets of rye and flowering canola fields, lakes with green meadows or forests coming to the shores. Tampere, an industrial centre in Finland, lies between two lakes, Nasi and Pyhajarvi. Where the city stops, endless forests take over. A friend of Arja lived also here, Marja. She worked in Stockholm with Arja in 1965, when we first met. Marja said again: "Your romance started like a dream." We all have 38 years later become a bit older, raised a family and hopefully also wiser. Marja's son made good efforts to become a sports teacher.

One of our first moves in Tampere directed us to the last resting place of Arja's mother. The cemetery was well maintained, a beautiful natural garden, standing out in comparison with many such places found in other parts of the world.

Standing in front of a grave of a loved-one is always a moving moment. It is difficult to comprehend, why we have to leave, when the time is up.

My wife visited the high school in Nokia for a number of years, a town close to Tampere. Nokia is also the birthplace of today's biggest mobile-phone manufacturer having given its products the town's name. Nokia originally made gumboots and car tyres diverting successfully to electronics in the 1960s.

A former school friend lived here with her family in the middle of the forest, next to her own lake. She came first to see us, before we paid her a visit. Not far lived also an old class-teacher, Juhani Valento. He had an obvious sense of humour telling his former student Arja: "You should write a book on how to get away from Nokia." As a French and Latin teacher, he addressed me also in French, farewelling us with "bon voyage".

Still in Tampere, there is the hillside of Pyynikki, overlooking the city between the two lakes, where a metal sculpture reminds of the Finnish poet Lauri Viita. An observation tower on the crest looks over the treetops, allowing a view to the forest and lake country. Pispala not far, harboured the house of Arja's grandparents, of whom I met the grandmother at our wedding in 1968. The house looked neglected and quite different with a pet-shop in its ground floor, 2003. Earlier the grandparents had a grocery-shop and the premises were well looked after. Our plans were not to stay now longer in the area, but to return after touring the north of Finland.

The first day further north gave us impressions of what lay ahead on a Finnish Lapland tour. Mainly forests and lakes continued, not much traffic on the way, only closer to a major city like Jyvaskyla a wider road system was introduced. Further north we came, the warmer it turned. In Lahti and Kuopio started the first hillsides of the north, allowing in winter serious ski-competitions. Our first day ended in Sonkajarvi in a typical block-house on a lake-site surrounded by a forest. Right through the mostly sunny night the temperature remained near thirty degrees Celsius, making a rest in the block-house fairly warm, because nobody was prepared here, what was called heat. Nevertheless, the feared mosquitoes of Northern Finland had not arrived that summer. Spring-time was too dry for the "beasts" to breed and summer became too hot to fly. Exceptional lucky circumstances for a Lapland visit!

Normal mosquito-years can make life unbearable, soldiers during the wars experienced a major battle with this plague. Despite the nice and neat accommodation, the early sun didn't allow much sleep. There was a table, chairs, beds with fresh linen, a cooking facility, fridge and curtains on the windows with shutters outside. A "thunder-post" (toilet) was usually in a small cabin, a distance from the accommodation.

The next day started with a swim in the lake's surprisingly warm water, due to the sun's good heating-job during the summer. Along the road to the north came the small places Iisalmi and Kajaani on a big lake-site and Kuusamo. They all were planned widely open with mixed buildings, both in a modern concrete-element system, or in the traditional timber construction. In the shopping-centre of Kuusamo we also bought a mobile phone to allow us to stay in better in contact with the civilized world, before advancing further north into Lapland's wilderness. Being close to the Russian border, we turned west towards Kemijarvi passing the sign of the "Arctic Circle" at 66.5 latitude, the start of Finnish Lapland.

*Arctic Circle, Lapland, Finland.*

*Reindeers in Finnish Lapland (North).*

The sign indicated also that from now on special attention had to be paid to reindeers on the road. They have free passage across the borders of Russia, Finland, Sweden and Norway with their owners, the Samens (Laplanders) have still today their own Sami language, different from the Finnish one. On festive occasions they wear very colourful dresses, often also during their daily harsh life in a contrast to the unforgiving nature up to nine months winter.

Only the politicians have marked in this area artificial borders, which are in Scandinavia open, but not to Russia.

Finland is considered within Scandinavia also a country of blond men and women, but there can be also found Finns with dark hair and complexions indicating often an ethnic connection to the Samens. My wife has actually a little bit of these characteristics making her the ideal representative for the proverbial "Finnish sisu", which can be interpreted as "steadiness and stamina."

Living with people of different backgrounds asks for tolerance, which opens a way to learn from each other for a better under-standing. My wife and I, are in many respects very different, but speaking on behalf of myself, I have learnt from her tremendously in our lives together. Forty years later since we met, I have become a different person in a continuous adaptation process with its ups and downs, but remaining on track.

Here in Finland on home-soil I found that my wife had shown through her own language stronger character-features in her temperament and joy expressions than outside Finland, which could be a personal sacrifice.

Despite the decisions we make in our lives, we cannot and shouldn't deny our origin. Sacrifices can build on strength, if they are properly received on another side.

Our tour continued to Sodankyla, where another day ended in blockhouse accommodation. From now on the sun did not disappear on the horizon any more at night, we had virtually 24 hours daylight with an even temperature.

In Finnish Lapland it went now well over 30 degrees Celsius and the further north, the warmer it became, something we did not expect.

Views towards the west around Ivalo unveiled snow-capped mountains in far Norway. Northern pines made up the forest here, growing however to a lower height. Occasionally the forest gave way to areas of tundra with only low bush and grass struggling for their existence.

Finland has also its "wonder of the world "in Inari, where the lake with the same name stretches over a large area with over 3000 forested islands in its waters and according to old legends is "as deep as it is long".

Despite sitting on latitude 69, which would be in the south right on Antarctica the area enjoys a similar climate like the south of Finland thanks to the Golf Stream's far-reaching influence. The silence in nature is a new experience and even the visitors to the souvenir-shops in rustic blockhouses cannot change this dominant feature. Nothing could stop even me from buying a good Finn-knife, which has the name of its maker engraved on the blade.

Lake Inari is during a good summer worth to consider for a peaceful holiday. The long sunny days give extra holiday-time for camping, wandering, boating, fishing and relaxing.

Utsjoki is Finland's most northern settlement at 70 degrees latitude. The Teno river forms the border with Norway, where Scandinavia continues up to the North-Cape at 71 degrees latitude. Mountains still covered with light forests rise also here in Finland. A modern bridge construction leads over the Teno river to Norway.

In the small settlement of Utsjoki lived a friend of my sister-in-law with her husband. The warm weather made people suffer in their well-insulated timber-houses. Many had set up in their backyard a "kota" (Lapland tent) with an open centre-top, which turned out to be a much better place than the firmly-closed house.

The night we spent in a blockhouse of a camping place in town, as we had made bookings prior to the visit to the Finnish couple Liisa and Arto. Drinking hot coffee in their hot house was in our view not a good idea. The Finns started to sweat until we suggested going outside where conditions were more favourable; Aussies know how to deal with the heat, became the message of the day. On the other side, the Finns could have told us, how to deal with the long arctic winter. Arto, the husband belonged to a local writer's association putting into words a dialogue between arctic nature and its human partners. Nature is here on a survival-edge, inspiring with its simple image to go back to the fundamentals of our existence, tracing and presenting it with poetry. Arto was working more with idealistic poetic expressions, whereas myself on the realistic philosophical one, we promised to exchange our work in the years to come.

The sunny night in the blockhouse remained at 36 degrees Celsius, which was unprecedented for the area.

## Norway

With close to no sleep, our tour went along the Teno river first to the south-west and then to Norway across a non-existing border.

The mountains rose higher, mixed forests still covered the slopes in lower areas. From the road salmons of good sizes could be seen to move in the clear cold waters of Teno river, an angler's paradise waited here, but not to be spoiled. Strict regulations were in place to preserve the environment and its habitat. As soon as we entered Norway, the weather changed dramatically.

Clouds covered the sky over Porsanger Fjord and the temperature dropped suddenly only to eight degrees. This change was incredible on such a small distance. No trees existed any more along the shores of the Fjord, rocky hillsides followed the Fjord into the Arctic Ocean. Houses of local fishermen sat on a naked rock, seagulls followed with their cry a shoal of fish in the dark silent water. Further out in the moving water appeared the back of a slow-moving whale heading towards the open ocean in a far distance. Patches of green moss were the only sign of vegetation on the shore-sides, no shells could be found. We had the impression of being on another planet with very little life.

*Tunnel under the Arctic Ocean.*

The road from the mainland to the island of Mageroyo passed through five tunnels, of which tunnel four went over a distance of 6890 metres to 212 metres deep under the Arctic Ocean, a very special driving experience: the entrance and exit were cut into steep mountain slopes dropping first steeply down to 212 metres under the sea to go up on the exit side again. Water dripping everywhere on the rock-walls reminded us that above was the Arctic Ocean. A feeling of a relief that we made it through the tunnel, didn't fail to take over. At one of the tunnel entrances, a herd of reindeers blocked the road, as if wanting to give their message to passersby. A local car driver became our saviour, taking on the reindeers and skillfully sending them off. I had little idea how to tackle this job—not having any reindeer experience.

The road between the tunnels is partly cut into the rock-walls along the fjord.

Once arriving on Magaroyo Island, a typical fisher-village nested in the protection of a hillside with its colourful timber houses standing individually on rock outcrops. The colours of these houses made here up for the missing colours in nature, signalling also to the homecoming fishing boats out of a distance.

The boats anchored in a small bay of the fjord. A steep climb across the island leads to North Cape, the most northern point of Europe at 71 degrees latitude. This became the furthest northern point of the globe we had been so far.

Dense fog added to the cold temperature making a drive on the narrow road hazardous, with occasional abysses to the left and the right. It seemed to become a tour to "hell" with the fog obscuring daylight. Whoever made it up to here had no choice but to pay the high visiting-fees to the North Cape, if wanting to see it. The fog of the day didn't allow us to see anything, an underground observatory gave instead views into the Arctic Ocean with fish and seals coming mainly to see the tourists. Celebrities like the Emperor of Japan and many others had left here their notes expressing also their recognition of how Norway has made it possible to reach such a wild place by road.

Most visitors had arrived here by bus, making it very difficult for other vehicles on the narrow road to get past.

Driving back from North Cape, we took on a direction after the tunnels to Alta on the Alta Fjord. The weather improved slightly, forest pockets turned up in a tundra region.

A church with a high chimney beside the bell-tower gave an unfamiliar appearance, indicating that heating was an important issue to gather people in a church. The Norwegian mountains reached the area, their peaks were covered with snow, adding to a marvellous view out of the fjord.

From now on we headed back to Finland driving southwards to Kautokeino with no traffic on the road. A small souvenir shop, still in Norway, had a busload of tourists on the small premises, when we arrived. The whole family of the business was on the shop-floor trying to cope with the demands of so many people at once. The shop-owners included their children in the service and the children again called their playmates out of the neighbourhood.

Everybody behind the service-desk tried to reach for the cash register to do his part, adding only to the confusion. Such an influx of customers must have been a piece of news for this small remote business. The efforts to help caused a complete stop, because the children learnt on this occasion how to operate the cash register. When our turn came up, I helped the girl on the register to itemise the amounts first on a piece of paper, sum it and then put it all into the register comparing the totals with that on the paper. As the totals amounted to the same, the girl was all in smiles and showed proudly the other three children how it was done.

One good thing came out of this lengthy operation, everybody took his time waiting for his turn, despite none of the visitors speaking Norwegian. It was by all means a pleasant situation, a possible influence through nature's solitude.

Towards Finnish territory, a wild deep rocky canyon followed a river course downwards approximately for two driving hours.

## Finland

The small settlement of Enontekio in Finland had its church tower separate from the main building making the place look special. Was the tower added later, when the money again allowed its construction? Not much later, the Muonio river marked to the south the border with Sweden.

*River Kemi-Joki, border to Sweden.*

Fir forests returned slowly and the further south we came to the Gulf of Bothnia, the more vegetation appeared. The hamlet of Pello has its own hero, showing at the entrance of a timber house the crossed pair of skies that the local long-distance skier Eero Mantyranta used in Olympic Games and World Championships, winning several times gold for Finland. A museum in the building commemorates his achievements. Finland as a nation with a relatively small population is proud of its citizens' successes; more than many other countries, the whole nation stands behind its sons and daughters who put the country onto the world stage.

Coming closer to the Gulf of Bothnia, the weather improved quickly bringing back the summer heat. The border river with Sweden had become near its mouth considerably wide like a large river. On its banks stood in man's height fresh green grass with an ocean of colourful flowers in it with white yarrows standing out in particular against the red willow-herbs and yellow gold-cups (crowfeet). Tornio at the end of the Gulf's shore brought back the modern civilisation of a Finnish town, still wide openly developed. Checking out the water in the Gulf delivered a surprise, the water here was fresh and not salty and so was the fish in it. Only further south the Baltic Sea changes the water to salt-water.

The mighty Muonio river pushes in its mouth the sea further back. Their own special marine life can therefore be found.

Oulu, next on the Gulf, impressed with a modern city-autobahn, allowing fast traffic in the area. Halfway further south towards Kokkola, we turned inland to Nivala, where a sister of our friends in Australia lives with her husband. The couple, Raili and Kalervo, were delighted to have visitors from Australia.

They lived also in a typical Finnish country fashion, supplying as much as possible out of their garden and everything grew well. The summer day was again hot and an outdoor stay at a table and benches reminded us a little bit of life at home with one slight difference being that in Queensland, Australia we can sit on our veranda all year around. People here adjust their lives accordingly, how to make the best out of the short summer with its long daylight hours. Work indoors is mainly left for the long winter, the work outside is done in summer, including holidaying with sunbathing and swimming. Finland has given its people an incentive, not to take all holiday in summer but instead in other times of the year with some additional time off.

An unexpected heavy thunderstorm came down in the area late in the day, something what would have been expected more in the tropics. Are these the signs of a climate-change, affecting every place on earth in one or other ways?

Kyosti Kallio, the Finnish President from 1937—1940, came from Nivala. A tomb in the town's cemetery remembers him today.

A modern industry of electronic components was established in the industrial park, diversifying in the area the employment possibilities from the forestry and agriculture.

After a relaxing break with the elderly couple, who didn't want us to go, our tour took us to the seaside, Kokkola. Another thunderstorm forced us to stop off the road and wait until the water on the road had gone. This must have been a result of the current hot weather. Kokkola was like a Swedish town on Finnish soil, many of its citizens had Swedish as their mother-tongue. Street signs showed first the Finnish and underneath the Swedish name.

Finland has a long history with Sweden, going back over 700 years. It was Russia in 1809, which took Finland off Sweden. First in 1917 Finland gained its independence. A traditional relationship to Sweden has remained to a certain degree, not so much with Russia. It is a historical phenomenon that Finland has preserved through centuries of foreign occupation most of all the language, which can be related mainly to two facts: Finland was a farmer's society, resistant towards changes and secondly, the Finnish Reformation became an important pillar in maintaining the language. Everything in the shopping centre of Kokkola was Swedish, but everybody spoke also Finnish.

The next destination became the area of Hameenkyro, near Tampere, a picturesque region within Finland: lakes, mixed forests rolling over hillsides, green meadows with haycocks, scattered Finnish timber-houses mostly in red colour. On the way to Marja's summer-cottage in Osara we came past an old timber house, the family-home of her parents.

*Finnish home, Kantele.*

Together with her brothers and sisters they maintain the beautiful interior of the house with its antique furniture, central stove of Dutch-tiles, selfmade music instruments and grandfather clocks by Marja's late father. One sister's art-work has been added to the beauty of the family home. I was given the honour to play a Kantele, a multi-string zither, the Finnish national instrument.

The summer cottage was also a timber block house built into the forest of tall northern pines. A lake, where we regularly had a swim during the days of our stay, was just a stone's throw away. Such a holiday is so relaxing, because of the simplicity of the Finnish nature and homemade cooking, sharing small daily tasks with no time-table. Boat trips on lakes and exchange visits, made the day pass quickly. In the neighbourhood in another cottage lived the sister Anja with her eight-year-old son Ville, who invited us into his tree-house telling his stories. Every house has also its own sauna; it is a great experience to combine a sauna and a swim. As we had plenty of time available, our hosts Marja and her husband Pertti wanted to show us around the area. The nearby village of Hameenkyro has a 200-year-old timber-church with aisles to both sides, an organ in an excellent condition. Next to the church were big stone-plaques with endless numbers of fallen soldiers.

The village had also its famous son, Frans Eemil Sillanpaa, who received the Nobel Prize for his novel "Silja the Maid" in 1939. His parent's modest cottage could be visited next to an open-air theatre, where in summer regular plays took place. The simplicity of this home was astonishing, this was where he spent part of his childhood, most likely a start for his creativity.

On our way a cousin of my mother-in-law lived with his wife in a farm-house in the middle of the fields. The unannounced visit gave them a welcome break in their daily life and as this happens, they wanted us to stay much longer. Time together was spent first outside on a swing in front of a flowering potato field, before coffee was served inside the house. The happy moment brought out brilliant actor-talents of the farmer Matti, proving that there are many undiscovered talents around! He knew in particular to add with his humour, when the usual photo scene came up: "Women first on to the thin ice", and as he still, at 74, had fully-grown dark hair, he had to say this: "Nothing in the head, requires at least to have hair on it, like I do. Not enough intelligence gives us always something else instead, its "roots" always show up, even if a shave is needed twice a week, that day hasn't arrived yet, will you excuse me, please." More and more people wanted to see us, it became difficult for somebody like me to keep account as everybody was so forthcoming and friendly. The heat during the day was still around, making a stay in a house most of the time a sauna-like visit.

Family history surfaced usually during our visit and as we arrived from Australia, it was mentioned: the father of Matti went in 1904 to America, but returned, as many good Finns do, in 1925. When will you return to Finland, became a question, we didn't want to answer.

The region produced that summer very good strawberries as an excursion to a nearby farm demonstrated. We spent there some time picking our own organically-grown strawberries until the baskets supplied by a farmer family were filled. Picking mainly in one allotted row allowed us also a good taste—our stomachs could not compete with the baskets' intake. The reward of freshly-picked ripe strawberries waited back in the cottage with almost every meal at least for two days.

Another day's excursion brought us first to an old established farming community. The buildings all around a yard were built out of timber in a dark red colour. The door and window frames in white timber boasted tubs of red and white petunias under each window. The farm looked back at a 550-year family tradition, which is an extraordinary achievement. An art-exhibition took place in one of the buildings, where an artist of the farm had invited others to display their work, welcoming also visitors in an incorporated cafeteria.

It was demonstrated here that even another activity than farming within the family was bound to stay on the farm—a very strong community sense.

*Ossi Somma, "At the Gate of Dante's Hell".*

The people in the area must have been keen on expressing themselves through the art. On the roadside could be found in trees strange-looking objects by the Finnish sculptor, critic and satirist Ossi Somma. To understand his world-expressions required a good deal of fantasy: around his house in the forest were exhibits like a car-wreck with a pine growing out of it, reversed chairs on a slope towards a brook expressed that everything "goes down".

He called his "garden" with the statues, including skeletons, skulls and bones, "Dante's Hell"; what a shocking nightmarish view!

A very interesting exchange of thoughts took place and before we left, I was handed a booklet of his art with a personal dedication.

As we were on an artist-visiting trip, we also visited an organic-farmer and painter Osmo Rauhala (a distant relative of Marja). He was an energetic active family-man, who runs during summer the inherited farm and lives during winter partly in New York painting his Finnish stylistic simplified art and selling it apparently for a lot of money.

*At the home of Osmo Rauhala, artist.*

Lots of things go in our modern world today, we have only to bring nature somehow back to where it is displaced and make people believe in what they acquire that it is still a piece out of nature. A book with his art accompanied by excerpts on environmental philosophy was given to us in commemoration of our visit.

After a week in Hameenkyro, our tour continued to Pori, where another couple awaited our visit. It was really a good feeling to have so much attention during our stay in Finland. Sauna and a swim in a man-made lake of a quarry was also enjoyed in Pori. Living standards in today's societies have also some downsides that bore heavily on this couple, when their talented daughter became hooked on to drugs, paying the ultimate price.

No matter from which angle this problem is looked at, we are too weak and soft to prevent it, only drastic measures at the appropriate level can protect the most vulnerable in a community.

In Masku, near Naantali, waited on the seaside another couple in a cottage for our visit. The fun started already at our arrival, when introducing ourselves: my wife Arja Kari and our hosts Arja and Kari provided during our stay some confusion. Beer, champagne and a barbecue helped instantly to get over it, with a sweat-out in the sauna and a swim to follow. It was quite easy to get used to this life, but also time to move on.

Naantali in the south-west corner of Finland is a very old town, which has maintained its historical image through centuries although modern buildings could be found as well.

Friends, who had visited us before in Australia, lived in an apartment block, where the balcony was completely behind glass so that an outdoor-living could be enjoyed for most of the year. Finnish homes are usually of a high standard. Naantali was not far from Turku to return to my sister-in-law's house in Kaarina. Our circle through Finland closed here, the rented Renault did its part, not leaving us stranded even once.

The next couple of days went in Turku on a familiar path: making up for not enough sleep, shopping, swimming in a nearby arm of the sea. As long as the rented car was available for us, other visits could be followed up like to my wife's childhood home, which her father Petteri had built in Hirvensalo over 50 years earlier. The retired architect Esko Aho lives with his wife Tarja, a retired German and French teacher, on the property today.

A long old-grown garden leads to the sea with a boat anchored on a footbridge. The house is restored with additional changes, as my wife found out, when asked to come in. All the new interior work with timber had been done by the architect himself. The basis of the house remained the same, originally built to last for a long time. It became another homecoming moment to my wife's childhood with lots of happy memories. Even the painted tipplers in their funny mood on the sauna-building wall were still "drinking beer" with the same colourful expressions, unabated like many years before.

Even in the neighbourhood we could knock at the door and enter into a conversation with residents, who had bought the property from the 95-year-old lady, we visited earlier. A current photo taken on the property became a present to her.

*Signe and Arja, Turku.*

At the time lay on the Aura river quays anchored a great number of Tall-Ships from countries around the world. The biggest of them came from Russia, the oldest sailing ship entirely built of timber was the Finnish Tall-Ship "Sigyn", built in 1887. Hot summer weather brought big numbers of onlookers to the quays. Some ships allowed on board visits. All were kept in an immaculate condition, fit for sailing with their impressive masts and sails, everything on board to the last detail was kept polished and clean in a modern show of a shipping-history.

A plan came also together to retrace the moment 38 years earlier, when we met for the first time in Stockholm-Sweden. On our way to the Turku harbour we dropped in to see Arja's old friend, Tuija. This was Arja's oldest friendship going back 56 years. It was a great experience to meet Tuija again, because she had experienced so much bad luck in her life and still kept up her cheerfulness and steadiness, despite having lost: husband, both parents and the son at the age of 30, all through sickness and she lost her own battle for life barely two years after our visit.

Could this have been a result of the Chernobyl nuclear-disaster of 1986? It does happen often in life, some people get all the bad luck, while others, even when challenged, remain on a lucky side.

## Sweden

*Our ship to Finland.*

A big ultra-modern ship took us from Turku through the marvellous archipelago in front of the coast of Finland across the Baltic Sea to Stockholm. Being on our tour-around-the world, we fulfilled our dream by having a luxurious cabin in the upper ship's classes, that gave nice views to the outside.

Sunset at the horizon became a spectacle, sending the last red sunlight across the glittering sea interrupted by forested islands. The ship had the latest automated satellite navigation system enabling her to find the tricky passage between the archipelagos. Exactly on time, and with blue skies, we arrived in Stockholm. This city hasn't lost its beauty in all those years. The waterways were still the same, the massive Royal Palace with one more room than Buckingham Palace in London, opposite the island with the anchored sailing-ship on the shore, where we met for the first time. Sea-arms keep large parts in the city open, where boats invite sightseeing—tours. During one tour we could also see the latest modern face of a city-development in Stockholm.

The hot summer weather transferred our day into a special event lending the place a southern European lifestyle. Climate can change people's habits without transition, we all like summer more or less in the same relaxed way.

Nobel Park showed all in Sweden growing trees, whereas in Drottninggatan, the city-centre, all the people from different nationalities meet today.

Even number 66, former Fralsnings Armee Hotel (Salvation Army Hotel), where Arja worked during the holiday in 1965, was still around.

The reconnection to our first joint past in Stockholm turned out excellently. All we could wish for our future, was to have another 38 years together.

One full day's program in Stockholm made us tired enough to go back to another ship and return across the Baltic Sea to Turku. A contact with the son of our friends, Pirkko and Kalevi, who worked as a scientist in Stockholm, was the only thing we didn't fit into our schedule.

## Finland

The date of August the second told us that our days in Finland were numbered from now on. A farewell atmosphere started to set in. The only time left for us to say goodbye to the 95-year-old lady was at our arrival in Turku. We didn't leave without assuring her to be back on her 100th birthday and wished her to stay well.

Two visits to the young families of my sister-in-law's daughters were still on the list and had to be tackled in a short time. They lived in their own homes, saunas included.

*Turku; Raija, Tuire, Arja, Tuija.*

Whoever still wanted to see us, had to come to Kaarina. Tuija and her sister Tuire came to visit my sister-in-law, her husband and us. Our farewell dinner happened in a joyful atmosphere with old and new memories exchanged without recognising the serious health-status of Tuija. As this became the last face-to-face meeting with her, only the strong memories were left to us.

When returning to Helsinki my sister-in-law and her husband farewelled us at Kaarina bus-stop: "It was so nice to have both of you with us, we will miss you and it will take time to get used to the empty house."—"It is your turn now to come and see us in Australia, that should help." One stumbling point could become that the sister-in-law is scared of flying and wants rather to stay firmly on the ground.— "Look, how our mother came twice to see us in Australia, the last time at the age of 85."—Only the future will tell, whether she is going to make it to Australia. Arja's former childhood friend, Anja, picked us up in Helsinki recognising us out of her car despite many years having passed since we saw each other. Anja lived with her husband, Antti, on the eastern outskirts of Helsinki in a fabulous house of their own. A lot of glass allowed daylight into the premises. Tropical plant-specimens lent to the interior a special atmosphere like we have around our house back home in Queensland. The hosts' daughter had come from Italy for a visit with her "bambino" and Anja's old mother as well. A nearby park offered, besides walks, also activities on outdoor-exercise equipment and all this not far from the waters of the Baltic Sea.

Helsinki, the capital of Finland doesn't stand behind, what a modern city can provide: modern Finnish architecture is expressed in the unique Finlandia Congress Centre, which can be changed into any event with shortest notice, whether a conference, concert or sports event (even ice-hockey). This is a good example of a rational Finnish fantasy carried further by ingenuity.

Antti brought us to the doorsteps of Pirkko and Kalevi on the other side of Helsinki, in Nikkila, in the west. Their children had also arrived for our farewell, the son Seppo from Stockholm and the vet-daughter Mirjami from Helsinki.

*Sipoo; Kalevi, Pirkko, Sampo, Arja, Seppo.*

Time allowed us to organize a trip to Porvoo, another old Finnish town located at the sea, east of Helsinki. The town has largely preserved its old centre with the cathedral on the highest ground. A sailing-ship hanging from the ceiling made the cathedral special, pointing towards a connection with the "Hanse" history of other towns along the Baltic Sea. A ship in a church can also be found in the Hanse cities of Germany: Bremen, Hamburg, Lubeck, Flensburg, Rostock. On the day of our visit a concert was given on the large organ of the church: Praeludium et fuga in a, Aria opus 51, Concerto in G (allegro), all from J.S. Bach, performed by Michael Helenclund. Bach, being my favourite composer, absorbed all my attention, lifting one's mind into higher fields. It was a great farewell for us from Finland. We would have liked to take all these kind people we met with us to Australia, but the memories will follow us for many years to come. August 6 was the day of our departure from Helsinki Vantaa Airport, destination Munich.

## Germany

The weather during the flight was exceptionally fine, but an unexpected surprise awaited us at our arrival in Munich, which suffered under a sweltering heat. The day reached 40 degrees Celsius, reducing the level of activity to a visible calm everywhere, the air-port looked deserted. A rental car from the airport gave us instant independence. In Augsburg lived one of my brothers' family, only a quick drive away from Munich via the Autobahn. Hans was also the first one we had met during our visit to Transylvania in 1978. Since then, three brothers and one sister had moved to Germany starting a fairly good existence with substantial financial help from the German government.

What a development, we left Germany and they moved in, receiving all the help they could think of. Was this the government's propaganda for short political gains? When family members meet, these things have to stay aside, there are more important ties making up a family.

For German conditions, the two houses of brother Hans were quite representative, what looks like a great achievement for a tailor in only a few years. Anyway nothing would have stopped us from having a good time together. My full-brother Michael came especially for the occasion by bus from Transylvania.

At the local bus-station I had to wait for hours, because the bus was running late. During this waiting time a man spoke to me and as it turned out, he was a Romanian surgeon trying to establish himself in Germany. He was waiting for his fiancee. Discussing with him in German, English and French, I found out that he was quite knowledgeable also in his medical field. Not every German would match his medical profile. The gentle-man spoke also about the present difficulties people experienced in Romania. Even he couldn't make ends meet because of the corruption already out for European currency, meaning, only Euros paid for a living in Romania, despite not yet being a member of the European Union. Normal people not having access to the black-market of Euros had a struggle to make a living, especially before the entrance into the EU. With the human factor involved, the rule applied again: it had to get first worse, before getting better.

The nice young Romanian doctor joined me on the way back to my brother Hans in order to cut the waiting time shorter. Through the connections of this surgeon, the sister-in-law received valuable contacts for a personal health-problem. It shows that a connection to the right people can help a lot.

*Furth, Germany, all my brothers and sister.*
*Georg, Alfred, Hans, Martin, Michael, Elisabeth. 9. Aug. 2003.*

When my brother Michael finally arrived with the bus, a bigger family reunion was planned on the weekend in the sister's place near Nuremberg. The time between was used for other visits: to Hans' mother-in-law and mother (a sister of my biological mother), outside the family, Sofia and Jochen in Igensdorf, who visited us on their honeymoon in Australia in late 1988.

Their three children showed us photos from Australia that their parents had taken during their visit. In their fantasy also these three youngsters dreamed about Down-Under Australia.

The family house was quite different from a common house. Russia had supplied solid timber for the construction, based on a model-design. The house, being located on a hillside, rises from the ground level another two storeys, leaving interior views through the whole house in an open space with a staircase access. Solid beams with timber walls gave the house the warm wooden-appearance. From the veranda-platform, next to the house forested hills rose out of valleys and on the horizon to the east, the highest elevation of the "Bayrischer Wald" (Bavarian Forest), all densely covered with fir-forests.

Looking at each other's achievements, a tendency is often emerging: "The grass is always greener on the other side". This means that in Germany people can be found dreaming about Australia. Aussies also like to look at other places in the world, but return home with less dreams, because of a smaller population density, wide open spaces in an unparallel nature, a warmer climate and natural fortune supporting a unique lifestyle.

We took my brother Michael also with us so he could see something different from the poverty-stricken living conditions at the time in Transylvania. It was tempting for him to consider a move to the west with his wife and five children. This is a decision nobody should be talked into, because life in the west was by all means different from a life in Transylvania. Not everything in the west is a gain, progress has also got its price. My suggestion to my brother was: "Wait a bit longer and progress will catch up also with Transylvania, when Romania will join the European Union."

Today in 2008, I would go even so far as suggesting: the investment-climate in Transylvania has been internationally so attractive since Romania joined the EU that it is likely, many will return in the future from the west and help to rebuild the country also for the benefit of Romania.

At the family reunion in Furth, in the countryside near Nuremberg, I learnt that my biological family is well over 200 members strong both in Transylvania and Germany. A cousin even managed to gain a fortune with a hotel in poverty-stricken Transylvania, where he offers rich people, regardless of their origin, deer and bear safaris including hunting, followed up by Saxon-Transylvanian hospitality and tradition, for a price of course. His holiday-resort, called "Lutsch 2000", prepares, in some sense, the progress in Transylvania, showing the world its beauty, tradition and natural wealth. The cousin has created as an entrepreneur many jobs for the local community.

In Romania, where a car was beyond normal people's reach, he could offer to his guests four-wheel-drive Mercedes for their safari.

Somebody trying to stop him in his drive for wealth received simply a generous invitation and everything could be settled in a friendly way.

He was also convinced: "I will bring our people back from the foreign countries. The new Transylvania needs practical men and women, leaders with both feet firmly in the own country and not one foot somewhere else."

These were the words of a man who stood up against all the changes the country went through, holding on firm to the idea of a Transylvanian future. He could be called a man of action, but under very clever precautions, winning even his opponents for his case.

Listening to this information out of first hand in the family I started to feel that I would like to go one day and see all this myself. At that time it was not possible to take a rental car to Romania and to rent one in Romania remained unanswered; a rental agreement was facing too many risks in the country.

For such reasons and mainly the time-loss as a result, caused us to abandon this leg of our round-the-world tour. I wanted to see my native country another time with special time dedicated to it.

It was decided to spend, instead, a couple of days in Paris to give our tour an appropriate finish.

The family reunion of five brothers and one sister with most of their families took place outside the house at long tables and benches, because the temperature had risen again to 40 degrees, incredibly hot for German conditions. Unfortunately the mother, my biological mother's sister, could not be convinced to join us because of an argument with her daughter. How stubborn can we sometimes be! Bearing a grudge against somebody, especially in the own family, should be declared senseless and rather forgotten.

If such a family reunion could be repeated in the near future, we were then all older and our stories would be different again. Let us enjoy the moment and carry all the good memories with us. My brother Michael remained a few more days with the family of Hans, before returning to Transylvania by bus.

His daughter of the previous marriage lived with her family further north in Germany. A pity, we couldn't fit this visit into our program as well.

The farewell was quite emotional, because nobody could say for sure whether we would see each other again, especially because Australia remains for most family members too far away. Strong wishes however can support us in reaching new horizons.

The party went on almost through the whole night, leaving us with hardly any sleep to drive early in the morning to Munich Airport and catch our flight to Paris. Getting out from the countryside through roadworks early Sunday morning on to the Autobahn, became a difficult "exercise", cutting our time dangerously short.

## France

News still at Munich Airport informed us to expect "Saudi-Arabian conditions in Paris". Views from the aircraft supplied a picture of a sunburnt country, as we know from parts of Australia. Paris—Charles de Gaulle—International was busy on our arrival with passengers from all over the world. Paris is still today the most visited city of the world.

*Tour Eiffel, Paris; Martin and Arja, Aug. 2003.*

*Hotel De Ville, Paris (City-Hall).*

French knowledge helped us to find our way into the city-centre first by bus Number 2 and then by metro Number 4. The heat became most unpleasant in the metro, no air-circulation reached the vast underground traffic-system, leaving the packed trains without fresh air. The metro-system still worked fast and to the clock, it was the people that had to adjust to the conditions. Everybody in the carriages was visibly sweating looking at each other with rather sorrowful faces. Not only fashionably dressed men and women, but also other appearances reflected on a multi-cultural society, pushing their luck constantly to get on and off at the fast approaching stations. It looked like a perfectly-working "chaos", nobody was really in anybody's way, everybody pushed and gave in at the same time to get past each other. Up on the street, people on foot and traffic in the "rues", "boulevards", moved constantly, but didn't succeed to leave the heat behind.

Abotel Beaunier Hotel became our destination, from where we planned our stay. The heat of the day got trapped also in the hotel building, making the night especially unpleasant. Only a cold shower helped to replace, for a short time, the air-conditioning system. Paris was not prepared for such an onslaught of heat. The old and very young suffered most calling all day and night for the help of the ambulance-services, of which the sirens constantly filled the air.

During that time of our stay it was said that 11,000 people died in Paris through the effects of this heat. My wife and I were fortunately not affected by the heat. We walked most of the time easily daily up to 30 kilometres, covering only larger distances with the metro. Once you have understood the transport-system of Paris, it is very easy to move around. Paris is full of sights of interest, to see them all amounts to a big undertaking. It is better to pick a number of sights and concentrate on them in the available time. This was exactly, what we did.

The centre of Paris hadn't changed at all since my last visit many years earlier. It is fascinating how the far-reaching planning centuries before had created a city-centre, still working today with its roads, especially as in those days the population was much smaller and there were no cars on the roads.

Having said this, I also want to stress that this achievement of the past was largely built on sacrifices out of the country, which the respective power-system exploited through taxes, becoming ultimately the trigger for the French Revolution, a rebellion against the established rules of exploitation.

It is a human dilemma, for what we do, we always have unbalanced our existence with it. Our intellect is not developed enough to act non-controversial.

Our sights of interest were for the four days of our stay in Paris: The Grand Louvre, Place de la Concorde, Champs Elysees, Arc de Triumph, Tour Eiffel, Grand Opera, Hotel de Ville, Notre Dame, Sacre Coeur, Versailles.

*250-year old carousel at Mont-Martre, Paris.*

*Versailles, Paris (42 degr.Cels.!)*

I'd like to highlight a couple of notes relating to these sights: Le Grand Louvre: undoubtedly the largest art gallery in the world, each building of the U-shaped palaces contain a wealth of art treasures "collected" from around the world. A glass-pyramid in the centre forms today the entrance from underground into the vast building complex.

If you want to see people from all parts of the world in one place, go and visit the Louvre. The good thing about the Louvre was also that many of the buildings were air-conditioned, making a visit pleasant. Ancient Mesopotamian, Persian, Egyptian, Chinese, Greek, Roman cultural exhibits can also be found, just to mention a few outstanding items like the colossal painting: "Coronation of Napoleon I" by Jacque Louis David and the most valuable painting of all, Leonardo da Vinci's "Mona Lisa", painted 1503—1505. We did not have to look far for the "Mona Lisa", it could be found where most people were gathered.

The famous smile of her's, "that slight opening of the lips at the corners of the mouth were considered in that period a sign of elegance". "Venus de Milo" is a famous Greek statue found in 1820 by a peasant on the island of Milo in the Cyclades, "this statue has come to be considered the prototype of Greek feminine beauty". Somewhat more than six-feet high, with its arms broken off, it belongs to the Hellenistic Age, towards the end of the 2nd century B.C.

Leaving the Louvre, the gardens of the Tuileries direct a visitor towards the Champs Elysees, while passing first Place de la Concorde, a constant traffic in multiple lanes rushed around an Egyptian obelisk; the fountain next to it was filled with people seeking relief from the heat. People of Paris can be watched in the gardens of the Tuileries, how they enjoy themselves with sun-seeking, picnics, bringing their children outdoors, babies in their prams, connecting to others, some youngsters showed off with acrobatics, others made music, in between ice-cream-wagons sold their sweet cold in the heat of the day. Even a big orchestra from Holland had arrived and practiced in the open free of charge. Water together with ice-cream, a precious commodity, could be bought on many occasions also outside regular shops. Who looked for the city water-taps, could have the water for free, if prepared to join a queue. The Champs Elysees starts with the horses-statue of Marly, four lanes on each side leading straight across towards Arc de Triumph. Rows of elm-trees losing already their leaves under the hot drought-conditions, patrician houses behind and street cafes in front, each individually marked off with plants and flowers, make this one of the busiest and most colourful city-avenues.

Across the Seine river, which passes through Paris with its many marvellous bridges, lies also the Eiffel Tower, an engineering masterpiece erected for the occasion of the World Expo 1889. "If the symbol of Rome is the Colosseum, then Paris's symbol is without doubt the Eiffel Tower, it seems to triumph over all the older monuments of the city through its more dynamic and modern construction through steel." The tower rests on four enormous pylons from where elevators carry visitors up to the first platform at 62 metres height, from where another two platforms follow in 124 and 300 metres heights.

Stairways lead from the first platform further up, giving increasingly a bird's-eye view across the city. The new face of Paris with modern high-rise buildings and architectural creations can be seen in the distance: the "Grand Arche", or the "Geode" called "Villette", a vast hemispherical projection hall.

Returning to the other side of the Seine river, one can walk through streets where buildings are shaped to a street course, with two roads meeting on a sharp angle, the building runs into a sharp point. Over centuries all spaces have been used to its maximum, leaving however open spaces and parks, which make Paris so attractive.

*Opera, Paris.*

The Opera is the largest theatre for lyric in the world. Its rich decoration of columns and arches on the outside introduce you already into its much richer interior: polished coloured marble-columns, a central stairway leads greatly to the theatre, side-corridors providing also access and exit.

Noticeably, seven great musicians have been placed on top of the outside entrance-façade with a bust of Mozart in the centre. On the side of the Opera is the famous coffee-restaurant "Café De La Paix", one of the most exclusive ones in the world. In the guestbook the names of important people and celebrities can be found. Despite not being commonly known that it could be done, we also paid a visit to "Café De La Paix" and had a cup of coffee with a glass of water. The price underlined the exclusivity of the place. When I had a glass of mineral water 38 years earlier, tables and chairs were also outside, but not any more.

Near the modern glass complexes of "Les Halles", the small restaurant "Au Chien Qui Fume" (The Smoking Dog) served us in style on our 35th wedding anniversary, the 11th of August. Late in the afternoon we were still earlier than their regular customers. It must have been because of the heat that people went out later in the day. The waiter must have misunderstood, when he congratulated us on our marriage. The main thing was that we enjoyed the French-cuisine tradition to serve food items separately and not mixed together and that the waiter was left with the impression having done his contribution to a "newly-married couple".

During our walks through city-quarters we went also past "Place Du Tetre", where artists sit outside on stools in front of the easel, putting their colourful impressions on canvas. Artists created here their own environment and atmosphere in a close-knit community. Passersby looked at the canvasses and the artists at work, buying eventually something they particularly liked.

Taking a photo was out of question, somebody quickly put out their hand in front of your camera: "No photos are taken here, you can buy our art work!"

In our view some good art work could be seen here, prices were rather high, but negotiable.

Overlooking the whole of Paris stands majestically Sacre Coeur on the top of Montmartre hill. Long steep stairways lead up to the curiously-styled church, a mixture of Romanesque and Byzantine, the central-dome overlooking the four smaller corner-domes. The whole church is in a white colour and can therefore be seen from far away. The central-dome holds the 19-tonne "Savoyade" bell, one of the biggest in the world and when it rings, it can be heard with its heavy tone across Paris.

At the start of the stairways stood a 250-year-old beautifully maintained carousel, designated to children with its colourful wooden horses, sledges, swings, swans, all hanging from the carousel ceiling and turning with the music slowly, proper for its age. We haven't before seen a carousel of this age and in such a beautiful condition.

Paris has chosen for its municipal headquarters a magnificent residence with the "Hotel De Ville". To mention just one museum, the "Orsay-Museum", on the left-bank of the Seine river, "defined as the most beautiful museum in Europe". It exhibits the art work of Henri Toulouse-Lautrec, Paul Gauguin (Tahitian women), plus Vincent Van Gogh (The Church of Auvers).

Notre-Dame is located on an island of the River Seine in the neighbourhood of the "Palais De Justice" (Justice Palaces) and its history goes back into the 11th century. Twenty-eight king-statues of Israel and Judea reside above its portals. The portals are Gothic, the two towers were never completed—only their spires are missing. Entering the interior of the cathedral, one is immediately struck above all by its dimensions. At each end of the transept are rose-windows containing splendid stained-glass pieces dating from the 13th century.

Our time in Paris was filled with all this sightseeing, and one we didn't want to miss was Versailles, on the outskirts of Paris. In the train going to Versailles on the opposite bench to us sat a Frenchman returning from the city, after having checked how his old parents were faring from the heat wave: "It is a disgrace, how many elderly people are left on their own without the support of the family. Our younger generation is busy holidaying, therefore it is no wonder that too many are alone. It is a shame for the whole nation, so many elderly people have died so far. I am now comforted, my parents are all right."

Versailles is today a living-museum of bygone royalties with a huge terrace-platform above the geometrically laid-out gardens stretching far to the horizon. The heat on the day of our visit was an excessive 42 degrees, which didn't keep the people-masses away. Queues waited at the palace entrances to gain access to the cooler interior of the buildings. The waiting game appeared to us far too costly, therefore we concentrated more on the surrounding gardens.

During a visit almost 40 years ago, I was only with a few visitors inside and had the best opportunity to see the interior splendour: Royal Chapel, Opera Royal, State Apartments, Royal Private Saloons (Venus, Diana, Mars, Mercure, Apollon, De La Guerre), Hall Of Mirrors, where the treaty of Versailles in 1919 sealed the fate of post First-World-War Germany, Queen's apartments, Gallery of Battles, Kings Apartments, Dauphin's Apartment.

Nothing was spared to equip the palaces with a sophisticated decoration: furniture, paintings, goblins etc. The excessive luxury on one side and the destitution of a vast majority of people on the other side fuelled with time the French-Revolution. It is difficult to listen today to a "cultural glorification" of corrupt regimes, which have used the sacrifices of too many others exclusive for their own benefits. It is a historical fact that humans went also through cycles in the past, not always supported with an intellect; we are still reluctant to leave things as they are and change often only as a last resort; "don't rock the boat, if you do, you are our declared enemy".

The 14th of August was our departure-day from Paris to Australia via Singapore. To sum-up our stay in Paris in one sentence: Paris was worth a visit ("Paris vaut bien une messe"). The trip from Paris to DeGaulle-Aerogare 1 went without any hiccup. Generally speaking, not even once did we feel insecure during our stay, uniformed police were hardly visible, life in Paris must have regulated itself to a large degree through its own people. We saw neither an accident, despite Parisians driving cars with temperament, fast, looking for overtaking-spaces and using the horn in the traffic as a communication.

Another particularity of the French car-driving was, when parking, don't put your hand-brake on, because often the car in front or behind you pushes its way out of a parking position. The cars with the damaged bumpers were the ones, which had the hand-brakes on. It is nowadays not so widely common, but a remnant of the past.

Having arrived at the airport, the usual arrangements with seat-allocations took place. Due to the large numbers of passengers at the airport one could expect, we had arrived with plenty of allowance for our dispatch and it still happened that only to the last minute of our departure a hiccup could be solved: my wife accidentally received a boarding-pass of a Japanese-mister. Until the mix-up could be sorted out, time for departure came to a hair's breath, the "transformation" from a "Japanese" to an "Aussie" could finally be arranged.

Luck must have been also with us while we waited in Aerogare 1, because only a few days later we heard in the news in Australia that this building had suddenly collapsed for no reason, burying a number of people in its rubble; again our time was not yet up.

Soon after take-off, flat land could be seen outside Paris, making no difference between the yellow colour of wheat and grass fields. The long-distance flight-route went over Iran, Afghanistan, Pakistan, India, Malaysia, Singapore, giving spectacular regional views during daylight hours from the aircraft, a Big-Top 747-Boe-ing. Teheran appeared at night clearly underneath with its ocean of lights. Afghanistan and parts of Pakistan looked from the air like mountainous desert-countries, whereas suddenly over the Ganga river in India the land turned green, remaining like this until Singapore with an interruption over the Bay of Bengal. Palm forests and many running waterways through this "green hell" appeared, when the plane gradually descended to Singapore-Changhi Airport after a 13-hour non-stop flight from Paris. A walk in the beautiful air-conditioned airport to the next terminal became a welcome exercise after so many hours locked into an aircraft-seat. Experience teaches us also today, how to cope best with long-distance flights: circulate feet, move legs and arms regularly and if possible move also around in the plane from time to time, in the back is often room for a couple of pump-ups from the floor and knee-bending.

The plane left Singapore for Brisbane in the morning, arriving on Friday, the 15th of August at 8.10pm. Our round-the-world tour had come to a successful end, a dream had been fulfilled.

The French author Jules Verne described in his science fictions also in 1875 a fantasy-journey around the world in 80 days. Only in a fantasy somebody could at that time engage in such an adventure. Today it is not so much a fantasy, but a decision of other criteria: time, that bit of money, still good planning backed up with a good health. With luck, an adventure like this can flow into a lasting experience, in which we have not met only new conditions and people, but also reconnected to old acquaintances.

Only by going out, we can make this level of experience and when returning, a new view has developed towards what we call home. Our home was still in the same place, looking a bit different after almost three months away.

What had changed, the home or us? One thing was for certain, home-coming was better again than leaving.

## Back Home

Realities of the daily-life caught up with us immediately, but not necessarily spoiling what was gained on our tour. Achieving a smooth transition to the demands, that had not gone away during a break like this, depends on a personal ability to recognise the new tasks back at home, organise the priorities and start to deal with them one by one. Home under the supervision of our youngest son Micki could be soon ticked-off from a priority list.

At work I received a warm welcome with a big sign: Martin welcome back. My "mates" at work were not forgotten during the tour, they all received their post card. This might have helped them not to forget me.

An immediate task was to develop and build modern production equipment in house for the new generation of car air-conditioning heat-exchangers laid ahead.

Australia, as a relative small industrial power-house, has to do more home-work, because the capital-layout for overseas' technology is very expensive. Also with this in view, some outstanding results were achieved under the leadership of my boss, Bevan, in the three years until my retirement at 65. The company had, in some aspects, beaten in their own game the Japanese, who were the licenser of their technology to us.

Why time passes quicker, when we become older, I really don't know. The next three years went in a hurry. At home a couple of projects on our property were also tackled at the available time: the extension of three bedrooms for the home-coming growing family, cutting out problem-trees, getting rid of the grass, landscaping with mulch, creating walkways, cleaning and fencing of the dam, house renovations, building a veggie garden raised from the ground; everything designed to ease life in the years to come.

Towards the end of my career with the company, Micki the youngest of our children also joined us in the team. The company he was doing his apprenticeship with had gone into receivership, but thanks to the helping hand of my boss, Micki could finish his time with us. Good Aussies don't let their mates down!

In 2004 we had also a special visitor from Germany—Dominik, from Wernau, near Stuttgart, our last residence in Germany. He is an architect, trying to follow in his father's footsteps. The family took in our German-shepherd, Mars, when we left for Australia. Being grateful for this special friendship with this family, it was understood that we return our favour to their son. Despite our best intentions and support, Dominik could not stay in Australia because he didn't listen enough to our advice and had, like so many others, to return to Germany disappointed. A German way of thinking doesn't necessarily succeed in Australia. The country still asks for people that can stand up to the challenges facing a migrant. Dominik, being single and over 40, didn't help his case, as he thought that Australian opportunities were waiting for him to be picked. It became once more evident, if somebody wants to live in Australia, he is well advised to stick to the rules Australian migration has put into place. Personally, we regretted this unsuccessful outcome with Dominik.

The years have continued with a persistent drought, which most parts of Australia have not seen in a living memory, including Queensland. The higher evaporation rate of the continent can dwindle water resources very quickly. Our rainwater tanks and the dam regularly reached critical supply levels. Our garden would not have survived without additional water. 2007 was the eighth consecutive year with very little rain, making the work in the garden more and more time-consuming.

Despite the threat of weather changes from the Antarctica, Aussies keep up their hopes: the wet will eventually return in 2008. In the meantime we have to be patient and learn to economise precious resources like water.

Ultimately "we are not only in our local boat, but all in the same boat on our planet earth." Every possible effort should be made to keep our boat afloat. The consequences from not doing so, or not enough, become irreversible; a "sinking boat" is more difficult "to keep on a course".

Before turning 65, I handed responsibilities gradually to a team of a younger generation to allow a process of a selection to develop, who would be the suitable successor with the support of the team. It should only be regarded natural to step back in time and hand the reins over to a well-prepared younger generation. I gave the team all my support, which in return also helped me to perform my job not as a single-performer, but in a team and with their support. Operating in a team-environment supplies that important control-mechanism which builds on good results, as long as the team leader fills his position responsibly and effectively.

As the first retiree in the company's history of just over 20 years, I was given a memorable farewell party with a number of special gifts. Wishing everybody a continued future with the company in the face of growing difficulties in the Australian manufacturing industry, I stepped aside into a new period of life.

## Retirement—As a Writer

What is generally called retirement should be seen as a new chance to live a life with all the gains in a widest sense, depending also on how much was "deposited" on an "account" of health, focus on friends and family, and a reasonable planning for a future. With "deposits" on such "accounts", only then in retirement is a future secured. We can build a lifetime, or leave it to coincidences. Sooner or later everybody has to turn into his own master, which is also given with the circumstances surrounding him. A scale of achievements is as endless as the number of individuals.

How does such a view translate into conditions of an under-privileged majority in the world? My understanding relates also to it, but with the difference between living standards, still allowing to achieve relative freedom in a retirement as long as conditions do not prevent this from happening.

It is important, however, to find a balanced direction out of the past for a new life-span. The answer lies in simplicity towards our expectations. Spending all we have gained in a life so far wouldn't be satisfactory. We should look back at our life and try to learn out of a distance from it. Continuing to "shovel" more wealth and power loses its sense with age, because we can't take anything with us on our "final journey". The time arrives for everybody, when we will be asked to answer: has your life been worthwhile?

How would my current answer be? Life continues with only minor changes: the children have grown up with our initial support, it is now up to them to live their lives, extend the family-ties and not to forget the mutual help.

The task to get early up to work and return late home has changed. The time has to be filled with own decisions. I enjoy having more time at home and doing many things I had to rush before: working on the property, hobbies, but also to find new activities like writing, which never was given proper attention because of a lack of time. Now with time available, writing has taken a foothold, not only in my life, but as I found out only now that my wife Arja could join me and we have found a new common ground. She has read a lot during her life and can contribute with her pre-editing to my ideas.

As we have worked in the past together, we continue to do so. Writing today calls for the use of computers, but I write still the very first script by hand and then type it, together with my wife, into a computer-file, which undoubtedly allows changes and corrections much easier than on paper. After a script is completed on the computer, we then take our time and go completely again through the script to improve it.

To go out and find somebody to look at a script: reviewing, editing and proof-reading, line-editing, designing, printing it—all this is a challenge.

As my Latin-teacher told me at school once: "A blind chook occasionally finds also a corn". It must have been such an occasion, when the publisher of this book expressed his immediate interest in my first presentations. I found the concept of this publisher great: there are many people with stories and ideas not recognised, because they are not known to a public, thus meaning, there is an unknown potential of writers not being recognised. Give them a chance to bring out what they want to say, a team of qualified proof-readers judge it and decide whether to go ahead and give it a first "polish". Most people reading a book wouldn't have a real idea of the amount of thoughts, energy and time going into a book, before reaching the public. But this is also the secret of a success: the better the homework is done on a book, the better it will be received in a world of fussy readers.

Writing about all what came across my mind and how it translated into messages for a wider readership has become a new direction in our lives—my wife's and mine. Starting on a humble basis 52 years ago in a clinic-environment, where I filled my time with writing, this is now continuing from 2007 onwards hopefully into many years to come. If my life were depending on what I still have to write, probably another 50 years would be needed. As this is not realistic, I restrict myself to the time, which allows me to continue to write.

There is a Latin adage: "Mens sana in corpore sano" (a healthy mind in a healthy body), and a Greek- one: "We have also to do something good for our body so that a soul likes to live in it".

Referring to these words, the writing and reading cover the mind to a large degree, the body again receives its attention with a daily swim, gymnastics and regular work on the property.

Animals and plants can also give us one important message: an active, healthy, long life asks for a regular pattern. Why do animals and plants relate to it? To adjust our lives to a regular pattern with them, feeds back on us; they all respond to an exact time-table organising us in a natural way. Whether it is the parrots, dogs, cats, or donkeys, they must have a built-in clock telling us daily routines, even plants respond best to regular care.

Meaning in our case: a regular life gives us the best return. Maintaining appropriate activity levels, followed by a regular rest-time, educates our body to a time-table, which feeds back to our mind and ultimately on to our health.

I remember an interesting critical comment to a healthy life: passing away, why should you have a perfect body, when it is more suitable for a run-down one.

I disagree with this view because it ignores the existence of a quality in our lives; a healthy body can deliver this better, regardless of a life-span.

I acknowledge the existence of many views, but it is a secret in life to embark early enough on perceptions, specific to our "physique", which can deliver this quality in our lives.

This is not happening instantly, it might be an end-result of a process, we have to go through; no gain without pain!

Who avoids that path and embarks on smart-sides in life, misses however the real heydays of life. Only what we invest, can be expected in a return.

In life we should develop, if possible, views from the present to look back into the past and also into the future. An autobiography is mainly based on a life in the past, a view into a future should also be a part of it, because we live only as long as our lives are projected into a future, the space of time is of a secondary nature. It doesn't matter, how many times we experience that our planning turns out different, a strong view towards a future still has to be maintained in order to overcome present hurdles.

Everything in our lives asks for a balance, which has to be addressed and found. Where does now a future lie after this auto-biography? To establish first a life with the old and new elements and then start going out accordingly to the opportunities available at the time.

It is my hope that our lives will become another volume of a "journey of a lifetime" from now on.

# EPILOGUE

"We should plant a tree, have a child and write a book in a lifetime" says a Chinese adage. Judging my autobiography from there, I have given my answer and want to add to it: life doesn't stop after that.

> *"We have always got enough time, when we know how to use it".*
> (Goethe).

"Journey Of A Lifetime" volume 2 is a continuation of a life, in which also people around us have reflected on my and my family's existence. Extraordinary circumstances have asked for strong commitments, which had become a good school for every family member. We are not "non-paying spectators" in our life journey. We have come to an understanding with our life-situations, we were asked to respond, which has been done to the best of our knowledge. What makes our existence is that everybody produces different answers in a life.

Truthful writing was again the key for a dialogue with a reader. Every book has its final chapter and so ends ours in Down-Under Australia.

www.ingramcontent.com/pod-product-compliance
Lightning Source LLC
Chambersburg PA
CBHW030225100526
44585CB00012BA/227